IOWA PUBLICATIONS IN PHILOSOPHY

IOWA PUBLICATIONS IN PHILOSOPHY
VOLUME 1

ESSAYS IN ONTOLOGY

EDWIN B. ALLAIRE
MAY BRODBECK
REINHARDT GROSSMANN
HERBERT HOCHBERG
ROBERT G. TURNBULL

UNIVERSITY OF IOWA
IOWA CITY, IOWA
1963

MARTINUS NIJHOFF
THE HAGUE
1963

PRINTED IN THE NETHERLANDS

EDITORS' PREFACE

The Iowa Publications in Philosophy is a series of analytical studies – essay collections, monographs, books – in ontology, the history of philosophy, the philosophy of science, and other branches of philosophy. The authors of the present volume are all closely connected with the Department of Philosophy of the State University of Iowa; May Brodbeck of the University of Minnesota, Reinhardt Grossmann and Herbert Hochberg, both of Indiana University, as former students; Edwin B. Allaire and Robert Turnbull, as members of the department. But it is not anticipated that the authors of subsequent volumes will all be associated with the Iowa department, whose senior members will serve as the editors of the series.

CONTENTS

AUTHORS' NOTE

Essays IV, VII, XII have not been previously published. The others appeared originally as follows:

I "Existence, Independence, and Universals" in *The Philosophical Review*, 69, 1960, 485–496.

II "Bare Particulars" in *Philosophical Studies*, 14, 1963, 1–8.

III "Elementarism, Independence, and Universals" in *Philosophical Studies*, 12, 1961, 36–43.

V "Conceptualism" in *The Review of Metaphysics*, 14, 1960, 243–254.

VI "Sensory Intuition and the Dogma of Localization" in *Inquiry*, 5, 1962, 238–251.

VIII "Ockham's Nominalistic Logic: Some Twentieth Century Reflections" in *The New Scholasticism*, 36, 1962, 313–329.

IX "Berkeley's Idealism" in *Theoria*, 29, 1963.

X "Frege's Ontology" in *The Philosophical Review*, 70, 1961, 23–40.

XI "Moore's Ontology and Non-Natural Properties" in *The Review of Metaphysics*, 15, 1962, 365–395.

XIII "Of Mind and Myth" in *Methodos*, 11, 1959, 123–145.

XIV "The Philosophy of John Dewey" in *The Indian Journal of Philosophy*, 3, 1961, 69–101.

The necessary permissions by editors and publishers have been granted and are gratefully acknowledged.

INTRODUCTION

Certain words are crucial in ontological discourse. 'Exist', 'individual', 'particular', 'universal', 'simple', and 'independent' are obvious examples. These essays examine how philosophers have used some of those words. The purpose of the examination is to make sense out of the ontological doctrines in which the crucial words occur as well as out of the arguments that have been made for and against the doctrines. This common purpose is one good reason for bringing the essays together. Nor is it the only one. The several essays share an awareness of the dialectical connections among the several issues with which they deal. Also, the realism-nominalism issue is the central one; and the essays are all realistic. That is another good reason for bringing them together.

The authors believe that they share a method. If they are right, then there is a third good reason for bringing them together. But it seems pointless to attempt here a statement of the method. A method is best judged by watching it in operation.

Even though the essays are all realistic, their defense of realism is both varied and complex. For this there are three reasons. First, none of the essays defends uncritically any traditional position. Rather, each defends some proposition or propositions which by the method may be shown to be connected with some traditional position. Second, they all put less weight on the proposition itself than on the intellectual motives which have led philosophers to propound it and on the arguments by which they support it. Third, they all make a special point of exploring the dialectical ramifications of the realism-nominalism issue. That is why the common purpose will be best served by allowing each essay to speak for itself.

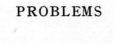

PROBLEMS

I. EXISTENCE, INDEPENDENCE,
AND UNIVERSALS*

EDWIN B. ALLAIRE

Consider a visual field which contains two red spots (of the same shade). At least two sentences are true of it: (a) "This is red" and (b) "That is red." One question which ontologists frequently ask themselves, when considering such sentences and what they refer to, is: What is the meaning of "is" in (a) and (b)? How one answers this question determines in large measure whether one is a nominalist or a realist.

The realist claims that the "is" in both sentences is the predicative *is*. Accordingly, his analysis runs as follows. Each spot is a fact which consists of an individual and a character standing in the exemplification relation. The individuals are referred to by "this" and "that," respectively; the character(s) by "red." Thus, the individuals are different; the character(s) the same. Upon the realist's analysis, therefore, there are in this situation three existents. Or, to say the same thing differently, diversity and non-diversity are primary. This, in fact, is one of the basic considerations which guide his analysis. For to him it is obvious that the spots are, as one says, numerically different – that is, two – and are yet in one respect the same.

The nominalist is less explicit regarding the meaning of "is." Implicitly, though, he assimilates it to the "is" of identity. Upon the nominalist's analysis there are but two existents, the two red spots. Thus he maintains that "this" and "that" name the two existents *properly*, whereas "red" names them *commonly* or indifferently. However, even though "this" and "red" both name the same existent, the meaning of "is" in this case cannot be that of non-diversity, that is, literal sameness. For, if it were, there would be only one spot and not, as there are in fact, two – a fact which no ontologist can afford to lose sight of. It follows that if the nominalist wishes to maintain that there are only two existents, he must also maintain that they are both complex. Or, to say the same thing as it was said above, the nominalist

* *The Philosophical Review*, 69, 1960, 485–496. *Reprinted by permission.*

like the realist must maintain that diversity and non-diversity are primary. That the nominalist does maintain this is implicit in his admission that the application of "red" to the *two* spots is not arbitrary but somehow grounded in the fact that they are both red and not, say, one red, one green. This means that the sameness (qualitative) as well as the difference (numerical) of the two spots is grounded in the spots. Now four comments.

1. In both analyses the existents are named. Nominalist and realist both implicitly accept the following proposition. (N) *What is named exists.* According to the realist, however, "this" and "red" name different things, namely, an individual and a character, respectively. According to the nominalist, "this" and "red" both name the same thing, namely, a red spot. (So do "that" and "red.") This is as it should be. For the realist accepts the existence of characters (universals); the nominalist does not. According to the latter, red does not exist; only red things do.

2. The realist accepts another ontological proposition which the nominalist does not. (S) *What exists is simple.* The full dialectics of this notion is extremely subtle.[1] It is, in fact, at the core of much current criticism of logical atomism. However that may be and however many strands the notion of simplicity may contain, in one clear and significant sense the nominalist is willing to accept a complex entity – namely, our red spot – as one existent. Thus he must at least implicitly reject (S).

3. (S) and (N) jointly yield another proposition. (SN) *What is named is simple.* The realist accepts (SN). The nominalist must reject it; for, though he takes "red" to be a name, what it refers to is in at least two senses not simple. Like "this" and "that," "red" refers to something complex. This is the first sense. Unlike "this" and "that," "red" refers to two existents. This is the second sense. In contrast, the realist asserts that "red" refers to one and only one existent, the character red, which, like all characters, can be exemplified by several individuals. So, too, with "this" and "that." Each refers to one and only one individual.

4. According to the realist the "is" in both (a) and (b) is the predicative *is.* The meaning the nominalist assigns to it has not yet been

---

[1] Some realists construe "simple" as Moore did (in *Principia Ethica*). Briefly, a *simple* is the referent of an undefinable term, e.g., "yellow"; a *complex* the referent of a definable term, e.g., "horse." The referents of the former are said to *exist*. These explications would appear to uncover the core of the ontological enterprise. Again briefly, that enterprise is to show what is made of what and tends to claim that what is *composed* does not, in this special sense, *exist*.

clarified, except negatively. We saw that it could be neither the predicative *is* nor that of identity. Positively, the meaning that may plausibly be assigned to it is "part-whole." That is, (a) may be rephrased as "Red is a part of this." In other words, (a) may be analyzed by saying that "this" refers to a whole of which red is a part, "red" referring to the part. A nominalist who accepts (N) cannot, however, propound this analysis. For it would be tantamount to saying that universals exist. Our nominalist may, therefore, try to discard (N), replacing it by (N'). (N') *What exists is what is properly named* (named, that is, by a proper and not a common name). Then he could accept the suggested analysis (part-whole). This analysis has indeed the merit of at least rendering intelligible the meaning of "is" in (a) and (b), a merit which the more traditional common-name doctrine lacks. It also fits more closely the over-all nominalistic pattern. For the nominalist wishes to maintain that only individuals exist. (N') is a convenient explication of this claim. It must not be overlooked, however, that upon this gambit, as upon the other, the nominalist's individuals are radically different from the realist's. The realist's are simple, the nominalist's complex, consisting of both the realist's individuals and characters.

These four comments show what the basic difference between nominalist and realist implies. More importantly, they are meant to show that the nominalist's attitude toward (S), (N), and (SN) is not determined by a claim concerning the constitution of the spot that differs significantly from the realist's. For in both analyses diversity and non-diversity are primary and there obtains in both a (logical) relation between the two constituents of each spot. The nominalist's reluctance to admit the existence of universals must, therefore, not be ascribed to his attitude toward (S), (N), and (SN). Rather, it is the other way around. His nominalism determines his attitude toward (S) (N), and (SN). If this is so, as I believe I have shown, then one must ask oneself: What is the cause of the nominalist's reluctance to acknowledge that universals exist? That is, why does he insist that only the complex entity (the spot) exists while its constituents do not? Historically speaking, his insistence or, if you please, his position echoes the classical doctrine of hylomorphism. If made explicit, this position is unobjectionable as a choice of terminology. We continue our probe, however: What are the (terminological) consequences the nominalist tries to avoid by insisting that universals do not exist?

One of the deepest roots of nominalism, the one which I hope to unearth, emerges in the nominalist's claim that, while red things exist, red does not. Few would deny what underlies this claim. One is never acquainted with red alone but always with something that exemplifies red. This is the common-sense core of nominalism. The question is: Is this core incompatible with the claim that universals exist? The nominalist apparently believes that it is. I now hope to show that his belief is mistaken.

The heart of the matter is the notion of independence. The nominalist is implicitly guided by still another ontological proposition. (I) *What exists is independent.* Unhappily, the nominalist fails to distinguish the several meanings of "independent." That is why he is misled by spurious arguments of the following sort. "What exists is independent. Characters are dependent. Hence, characters do not exist." This is a crude paradigm of his confusion. I call him confused because "independent" does not mean the same thing in the two premises of the spurious argument.

Four uses of "independent" are relevant. They occur in the following sentences. (I1) There are *independent* entities. (I2) An individual is *independent* whereas a character is *dependent*. (I3) Neither individuals nor characters are *independent* of each other. (I4) Atomic facts are *independent* of each other. Each sentence is the crux of a philosophical controversy. The atomist-holist controversy centers on (I1).[2] (I4) is the focal point of the synthetic-a priori issue.[3] Both (I2) and (I3) are central to the arguments concerning the ontological status of characters and individuals.[4]

Every atomist (pluralist) accepts (I1), asserting it in the teeth of the holist's (monist's) claim that only the Absolute is real. The issue is whether or not there is more than one "independent entity." To recover this meaning of "independent" it will be profitable to consider the following proposition. (P) *A thing is what it is independently of all the characters it exemplifies and of all the relations in which it stands.* Not surprisingly, (P) is at the heart of the "internal relations" struggle. That struggle, however, does not concern us directly. The point is that either explicitly or implicitly (P) is frequently embraced by philosophers who wish to maintain, say, that a physical object is "more than"

---

[2] This controversy in its contemporary dress is discussed by Gustav Bergmann, "The Revolt Against Logical Atomism," *The Philosophical Quarterly*, 7, 1957, 323–339 and 8, 1958, 1–14.
[3] For an analysis of this issue see Edwin B. Allaire, "*Tractatus* 6.3751," *Analysis* 19, 1959, 100–105.
[4] Cf. Gustav Bergmann, "Frege's Hidden Nominalism," *The Philosophical Review* 67, 1958, 437–459.

the "class" of its properties (and relations). That is, one holds (P) in order to be able to deny that a physical object can be "defined" in terms of its properties (and relations). There must be something in which those properties (and relations) inhere. Furthermore, that in which they inhere "is what it is" regardless of what in fact inheres in it. Consider the sentences "Socrates is white" and "Socrates is red." Assuming that "Socrates" refers to what properties inhere in, it follows from (P) that both sentences are about that same thing and that no matter which of the two is true Socrates is not altered, that is, not different. Only the facts would differ. Or, to say the same thing differently, to accept (P) is to maintain that the "meaning" of "Socrates" remains the same regardless of what true (or false) sentences "Socrates" occurs in.

(P), however, does not assert that Socrates, in order "to be what he is independently," must not have any properties (or relations). Nor does it even suggest that Socrates may ever be without properties. That is not the point. The point is, rather, that no matter what properties a thing may have, its "essence" is not changed, though, to be sure, the fact may be. Another way of expressing this meaning of "independent" is to say that there is no logical connection whatsoever between knowing what the word "Socrates" refers to and knowing in which sentences (true or false) it occurs.[5]

In its broadest sense (P) does not apply only to what are usually called individuals or substances. An extreme Hegelian, for example, who like all Hegelians must reject (P), is yet willing to allow "thing" to refer not only to individuals but also to characters and whatever else there may be. For one who denies (P) thus broadly interpreted, "individuation involves negation." Again, this is individuation in the broad sense, which includes distinguishing an individual from its characters as well as two characters from each other. To know green, according to the extreme Hegelian, one must therefore know everything that green is not. Or, to put it a bit captiously, to really know anything one must know everything. That something is wrong here, that indeed "language has gone on holiday," many will allow. What exactly is wrong is another story, one which need not detain us. The following suggestion, however, is relevant to the meaning "independent" has in (I1). One mistake which, according to some atomists,[6]

---

[5] There is, however, an intimate connection between knowing the referent of a word and knowing the syntactical rules which govern its use. Cf. Gustav Bergmann, "Ineffability, Ontology, and Method" in *The Philosophical Review*, 69, 1960, 18–40.

[6] Cf. Bertrand Russell, "The Philosophy of Logical Atomism," reprinted in *Logic and*

the Hegelians make is their failure to distinguish between knowing what a word refers to (in one sense of "meaning") and knowing true sentences in which it occurs (another sense of "meaning"). If these senses of "meaning" are not distinguished, then the claim of the Hegelians that to know (the meaning of) anything one must know (the meaning of) everything can easily lead to the absurdity that to know, say, the difference between red and green one must know everything. In this connection the following passage from the *Tractatus* is worth examining.

2.0122 The thing is independent, in so far as it can occur in all *possible* circumstances, but this form of independence is a form of connexion. (It is impossible for words to occur in two different ways, alone and in the proposition.)

Here we encounter an explicit use of "independent" in the sense of (I1).[7] Wittgenstein's point, I submit, is that what is meant by the "independence of the thing" can be clarified by saying that its name can occur in any sentence provided only that the "type rule" is observed. This rule, however, is held to be purely syntactical. That is, the formation rules of the language depend on the shapes of the sign and not on what they refer to.[8]

Let me restate the main features of the first meaning of "independent." First, to say that an individual or a character is *independent* is to say that the word referring to it can occur in any sentence provided only that the syntactical rules are observed. Second, a thing is *independent* in the sense that there is no logical connection between what the thing is and in what facts it occurs. Or, to put the matter linguistically, there is no logical connection between the referent or meaning of a word, in one sense of "meaning," and true or false sentences in which it occurs. Third, the *independence* of a thing is expressed by saying that the word which refers to it is a "mere label" (a name) and that the formation rules on which its place in sentences depends are syntactical, not semantical. Fourth, the thing's *independence* can also be expressed by saying that what a word refers to (its meaning in one sense of "meaning") is not altered by its occurrence in sentences which were not previously known to be true.

(I1) is, of course, intimately connected with (S). The logical atomists

---

Knowledge (London, 1956), pp. 203–204. Lectures II and III of this essay are worth reading in connection with the several meanings of "independent." For Russell's confusions are transparent and instructive.

[7] Whether the early Wittgenstein was a nominalist or realist is controversial. What he means in 2.0122 does not, however, depend on his being either. For no matter what the primitives of his improved language are, they certainly are mere labels.

[8] See note 5.

all embraced (S). Naturally, they all believed that there were "independent entities" in sense (I1). Often (S) itself carried this weight for them. However, the connection extends further. If there were no (ontological) simples which could merely be labeled by linguistic simples such as "this" and "red," there would plausibly be at least a quasi-logical connection between the referent of a word and the facts expressed by true (or false) sentences in which it occurs. To grasp this, consider that, if the linguistic simple "this" is to refer to a complex entity, knowledge of what it refers to would in some sense depend "logically" on knowing the constitution of the entity, which distinguishes it from others, that is, on knowing facts expressed by sentences. Since the nominalist maintains, at least implicitly as we saw, that "this" does refer to a complex entity, he is in danger of asserting such a "logical" connection. For, as we also saw, upon his analysis the referent of "this" contains the referent of "red." This may explain why some nominalists prefer the fuzzy common-name doctrine to the part-whole analysis.[9]

Whether the logical atomists' program can be realized is controversial. The language they undertake to construct would of course contain no primitive descriptive terms which are not mere labels. The point I wish to make, however, does not depend on whether the program is realizable, that is, whether such a language can be constructed. My point is rather that, whether or not it is, both the realist and nominalist must consistently believe it to be realizable. For if they do not, then, as I have shown, they implicitly deny (I1). And, as I have also shown, the denial of (I1) leads to monism, that is, to the obliteration of distinctions on which both nominalist and realist insist.

That concludes the discussion of (I1), the first use of "independent." I turn next to the third, (I3).

The "form of connection" of which Wittgenstein speaks in the quoted passage (2.0122) and which he himself so poignantly explicates is closely related to (I3). Wittgenstein's point is that a language cannot even be a candidate for the role of ideal language (L)[10] unless there is a sharp distinction among its words and its sentences. Words are not sentences, they only occur in them. That is why words "cannot stand

---

[9] It is to be noted that upon both nominalistic analyses the referent of "this" cannot be "defined." For "this" in both cases refers to a whole, only one part of which is or can be named. The individuating constituent, if I may so express myself, is not named. Again, one hears the echo of the hylomorphic doctrine.

[10] As was shown above, the thesis of this paper does not depend on whether or not such a language can be constructed. It merely depends on both nominalist and realist admitting that it can. For in so doing they both embrace (I1).

alone." The formation rules of L are such that only strings of words count as sentences. This restriction on L, however, is weaker than (I3), which maintains that no character word can occur in a sentence without having first occurred in an atomic sentence of the form "fx." Let me sharpen this. There are two points which, though they are closely related, must be clearly distinguished. First, there is the interpretation of L. In this context (I3) merely means that, say, no color word can be introduced into L as a primitive term unless its referent is first exemplified by an individual. That we never do know what a color word refers to unless we have once seen the color exemplified is undeniable indeed. Second, one may know, in some sense of knowing, without actually being acquainted with the color red, that "red" refers to a color. But then this kind of knowledge can be accounted for without disrupting the import of (I3). That is why the two points must be distinguished.

(I3) is the heart of the realism issue. One who denies both (I3) and Wittgenstein's thesis in 2.0122 I would call an extreme Platonist. One who merely denies (I3) I call a Platonist.[11] Aristotle certainly accused Plato of denying (I3) with respect to the "Forms." Whether he also accused him of denying the weaker requirement is difficult to say.[12]

(I2) takes for granted that the exemplification relation is asymmetrical and that individuals are the lowest-level items, that is, that individuals are referred to by terms which occur only in the subject place. (I2) thus rests on the type distinction. Many metaphors are associated with this meaning of "independent." Some deserve mention, for they contribute to the nominalist's perplexity. First, an individual (or substance) is often said to "need no support" while a character does. Second, it is said that characters "cannot stand alone" while individuals can. The latter metaphor may tempt one to claim, as Russell once did,[13] that the world could consist of only one individual and nothing else. Clearly such an individual could not be of the realist's sort. Russell, therefore, made it an individual of the nominalist's sort, that is, one which "contains" characters. Third, since words referring to

---

[11] It is interesting to note that both types of Platonism in their relation to the doctrine of simples are a major concern of the later Wittgenstein. Cf. *The Blue and the Brown Books* (Oxford, 1958), p. 17, and *Philosophical Investigations* (New York, 1953), Secs. 37–59. Secs. 57 and 58 are especially interesting in this regard.

[12] Wittgenstein's thesis is sometimes expressed by saying that "thought is propositional." This means that the object of awareness (in the generic sense) is always referred to by a sentence. Cf. *Tractatus* 2.0121 and 3–3.144.

[13] Russell, *op. cit.*, p. 202. For a discussion of Russell's individuals see J. O. Urmson, *Philosophical Analysis* (London, 1956), pp. 54–57.

individuals occur only in the subject place, they are often called "proper names." [14] This may tempt one to believe that a predicate term, say, "red," is a different *kind of name*, and not just a name of a different *kind of thing*. This, I submit, is one reason why the nominalist calls "red" a common name. Fourth, in the hylomorphic scheme a substance is a composite of form and matter, neither of which exists. Some medieval philosophers who held this doctrine believed that a substance could exist without accidents, that is, they denied (I3). One reason was their concern with immortality. A contemporary nominalist who takes his cue from these philosophers obviously is misled. Furthermore, the composite substance of the hylomorphic scheme is, of course, not really a thing but a fact, namely, a "form informing matter." The nature of the informing relation remains obscure in the hylomorphic scheme, just as the meaning of "is" in (a) and (b) remains obscure upon the common-name analysis. Nor is this an accident. The doctrine of common names has its historical root in the hylomorphic scheme.

The explication of (I4) is standard and familiar. In L no (atomic) sentence of the form "fx" (or "rxy," and so forth) logically entails any other. This and only this is the meaning of the *Tractatus* thesis that (atomic) facts are independent of each other. Accordingly, one may say that it is logically possible (in the sense explicated by the truth tables) for the world to consist of only one atomic fact. This suggests that, carelessly construing "independent" as "capable of standing alone," one may be tempted to propound a fact ontology: that is, an ontology according to which only atomic facts *exist*. (I) and (I4) create a similar temptation; for taken together, they yield the same doctrine. Moreover, there is a significant connection between (I1) and (I4). One possible way of securing the privileged status of "a priori truth" for certain sentences is to claim that, in some (to me) obscure sense of "follow," their truth follows from the "meaning" of the words which occur in them.[15] This claim I have shown to be incompatible with (I1).

One is never acquainted with red alone but always with something exemplifying red. This is the common-sense core of nominalism. Is it compatible with the existence of universals? The nominalist answers that it is not. I have in this paper set myself the task of showing that his answer is mistaken. To accomplish the task I maintained that one must distinguish among four uses of "independent" and the philo-

---

[14] "Proper name," in so far as it is used philosophically, I call a metaphor. For I do not know what it means to be a name without naming one and only one thing.

[15] See note 3.

sophical issues which they control. Having made the distinctions, I now return to the task.

The realist holds that individuals as well as (some) characters exist because both are independent in sense (I1), because they are simple (S), and because they can be named (N). But the realist must also know how to distinguish between these kinds of existents. The distinction he secures by accepting (I2). Nor need he maintain that this is the only difference between individuals and characters.

What does the realist claim with respect to (I3) and (I4)? If he wishes to avoid the pitfalls of either Platonism or extreme Platonism, he will be wise to adopt (I3). One who adopts (I3) in this spirit may be called an "empiricist." At least, that is one reasonable specification of that overworked word. With respect to (I4) the realist is free to choose. His choice, if he knows what he is about, will depend on the position he takes in the analytic-synthetic controversy.

If I am right, then I have already solved the task I set myself. One need not reject the common-sense core of nominalism in order to hold that universals exist. The nominalist thinks that one must. It remains to exhibit the anatomy of his belief. To do that one must keep two things in mind. One is that the nominalist is mesmerized by his desire to prevent universals from flying off into Plato's heaven. The other is that the nominalist, as I portray him, fails to distinguish the four meanings of "independent."

There is indeed a sense in which only individuals are independent, namely (I2). This gives the nominalist his start. Yet a clever nominalist is fully aware that universals are in some sense presented to us. Thus he puts them in his individuals, which become, therefore, qualitied things. In this fateful move he receives aid and comfort from (I4). To see that, one merely has to consider that to speak of a qualitied thing is to speak of a fact, namely, of a thing having a quality. At this point, therefore, the nominalist takes advantage of all the verbal suggestions contained in such phrases as "standing alone" and "needing no support." If one wonders whether in thus attributing to the nominalist an implicit fact ontology I am not going too far, I would say this. On the one hand, a consistent nominalist must deny that the "is" in (a) and (b) is the *is* of non-diversity. On the other hand, he must maintain that (a) and (b) refer to two things rather than to two facts. If one now wonders that so awkward a predicament was not noticed for so long, I reply that the spurious doctrine of common names may well have kept one from noticing it. After all, nominalism has a distinguished history.

I should like to close by answering a general objection that may be raised against this paper. The objector, I imagine, calls my explications arbitrary. Why, for instance, select (I1), rather than (I4), for the explication of the philosophical proposition that what exists is independent (I)? My answer is two-fold. First, if one says that what exists is independent, he uses "exist" as well as "independent" philosophically. Such uses, just as those which some call ordinary, have their context. I believe I have shown that the context which most closely relates "existence" and "independence" is (I1). Second, if a philosopher wishes to use his words so that facts and only facts exist because they and they alone are independent in the sense of (I4), he may surely do so. All we may expect from him is that he tell us exactly how he uses "independent." Once such explications are given and the distinctions made, what is there left to argue about?

II. BARE PARTICULARS *

Edwin B. Allaire

Consider 'this is red', asserted truly of a colored disc. Some philosophers claim that the sentence refers to a fact consisting of two (kinds of) entities, an individual (bare particular) and a character (universal), referred to by 'this' and 'red', respectively. They claim further that the two entities stand in the exemplification relation, represented by 'is'. Currently, that claim is widely rejected. Underlying the many arguments supporting that rejection is a rather simple idea which Russell once expressed.[1]

One is tempted to regard "This is red" as a subject-predicate proposition; but if one does so, one finds that "this" becomes a substance, an unknowable something in which predicates inhere . . . .

Though awkwardly expressed, Russell's point is clear: The individual-character analysis is at odds with the empirical tradition. That is, if one claims that 'this is red' is a subject-predicate proposition *in the sense that 'this' and 'red' refer to unanalyzable entities of different ontological kinds*, then one has violated the Principle of Acquaintance (PA),[2] a basic tenet of empiricism. One is not acquainted with "a something" which could be construed as an entity of a kind different from red, except in the sense that *this* is a "collection" of the same kind of things as red; e.g., square and bright. The heart of Russell's point is thus that the individuals of the individual-character analysis are unknowable in the sense that one is not directly acquainted with them.

I propose to explore whether or not one can propound the individual-character analysis without abandoning the PA. In particular, I want to

* *Philosophical Studies*, 14, 1963, 1–8. Reprinted by permission.

[1] Bertrand Russell, *An Inquiry into Meaning and Truth* (George Allen and Unwin Ltd., 1948), p. 97.

[2] The PA states that the indefinable terms of any "ontological" description must refer to entities with which one is directly acquainted. Furthermore, "an unanalyzable entity" is explicated to mean an entity represented by an indefinable term.

discuss Bergmann's assertion [3] that "being acquainted with a red spot, and nothing else, one is presented not with just one thing but two, a particular .... and a character ...." If I understand Bergmann, he is maintaining precisely what Russell denies; namely, that one is on such occasions acquainted with an individual or, as he prefers to call it, a particular. His motivation is clear. He attempts to reconcile the individual-character analysis with the PA.

Before discussing his attempt it will be helpful to examine the dialectics which give rise to the problem. I will do that by commenting briefly on two other analyses of the disc.

(I) The disc is a collection of what has sometimes been called "perfect particulars." 'This is red', asserted truly of our disc, is analyzed as follows: 'this' refers to a collection of entities, one of which is referred to by 'red'. This latter entity is such that if there were two red discs, there would be two such entities (perfect particulars), each unanalyzable and numerically different from each other. (II) The disc is a collection of characters (universals). 'This is red' is analyzed as in (I), except that the entities are such that if there were two red discs, the two collections would have one member in common, i.e., one member which is literally the same.

Each of these analyses encounters an immediate and, I believe, insurmountable objection. Consider two discs of the same (shade of) color, size, shape and so on. The objection to (I) is that it *cannot account for the sameness* of the discs since the members of the two collections are all unanalyzable and different from each other. In other words, though both collections contain a member referred to by 'red', (I) provides nothing they have in common since the members are unanalyzable as well as different. The objection to (II) is that it *cannot account for the difference,* since each collection has literally the same members.[4]

The individual-character analysis encounters neither objection. That is its strength. The difference of the discs is accounted for by each containing a different individual; the sameness, by each containing literally the same characters (as in (II)). The individual-character analysis thus allows one to solve the problems of sameness and difference, at least as they arise in connection with "things."

---

[3] Gustav Bergmann, "Strawson's Ontology," *The Journal of Philosophy,* 57, 1960, p. 616.
[4] Cf. Gustav Bergmann, "Russell on Particulars," *The Philosophical Review,* 56, 1947, 59–72. Reprinted in *The Metaphysics of Logical Positivism* (Longmans, Green and Co., Inc., 1954), pp. 197–214.

Speaking more traditionally, it provides a solution to the nominalism-realism issue.

Notice that a proponent of the individual-character analysis, or, as I shall henceforth call him, a realist, explicitly *grounds* (by means of entities) the sameness as well as the difference of the two discs. There must be entities to account for the discs being called the same, or less accurately, there must be a shared something in order to account for the same word ('red') being truly predicated of 'this' and 'that'. The objection to (I) is in fact sometimes expressed as follows. Since the two red entities of the two collections are different and unanalyzable, there is no way of accounting for their being referred to by the same word ('red'). So expressed the objection is misleading. Moreover, it tempts a defender of (I) to appeal mistakenly to a variant of the meaning-is-use doctrine.

The demand for grounding sameness is at present suspect. The suspicion makes (I) seem attractive. Consider two discs of *different shades* of red. In ordinary language, 'red' may be correctly used to refer to either. It appears that a realist, to be consistent, must also ground the sameness of the different shades. For, if he objects to (I) because it does not explain why the same word is used to refer to two "perfect particulars," he must take seriously the same objection in the case of 'red' when applied to different shades. Moreover, since each shade is simple and unanalyzable the ground (i.e., the shared entity) must be of a different kind. Thus, a third kind makes its appearance. For those of a Platonic stripe, this third is a "transcendent universal or concept." [5] Each shade is red in virtue of *participating* in the same transcendent universal, which is the proper referent of 'red'. Hence, either the PA cannot be maintained or we must be acquainted with ("intuit") concepts. The second alternative has been unacceptable to those who embrace the PA.

The realist thus seems doomed to Platonism. The proponent of (I) who denies the need for grounding sameness does not. This seeming advantage has had its effects. Recently, it has been argued that the root of Platonism is the mistaken way in which we sometimes look at language. In particular, the very attempt to ground sameness reveals the mistaken belief that there must be *a* referent to justify the use of a word. Not even the "referring use" of a word requires *a* referent, or so it is argued. What holds in general holds for 'red'. Hence, its use in

---

[5] For a discussion of concepts, see Reinhardt Grossmann, "Conceptualism," *The Review of Metaphysics*, 14, 1960, 243–254 and also pp. 40–49 of this book.

referring to different shades need not be grounded. Thus, we are told, "the sameness of the shades" merely means that they are referred to by the *same* word. Moreover, it is claimed, even in the case of things of the same shade, each exemplification of it is really different and unanalyzable. In other words, their sameness also consists merely in their being referred to by the same word.[6]

A defender of (I) may thus attempt to dispose of the objection that he cannot account for the sameness of "things" by arguing that the very attempt to account for it is mistaken. The attempt, he holds, inevitably leads to Platonism with all its horrors of transcendent entities. That shows why the use doctrine may be attractive to a defender of (I).

Consider again two discs of the same (shade of) color, size, shape, and so on. Suppose they are shown to you, one to the left of the other. If after a while you are shown them again, you will not be able to tell which is which. In fact, you will not be able to tell whether the two you now see are the two you saw earlier. You can only tell that the two you now see have all the properties that the two you saw earlier had. In other words, taken as such and in themselves, two perfect particulars of the same shade cannot be told from each other. That means that in this case at least the sameness is grounded. We know how the realist grounds it. It remains to be shown that he need not therefore ground the sameness of different shades in order to justify the use of 'red' for any of them.

My realist takes advantage of what the use doctrine has taught us; namely, that (a) from the fact that the same word is used to refer to two things it does not *always* follow that the two share an entity. (Indeed, we could decide to use just one word to refer to green and red.) On the other hand, it does not follow (b) that they *never* do. The proponents of (I) rashly infer (b) from (a). Their rashness, I have argued, may be due to their mistaken belief that even (b) commits one to Platonism. Some things, our two discs for example, are the same shade of color. This is not a linguistic fact; i.e., not merely the fact that they are referred to by the same word. They are the same in that they are indistinguishable as such, or, more precisely, one cannot differentiate them by their color alone.

Let us take stock. The problem of analyzing such things as colored discs arises in the context of the realism-nominalism issue. That issue,

---

[6] This explication of sameness may well explicate the *flatus-vocis* doctrine of some medievals.

we saw, cannot really be handled by accounting for the sameness in the discs in terms of the sameness of words. At *some* point sameness must be grounded in entities. To believe otherwise is to put upon the meaning-is-use doctrine a burden greater than it can bear. Thus, in our case, it remains the first task of analysis to single out the unanalyzable entities which account for the difference and the sameness of the two discs. The second task or step, as in all cases, is to employ the result obtained in the first step to explicate certain philosophical uses of words, thereby dissolving the traditional dialectics. The realistic analysis provides the required grounding. Yet, it is tainted. Like Russell, many philosophers claim that they are not acquainted with individuals. The heart of the matter is whether or not Bergmann's claim that one is in fact acquainted with individuals (bare particulars) is defensible or, even, whether it can be made intelligible.

An obvious objection is that the claim merely springs from the dialectical needs it satisfies and is not born out by a careful inspection of what is in fact presented. Indeed, Bergmann himself invites this objection.[7]

I, of course, have convinced myself that I am actually presented with two things. Yet I am loathe to rest the case on this conviction; for I am also convinced that a very major part of it is dialectical.

One cannot but wonder how one does convince oneself of such matters. In the light of what he himself says, one is indeed tempted to conclude that his conviction is dialectical rather than phenomenological, if I may so express myself. If so, then he has abandoned the PA. Whether or not under the pressure of the dialectic he has actually done that is not my concern. The point is rather whether or not the "description" he proposes can be defended independently of the dialectics.

Phenomenological description is prompted by philosophical puzzles. One turns to the former as a prelude to the dissolution of the latter. The dangers are obvious. One may think that one still describes when in fact one already argues. That makes all alleged descriptions suspect. The best one can do is elaborate them in several ways, always on guard against the various biases that might creep in. Once a description has been accepted, the puzzles must be solved by speaking commonsensically about it. In the course of thus speaking about it, one may well be led to reconsider it. After all, it was prompted by the puzzles. Nevertheless, one must not and cannot give away the game by maintaining that the description is forced upon one by the dialectics.

[7] Bergmann, "Strawson's Ontology," p. 616

Bergmann in the quoted passage comes dangerously close to doing just that. The most one could say is that the dialectics directs our attention toward what is presented. But it does not and cannot tell us what actually is presented.

A comparison may help to make the point clear. The later Wittgenstein, believing that the philosophical puzzles arise from the misuse of words, undertook to describe their correct use. The misuses are engendered by what he calls misleading grammatical analogies. Once these latter are recognized as such, the philosophical puzzles disappear. This is his basic idea. To speak as before, Wittgenstein's description of correct (and incorrect) use is the prelude to his solution of the philosophical puzzles. Are then his descriptions unbiased? There is no guarantee. Nor is it reasonable to demand one before hand. Wittgenstein's description proceeds directly from what he considers a puzzle and thus indirectly from what he considers an illicit use. Thus, the dialectics may have influenced the description. But once more, the best one can do is guard against the biases that may have been introduced. So, too, with phenomenological description. In this regard all philosophers are in the same boat. They all start from what they consider unproblematical or, as it is sometimes put, from what they hold to be commonsensical. With respect to their starting point they must always be vigilant. Once cannot do more; one must not do less.

I return to the issue: Can the realistic analysis be defended on phenomenological grounds? It will be well to distinguish between two uses of 'know'. First, there is the use of 'know' in which to know something means to be acquainted with it. Second, there is the use in which to know somethings means to be able to recognize it. In the second sense individuals as such or in themselves are unknowable. Consider again the two discs and the situation in which you are shown them twice. Since you can only tell that the two you now see have all the properties that the two you saw earlier had, it follows that if each consists of an individual and the several characters it exemplifies, the individuals as such or in themselves are not recognizable or, as I prefer to say, not reidentifiable. The characters are. To express the point differently, two individuals are merely numerically different whereas two characters are intrinsically different as well.

Russell held that individuals are unknowable. A defender of the realistic analysis may take him to have held merely that they are not recognizable, i.e., that they cannot be known in the second sense of 'know'. This, though, is not at all what Russell meant. Rather, in saying that individuals are unknowable, he used 'know' in the first sense. In turn, I hold with Bergmann that while they are indeed unknowable in the second sense they are known in the first. Accordingly, I cannot get away with just maintaining that they are merely numerically different. I must show in what sense one is acquainted with them. Not to recognize this obligation would be to confuse again the two uses of 'know'. Nevertheless, in pointing out that individuals are not recognizable, i.e., are merely numerically different, one has arrived at the heart of the matter. *Individuals are just those entities which do ground the numerical difference of two things which are the same in all (nonrelational) respects.*

Consider once more the two discs. When presented together, they are presented as numerically different. *That difference is presented* as is their sameness with respect to shape, (shade of) color, and so on. What accounts for that difference are the numerically different individuals. No character, nor group of characters can do that. Thus, to say that there are individuals is to say that things may be merely numerically different. No matter what description one proposes, the numerical difference of two things which are alike in all (nonrelational) respects must be accounted for. Consider (II). To claim that both discs are but collections of literally the same universals, does not account for the *thisness* and *thatness* which are implicitly referred to in speaking of them as *two* collections. That is, the two collections of characters – if one persists in speaking that way – are, as presented, numerically different. Clearly, therefore, something other than a character must also be presented. That something is what proponents of the realistic analysis call a bare particular. Or, perhaps better, that is their explication of 'bare particular'.

One difficulty remains. Bergmann claims that in being presented with one red spot one is presented with two things. That may be misleading. The most prevalent use of 'two' carries a spatial connotation. That is, if there are two things then they are spatially related. Yet, exemplification, the "relation" obtaining between a character and an individual, is obviously not spatial. Thus, the sense in which there are two things is merely the sense in which there are two characters (red and square) in the presentation of a red square. For, red and square are not spatially related. Nor is an individual and the character or characters it exemplifies. If one should insist that the two characters are in fact spatially related, arguing that they are *at the same place*, I merely ask him what he means by 'place'. There is only one answer I can think of which would help. A *place* as such is itself an entity. But, then, this answer makes places into bare particulars. This piece of dialectics is well known.

Consider again 'this is red', asserted truly of a colored disc. To what does 'this' refer? That it does refer to something is obvious. Nor does it always refer to the entity referred to by 'red'. That is, 'is' in this utterance does not always stand for identity. Hence, 'this' can only refer to one of two things; an individual or a collection of characters, one of which is red.[8] We know already that the latter alternative fails. For, in the case of *two* collections of characters the members of which are the same, the numerical difference of the two collections is left unaccounted for. The realistic analysis does account for it. Moreover, two individuals are presented in the sense that the two collections are presented as numerically different. That is not to deny though that individuals are *merely* numerically different from each other and thus not reidentifiable as such. That they are explains why they have been overlooked so often.

I have argued that one can propound a realistic analysis without abandoning the PA. Moreover, one can single out the bare particulars without using 'exist' philosophically, thus avoiding the dialectics of the nominalism-realism issue. In trying to do this, I described, or tried to describe, the sort of entity an individual is. Positively, individuals are the carriers of numerical difference as directly presented to us. Negatively, individuals are not rudimentary Aristotelian substances. Thus, they are not the sort of things Russell probably had in mind when he denied that they can be known. To the sort of thing he had in mind Locke's phrase, "a something I know not what," does indeed apply. To what I mean by an individual, it does not. To one who accepts the PA, Locke's phrase provides sufficient ground for rejecting the entities he speaks of. The individuals I want to keep from being overlooked are not such entities. That is why one need not abandon the PA in order to maintain that we are presented with bare particulars.

---

[8] As I have shown, the "perfect-particular" analysis (i.e., (I)) is unacceptable because it does not account for sameness.

III. ELEMENTARISM, INDEPENDENCE, AND ONTOLOGY *

HERBERT HOCHBERG

Elementarism is the thesis that all undefined predicates of an improved (ideal) language are of the first type.[1] Some philosophers adhere to an explication of ontology, (O_1), whereby the answer to the question "What exists?" is provided by the referents of the undefined descriptive (non-logical) terms of one's (implicit or explicit) ideal language. Proponents of (O_1) would then take the thesis of elementarism to assert the nonexistence of properties of properties. Recently Professor Bergmann has claimed that "the only philosophical reasons which one could with some plausibility adduce in favor of elementarism, or, rather, the only such reasons I can think of, are specious."[2] To produce philosophical reasons for a claim is, in Bergmann's terms, to show that it follows from one or several philosophical principles by themselves or in conjunction with commonsensical truths. "To accept a proposition as a principle is to refuse to defend it directly and to argue instead, first, that the things it mentions are all commonsensical, and, second, that without accepting it one cannot solve all the philosophical problems." The philosophical principle that Bergmann holds to be speciously involved in proofs of elementarism is the principle of acquaintance – the contention that all undefined descriptive constants of an improved language must refer to things with which we are directly acquainted. I shall not, in this paper, be concerned with the "specious" use of this principle that Bergmann argues against. What I shall try to show is that (1) a closely related principle supplies what may be considered a

---

* *Philosophical Studies*, 12, 1961, 36–43. Reprinted by permission.
[1] For discussions of elementarism see J. Weinberg, "Concerning Undefined Descriptive Predicates of Higher Level," *Mind*, 53, 1954, 338–344; G. Bergmann, "Elementarism," *Philosophy and Phenomenological Research*, 18, 1957, 107–114; L. Palmieri, "Higher Level Descriptive Predicates," *Mind*, 54, 1955, 544–547, and "Second Level Descriptive Predicates," *Philosophy and Phenomenological Research*, 16, 1956, 505–511); H. Hochberg, "Professor Storer on Empiricism," *Philosophical Studies*, 5, 1954, 29–31), and " 'Possible' and Logical Absolutism," *Philosophical Studies*, 6, 1955, 74–77.
[2] Bergmann, p. 108

reason for accepting the elementaristic thesis; (2) these considerations, in turn, may lead one to hold that O_1, by itself, does not provide an adequate basis for the explication of ontology; (3) these same considerations connect the elementaristic thesis with (a) the view that relations do not exist, (b) fact ontologies, and (c) nominalism.

I shall use the phrase "principle of exemplification," hereafter PE, for the two-part requirement (1) that all undefined descriptive predicates of an improved language, L, refer to characters that have been exemplified at least once and (2) that every particular named by a proper name of L has at least one primitive non-relational descriptive property. PE is thus a rule guiding the interpretation of L. A sentence will be called "syntactically atomic" if it contains no defined signs and no logical signs (connectives, operators, variables). Thus a syntactically atomic statement is of the form '---(...)' where '---' stands for an undefined predicate term and '...' stands for the subject term(s) (undefined predicate(s) or proper name(s)) of an appropriate type. A syntactically atomic statement S will be called "independent" if given that S is meaningful and true it does not follow from the rules for interpreting L that any other statement which is not a logical consequence of S is meaningful and true. A state of affairs is *atomic* if it is referred to by a sentence that is *independent*.

Let L be a phenomenalistic language. This means that the undefined signs of L name phenomenal entities and properties of such. L then contains independent sentences. For example, let '$^1f_1$' be an undefined first-level (non-relational) predicate and 'a' be a proper name of L. The sentence (α) '$^1f_1(a)$' is an independent sentence. Hence, the state of affairs it refers to is atomic. Where '$^2\phi_1$' is an undefined second-level (non-relational) predicate, the sentence (β) '$^2\phi_1(^1f_1)$' is syntactically atomic. But it is not independent and hence it does not refer to an atomic state of affairs. We can see why it is not independent in two ways – the second may be considered a specific case of the first. (I) For (β) to be meaningful and true PE requires that a sentence like (α) be true. For, in order for (β) to be meaningful '$^1f_1$' must be, and for this to be the case '$^1f_1$' must refer to a character that has been exemplified at least once. Hence there must be (have been) some particular such that a sentence like (α) is true. To put it another way, if one who coordinates statements of L to somebody's contents now coordinates '$^2\phi_1(^1f_1)$', then he either has, or could have, coordinated '$^1f_1(a)$' to an earlier content of that subject. To put it still differently, if what (β) asserts is the case then so is (was) what a sentence like (α) asserts. The acceptance of PE as a principle guiding the interpretation of an ideal language thus implies that (β) is not independent and hence the state of affairs to which it refers is not atomic. This, in turn, points up that a sentence's being syntactically atomic does not ensure that it is independent. (II) Essentially the same point is involved in a more specific form of the argument. Les '$^2\phi_1$' and '$^1f_1$' both first be presented to a subject *at the same time* and such that '$^1f_1$' exemplifies '$^2\phi_1$.' Then there must also be, by PE, an individual that is simultaneously presented and which exemplifies '$^1f_1$.' Hence, we know that if the state of affairs represented by (β) occurs, then, at the same time, so does one represented by, say, (α). Hence, (β) is not independent. Its not being independent provides, I suggest, one of the sources of the rejection of undefined second-level descriptive predicates by those who accept PE, O_1, and logical atomism. Logical atomism, whatever else it implies, has, I believe, implicitly involved the view, (A), that syntactically atomic sentences refer to "atomic states of affairs," or, in other words, that all syntactically atomic sentences are "independent." Yet, atomic states of affairs, as characterized above, are referred to by some but not all syntactically atomic sentences. Thus, as we saw, the concepts of "independent sentence" and "syntactically atomic sentence" do not jibe, and, consequently, (A) is rejected. But rejecting (A) destroys a symmetry between an improved language and "the world" that has always appealed, if only implicitly, to logical atomists. This may be thought to weaken the atomists' case. However, there is an alternative to rejecting (A). The alternative is to reject (β), and all sentences like it, as syntactically atomic. Elementarism provides a ground for such rejection, since, upon the elementaristic thesis, all second-level descriptive predicates would be defined. This suggests that logical atomism provides a "reason" for elementarism. It makes explicit what may have implicitly led some logical atomists to propose elementarism.

But this is not the whole story. Before proceeding three points should be noted about the argument that (β) is not independent. First, the connection between (β) and a sentence like (α) is not the result of an empirical law about phenomena and their properties. It follows, so to speak, from a "principle" of one's philosophy, PE – what, in a more traditional manner, might be called a metaphysical principle. Second, the connection between (β) and (α) is not that of logical implication. Neither (β) nor (α) logically implies the other, since neither '$^1f_1(a)$ $\supset$ $^2\phi_1(^1f_1)$' nor '$^2\phi_1(^1f_1)$ $\supset$ $^1f_1(a)$' is analytic. Rather, to repeat, from its being the case that (β) refers to a presented fact and from PE's being a principle or rule for interpreting L, it follows that what a sentence like (α) refers to is also the case. Note that in speaking of (α) and (β) I always referred to (β) "determining" a sentence *like* (α) to be true and not (α) as such. I did this because, strictly speaking, what follows from (β)'s being true and PE's being a principle or rule for interpreting L is that (γ) '($\exists$x)$^1f_1$(x)' is true. For, we only know that some particular exemplifies '$^1f_1$,' not that a does. I used (α), and the consequent awkward phrasing, to emphasize the point that if we know that the fact to which the syntactically atomic sentence (β) refers was presented then we know, by PE, that another fact, which could be referred to by a syntactically atomic sentence, was also presented. Thus, in a sense, PE may be said to "connect" facts referred to by syntactically atomic sentences. All this does not bear on (β)'s not being independent, since like (α), (γ) neither logically implies nor is implied by (β). Third, what was just said may be taken as an illustration of the point that "to follow logically" and "to follow from the rules for a language" are two notions and not one. For, from PE it follows that if (β) is true so is (γ). Yet, (γ) is not a logical consequence of (β). This shows the ambiguity of the phrase "language rule," since we may distinguish formation rules, transformation rules, and rules, like PE, which guide the interpretation of a language.

We saw that an undefined second-level predicate cannot refer to a constituent of an atomic state of affairs. This fact may lead some to hold that the existence of properties of properties is suspect. Elementarism expresses this contention. We may then consider an elementarist to implicitly assert the thesis that "to be is to be the component of an atomic state of affairs." The elementarist thus proposes an alternative explication of ontology, which we may put "linguistically" as follows: (O$_2$), to *exist is to be the referent of an undefined descriptive sign that can occur in an independent sentence*. Yet, there is a certain awkwardness in distinguishing among the undefined descriptive signs with respect to ontological significance – in asserting (O$_2$) at the expense of (O$_1$). But, in an elementaristic scheme (O$_1$) and (O$_2$) *might* amount to the same thing. For, in such a scheme only first-level predicates and proper names would be undefined descriptive signs. This, to repeat, may be thought to provide a motive and an argument for elementarism. Only in an elementaristic language *could* syntactically atomic sentences correspond to atomic facts.

Yet, even in an elementaristic language, (O$_1$) and (O$_2$) *need not* amount to the same thing. If one holds to the second part of PE, they will not. To see this consider the sentence (δ) '$^1R_2(a, b)$,' where '$^1R_2$' is a two-term relation sign of the first type and 'a' and 'b' are proper names. By the second part of PE, it follows that if (δ) is true then there must be two states of affairs referred to by sentences ascribing non-relational primitive properties to a and to b. Hence, by an argument similar to the one about (β), (δ) is not an independent sentence and, consequently, does not refer to an atomic state of affairs. Thus, on (O_2), '$^1R_2$' would not designate an existent, while on (O_1) it would; (O_2) may thus reveal a motive behind the rejection, by some, of relational properties as existents. It also establishes a connection between such rejection of relations and the similar rejection of properties of the higher types. This "ontological connection" has an interesting corollary. The Wiener-Kuratowski procedure for defining first-level relations in terms of classes involves, we recall, classes of higher types. Similarly, any attempts to define all higher type descriptive predicates in terms of first-level ones would certainly involve relational first-level predicates. This means that we seem to be forced to have either primitive relational predicates or primitive predicates of the higher types. Consequently, for one who holds to both parts of PE, some syntactically atomic sentences are not independent. Hence, (O_1) and (O_2) cannot jibe!

All this seems significant in that while (O_1) reflects one historical motif in classical ontology, *simplicity*, (O_2) reflects another, *inde-, pendence*. Some philosophers have thought of existents, in some ultimate sense, as independents. Those philosophers who propose to explicate ontology in terms of (O_1) have, I believe, ignored this other equally important theme. One strand of this theme may be thought to be reconstructed in the following: to be an independent entity is to be the referent of a sign that can occur in an independent sentence. Thus only individuals and first-level non-relational properties would be independent entities. Another strand of the explication of "independence" is reflected in the second part of PE. One might suggest that this principle expresses a basic ingredient in the concept of "individuality." For, by it, to be an individual is to be, in a sense, *independent* of the relations among individuals. The second part of PE makes that sense explicit.

One concerned with "independence" might point out that in yet another sense no component of an atomic fact is "independent." For, PE, party biculars *require* properties and vice versa. No particular is presented "bare" and no quality is presented unexemplified. This could lead one to hold that the only candidates for truly "independent" existents would be the referents of independent sentences – atomic facts. Such a one might then propose a further explication of ontology, (O_3), "to be is to be the referent of an independent sentence." This brings us to the connection with a fact ontology that I mentioned above. A proponent of (O_3) may then contend that atomic facts are not only independents but simples, since independent sentences, being syntactically atomic, do not contain other sentences as parts. This point, of course, makes use of a different sense of 'simple' from that used when we say, for example, that particulars are simples. Be that as it may, for such a fact ontologist two alternatives present themselves. He may hold that all independent sentences refer. True ones refer to facts and false ones to, perhaps, "false facts." But if he holds that the referent is the meaning of an independent sentence then he is forced to hold that a sentence means different things depending on whether it is true or false. This is unpalatable. Hence, he may separate the meaning from the referent of an independent sentence. He then no longer needs false facts, and may hold that only true independent sentences refer. Thus he is forced to the second alternative. Upon it a true independent sentence would have a meaning and a referent, a false one only a meaning. The meaning of a sentence would be the same whether a sentence was true or false. Thus a fact ontology would be "complex" in that each true independent sentence would, à la Frege, involve *two entities* – a sense and a referent – or, perhaps, *a complex* entity.[3] In any case making independent sentences the key to ontological commitment abandons an ontology of "simples" in the sense in which particulars are simples. For, one may hold that proper names mean what they refer to, whereas, as we have seen, a fact ontologist is forced to abandon the identification of meaning and referent. To avoid associating a meaning and a referent with a true independent sentence a fact ontologist might suggest that true independent sentences are not the only signs or sign combinations that refer. He may hold that while there are facts there are also things. The meaning of an independent sentence is then determined by the signs that make up the sentence – by the things that make up the fact. This would acknowledge that facts are *not simples* in that they are composed of individuals and

---

[3] This discussion does not presuppose that *all* descriptive signs, or sign combinations, of an ideal language require an entity that is their meaning – only those signs (sign combinations) whose meaning is not somehow specified in terms of others.

properties. But they would not be complex in the sense of being associated with two things, or one complex thing – a meaning and a referent. Such a fact ontologist could also remind us that individuals and properties, while simples, are not independents in one of the senses we have considered. Hence, to do justice to the various motifs of simplicity and independence we have considered, he might suggest that an adequate explication of ontology should be threefold, embracing (O_1), (O_2), and (O_3). Or, to put it metaphorically, one might say that there are different levels of existence which are revealed respectively by these three explications. To insist on the use of any one to the exclusion of the others would miss an important theme in ontology. On the other hand, we note that since the classes of entities selected, respectively, by (O_1), (O_2), and (O_3) are different, there remains an irreconcilable conflict. To put it cryptically, in all the senses of those slippery terms 'simple' and 'independent', all simples are not independent and all independents are not simple.

Two further points remain to be made. First, I spoke above of a fact ontology possibly involving a complex entity – a combination of meaning and referent. I spoke this way in order to point out a connection between fact ontologies and a familiar medieval pattern. In this pattern one distinguishes the essence and existence of an object. Existents are then objects to whose essence existence has been added. The essence provides the ground for the conceptualization of the object. Similarly, we have the meaning of an independent sentence, whether it be true or false. But if it is true, there is a further "component," the referent. In a fact ontology this corresponds to the *existence* of the essence. We may also note the similarity of fact ontologies to the Aristotelian pattern, where material substances are composed of form and matter. Since forms of material objects and prime matter are not independent existents, the "simplest" "independent" material existent are composites of form and matter. Aristotle's material substances are thus "facts" compressed into "things."

Second, I mentioned a connection of this discussion with nominalism. To see this consider a hierarchy of undefined predicates of types 1 through n, '$^1f_1$,' '$^2f_1$' .... '$^nf_1$.' Given a sentence (Σ) '$^nf_1$ $(^{n-1}f_1)$,' by the argument showing (β) not to be an independent sentence, (Σ)'s being true and meaningful "implies" that a sentence of the form '$^{n-1}f_1(^{n-2}f_1)$' be true. Similarly this latter sentence's truth requires a sentence involving a predicate of the next lower type to be true, and so on. The regress continues until we arrive at a sentence with a proper name. Proper names name individuals. Hence individuals may seem to anchor the chain of syntactically atomic sentences. This may lead one to stress the ontological importance of individuals. They may even seem to be the basis for there being independent sentences. Thus the notion of an independent sentence may reveal a thread, albeit a minor one, in the complex of motives that could lead a philosopher to nominalism.

IV. PARTICULARS AND TIME

REINHARDT GROSSMANN

Some philosophers agree that there is a connection between particularity and time: Particulars are in time; universals are not. However, they disagree among themselves about the precise nature of this connection. I wish to discuss some of the problems which give rise to their disagreement.

I

Perceptual objects are *continuants*. Phenomenal objects, e.g. sensa, mental acts, and the like, are *momentary* entities. A certain perceptual object A, being a continuant, may change its color from green to red and hence be green at one time and not green at another. Obviously, this situation cannot be described by the sentence 'A is green and A is not green.' The only satisfactory description introduces time in the form of moments: 'A is green at t_1 and A is not green at t_2'.[1] If one starts the philosophical analysis with continuants, one must introduce moments in order to describe a changing thing. Put differently, a philosopher who starts out with continuants, commits himself to *absolute time*. But time is *relational*. It follows that one must start not with perceptual objects (continuants), but rather with phenomenal objects, that is, with momentary things.[2]

This argument for phenomenalism is not sound. The ontological analysis of *things* shows quite conclusively and on its own ground that (logically) proper names must name *particulars*, rather than things.[3] According to this analysis, a perceptual object A, say, a colored disk, consists of a particular *a* which exemplifies certain universals. The

---

[1] Of course, time may be introduced through tenses. But this creates ontological problems of a different sort.

[2] Compare, for example, G. Bergmann: *Meaning and Existence* (Univ. of Wisconsin Press, Madison, 1960), pp. 182–188 and pp. 230–239.

[3] Compare Essays II and V of this book.

same holds for a so-called phenomenal object, say, a colored spot in a visual field. What we ordinarily call a (perceptual or phenomenal) thing, turns out to be a complex entity, only part of which is named by the proper name 'a'. Irregardless, therefore, of whether or not perceptual and phenomenal objects are continuants, philosophical analysis starts with neither. The argument could therefore not possibly establish that it must start with phenomenal rather than perceptual objects.[4] Our criticism shows, though, that we need not consider the distinction between perceptual and phenomenal objects, in order to discuss the connection between particulars and time.

But even though it fails, the argument contains a very important point. It seems to prove conclusively that particulars must be momentary entities, if time is relational rather than absolute. To be momentary means in this connection to be changeless. Hence there is a connection between particularity and *change*: If time is relational, then particulars must be changeless. Yet, a perceptual or phenomenal object may change, even though it consists of nothing else but a particular which exemplifies certain universals. We confront here an apparent inconsistency which ontological analysis must resolve.

II

Consider then, first, a "world" without change. It consists of two simultaneous things A and B. A has the property f_1; B has the property f_2. Assume further that A and B do not exemplify any spatial relations. Taking for granted that time is relational, ontological analysis yields the following constituents: (a) Two particulars, a and b; (b) Two properties, f_1 and f_2; (c) One temporal relation; and (d), the nexus of exemplification which holds between a and f_1, b and f_2, and between a and b and the temporal relation.[5] That there are *two* particulars, accounts for there being two things. Particulars differentiate between simultaneous things *numerically*. That a exemplifies f_1, while b exemplifies f_2, accounts for the *qualitative* difference between A and B. Properties differentiate among things qualitatively.[6] Turning from what there is to how we know what there is, our *recognition* of how

[4] This is not to say, of course, that there are no arguments for phenomenalism.

[5] There are further ontological constituents which are unimportant for our purpose. Compare G. Bergmann: "Ineffability, Ontology, and Method," *The Philosophical Review*, 69, 1960, 19–40.

[6] We could have assumed that both A and B have the property f_1. In this case, there would be qualitative sameness.

many things there are, rests on our recognition of how many particulars there are (simultaneously). Similarly, our recognition of qualitative difference, rests on our recognition of properties as being different.[7]

Next, consider a "world" with change. I shall call it the second. It consists, as before, of just two things, A and B. As before, A has the property f_1, B has the property f_2, and A and B are not spatially related. However, assume that B, instead of being simultaneous with A, occurs *later than* A. Just as in the first "world," then, A and B do not change. Nevertheless, there is change in the second "world." It consists simply in the fact that one particular occurs later than another.

Consider, finally, a third "world." Assume again that there are two things, A and B. While A *lasts for some time*, B occurs to the left of A and then disappears. What philosophical view will yield a correct ontological analysis of this "world"? Let us inspect four possibilities.

I. Starting from the assumption that time is relational, one could say that A consists of several changeless particulars.[8] These particulars must be momentary, because otherwise one can give a contradictory description of this "world." Furthermore, one may hold that a particular *lasts* as long as no change occurs. If there is change, for instance, when B occurs to the left of A, then there is also a different particular.[9]

But what precisely is a changeless or momentary particular? It is clear that a particular as such cannot undergo any change. We must mean, therefore, that one and the same particular cannot *exemplify* a certain universal at one moment and not exemplify this universal at another moment. Keeping this in mind, we can distinguish three different kinds of change. First, an entity may be said to have changed, if it exemplifies at one moment the non-relational property f_1 and at another moment, does not exemplify f_1. Second, it may be said to have changed$_2$, if it exemplifies at one moment a certain spatial relation and at another moment, does not exemplify this relation. Third, it may be said to have changed$_3$, if it exemplifies at one moment a certain temporal relation and at another moment, does not exemplify this relation. Now, a changeless particular must obviously fulfil all three conditions: It must neither change$_1$, nor change$_2$, nor, finally, must it change$_3$. To see this clearly in respect to change$_3$, assume that there

[7] Recognition of what property belongs to what particular rests on the nexus.
[8] Compare Bergmann's "Duration and the Specious Present," *Philosophy of Science*, 27, 1960, 39–47.
[9] This does not necessarily mean that we can only distinguish between particulars on the basis of change. See below.

are two things which do not change their properties and which are not in space. Assume that the first thing lasts, while the second appears and disappears. Even though the first thing neither changed its properties, nor its spatial relations, we must not hold that it contained one and the same particular, *a*, while a second particular, *b*, appeared and disappeared. Otherwise, we get again a contradictory description: '*a* is earlier than *b* and *a* is not earlier than *b*.' To avoid such a contradiction, a particular must be changeless in all three senses of 'change'.

From this follows that a particular can only last, until another particular occurs. But this means that a particular cannot last at all. For, if time is relational, as we assume, then there can be no duration without the kind of change which occurs in the second "world." [10] A particular cannot last, if I may so put it, because duration is generated by the occurrence of different particulars which exemplify the temporal relation of being later than (or of being earlier than). One particular by itself cannot last for even a small length of time; and if there occurs a second particular, then there is no longer the first particular. In short, particulars must be *instanteneous* and not merely *momentary*. The first view is thus unsatisfactory, because it asserts that there are changeless particulars which have a duration.

2. The second view takes its cue from the first.[11] The latter holds, as we just saw, that a particular lasts as long as there is no change. It does not hold, however, that we can only differentiate among particulars on the basis of change. Perhaps, the recognition of different particulars is immediate and needs, therefore, no further criterion.[12] The second view denies this possibility. First, it introduces the notion of an *event*. For example, A's being f_1 or A's being to the left of B are called events. Then it claims that we can distinguish directly between different events. Finally, it asserts that temporal relations do not hold between particulars, but rather between events. Now it is argued that one must differentiate between different particulars on the basis of distinguishable events. A particular lasts, as long as "its" event lasts. For instance, distinguishing between A's being (first) green and (then) red, one must assign different particulars to these two events. A's being green would involve the particular *a*, while its being red would involve the particular *b*. Since A's being green occurs earlier than its being red, one assigns the same temporal relation to the two particulars *a* and *b*.

[10] This is one explication of the assertion that change is the measure of time.

[11] Compare F. E. Dretske: "Particulars and the Relational Theory of Time," *The Philosophical Review*, 70, 1961, 447–469.

[12] We shall see, however, that particulars are not recognizable as such.

There are two fatal objections against this analysis. First, it assumes that there can be lasting events without change. But if time is relational, then there can be no duration, unless there are at least two events, one earlier than the other. This is of course the same objection which we raised against the first view. Secondly, and more importantly, the second view asserts that particulars must be differentiated in terms of events, while it can be shown that events must be distinguished in terms of particulars. Recall, for instance, the third "world." Assume that A has the property f_1 both before and after B occurs. According to the second view, there are then at least three events, namely, A's being f_1, A's being to the right of B, and A's being (again) f_1. Furthermore, these three events are temporally related. Now, the first and second events are distinguishable in terms of the spatial relation, but there is nothing that distinguishes the first from the third event. Yet, the proponent of the second view insists that there are three events, and hence three different particulars.

It may be argued that the first event is distinguished from the third event, because it occupies a different *temporal position*.[13] But this explanation introduces absolute time; and one of the purposes of the second view is to avoid such a commitment. Moreover, if there are moments, then temporal relations will obtain between moments and not between events.

It may be thought that events can be distinguished in terms of their *temporal relations*.[14] The first and third events, for example, would be different, because one occurs before the other. But how could the occurrence of a temporal relation differentiate numerically between two events, if its occurrence presupposes that there are *two* events? If it is replied that one and the same event cannot be earlier and later than another event, say, B's being to the left of A, then the mistake becomes even more apparent. If there are indistinguishable events, then there simply are no different events. Since the first event is indistinguishable from the third event, what justifies our speaking of two events, one occurring earlier and one later than B's being to the left of A? Furthermore, if it were possible to distinguish numerically between entities on the basis of temporal relations alone, then there would be no point to the second view. One would not have to differentiate among particulars on the basis of events.

Events must therefore be distinguishable by themselves, if the

---

[13] This is what Dretske seems to claim at one point (p. 461).
[14] Perhaps this is what Dretske means on page 461.

second view is to succeed.[15] But we saw that the first event cannot be distinguished from the third. There is only one way out: These two events must be different, because they contain different particulars. But this means that events are distinguished in terms of particulars, and not conversely. The second view is unsatisfactory, because it holds that particulars are to be distinguished in terms of events.

3. The third view accepts absolute time (and absolute space). According to this view, A contains a particular which lasts through time. Time consists of moments, t_1, t_2, etc. which are ordered by the temporal relation of being later than (or of being earlier than). Notice that our objection against the lasting particulars and events of the first and second view does not apply to the particulars of this analysis. For, to say that a lasts, means now that a exists at any given moment of a compact series of moments, ordered by a temporal relation. The objection could only arise, if it were claimed that moments themselves last for some time. Notice also that no moment can be numerically the same as any other moment. Two moments, presented to us at different times, if I may so put it, are never numerically the same. This shows that the question of numerical sameness cannot arise for *instantaneous* entities. It only arises, if the entity under consideration has a duration.

According to the third view, particulars have a duration. One can therefore ask whether or not a particular presented at one moment is numerically the same as a particular presented at a different moment. One can also ask how one recognizes that one and the same particular was presented at two different moments. A brief reflection shows that the recognition of particulars cannot be immediate or direct. For, assume that you see a green disk at a certain moment. A little later, you see again such a disk. If you have no additional information, you cannot tell whether or not the two disks are numerically the same. Hence, you cannot recognize the particulars "in" the disks as being the same or different. We may express this fact by saying that particulars are not recognizable as such.[16]

However, the third view holds that the numerical sameness of *things* is to be explained in terms of the numerical sameness of *particulars*. Since we cannot establish directly that one and the same particular occurred on two different occasions, we need to go back one step further: we need a criterion by which to decide numerical sameness of particulars. Traditionally and for things, *spatial-temporal continuity* is

---

[15] This is what Dretske seems to hold at still another place.
[16] Compare Essay II of this book.

often mentioned as the criterion of numerical sameness. Can we apply this criterion to the particulars of the third view? And what precisely must we mean by spatial-temporal continuity in regard to particulars?

Two things are obvious. First, if spatial-temporal continuity is to serve as the criterion of numerical sameness for particulars, then it must be directly presented to us. It must not, in turn, depend on some other criterion. Second, spatial-temporal continuity of a particular cannot be explicated in terms of the repeated occurrence of the *same* particular. We cannot say that it obtains whenever one and the same particular occupies successive moments and places. For this would presuppose that we can recognize particulars as such.

Particulars, as we saw, differentiate numerically among simultaneous things. How many things there are at a given moment depends on how many particulars there are at that moment. How many particulars there are, though, does not depend on anything else. Hence we know directly whether or not there is at least one particular at a given moment. But since this is all we can know on the basis of particulars alone, temporal continuity of particulars must be based on this kind of knowledge and on nothing else. We say that *the* particular *a* is temporally continuous, if and only if there is *a* particular at any given moment of a compact series of moments.

The explication of spatial continuity is quite similar. We know immediately, whether or not there is *a* particular at a certain place for a compact series of moments. We also know immediately whether or not there is (successively) a particular at any given place of a compact series of places. In the first case we say that one and the same particular remained at a certain place for some time; in the second case, that one and the same particular moved from one place to another.[17]

Numerical sameness of particulars can thus be explained in terms of spatial-temporal continuity. The latter must be explicated in terms of unrecognizable particulars, compact series of moments and compact series of places. We arrive, therefore, at the following version of the third view. (1) There are moments and places. Hence, time and space are absolute rather than relative. (2) Such moments and places form compact series. Hence, there are also spatial and temporal relations. (3) There are unrecognizable particulars. (4) Numerical sameness of such particulars is defined in terms of spatial-temporal continuity. (5) There are things which "contain" particulars. (6) Numerical

---

[17] This analysis would also apply if we assume that a thing changes its nonrelational properties.

sameness of such things is defined in terms of numerical sameness of particulars.

4. The fourth view rejects absolute time and absolute space. Time consists of temporal relations among particulars; space consists of spatial relations among particulars. Particulars are thus *instantaneous* entities. They have no duration; nor do they have an extension. Since it makes no sense, as we saw, to raise the question of numerical sameness for instantaneous entities, this question cannot arise for particulars. One and the same particular cannot be presented on two different occasions. Numerical sameness of things is explained in terms of spatial-temporal continuity. The latter is explicated in terms of compact series of particulars. The explication is in all essential respects similar to the one proposed for the third view. For instance, when a certain thing moves from one place to another, then there is a compact series of particulars, ordered both by temporal and spatial relations.[18]

Compare this view with the other three. It is clear, I think, that it can account for all the facts which the third view explains. But it avoids the ontological commitment to absolute time and space. This alone should highly recommend it. Moreover, it does away with the lasting particulars of the third view. Numerical sameness of things is not explained in terms of numerical sameness of lasting particulars. Rather, it is explained directly in terms of instantaneous particulars and so-called spatial-temporal continuity. The fourth view also avoids the unacceptable notion of a lasting entity in a world in which duration must be created by a temporal relation between different entities. In this respect, it is superior to both the first and second view. I submit that the fourth view describes accurately the connection between particulars and time.

III

There is, however, one weighty objection against this conclusion which we have not so far considered. A philosopher, who accepts the so-called principle of acquaintance, may object that we are never acquainted with instantaneous entities.[19] I think that at least some versions of this objection can be met.

---

[18] It is clear, I trust, how this view applies to the third "world." However, two things should be pointed out. First, in a spatial world, there could not be just one thing. Second, it follows from this view that in the case of interrupted observation, there is no inductive or deductive argument for numerical sameness.

[19] Compare Bergmann's "Duration and the Specious Present," pp. 44-45; and Russell's *Our Knowledge of the External World* (London, 1926), p. 121.

Most philosophers who accept the principle, use 'acquainted' in such a way that we are only acquainted with phenomenal entities. They have a number of philosophical reasons for this restriction. To mention just one, the traditional philosophical problems of perception seem to require a phenomenal starting point.[20] Be that as it may, I shall give a different interpretation to the principle of acquaintance. I shall say that we are acquainted not only with *phenomenal* objects, their properties and relations, but also with *perceptual* objects and their properties and relations.[21] Are we acquainted, in this sense, with instantaneous particulars?

If the fourth view is correct, then every lasting thing consists of an *infinite* number of particulars. Now, the objection that we are not acquainted with instantaneous particulars may simply mean that we are never acquainted with such an infinite number of entities. It may be thought, for instance, that the fourth view requires that we are acquainted first with one particular, then with the next, then with the next, and so on, with infinitely many particulars. But this is not what the fourth view holds. Since such a series of particulars is *compact*, there are no two *successive* particulars. Then again, it may be objected that an infinite series of particulars must really take a "very long time" to occur. This objection rests on the wrong notion that particulars are very short-lived entities, while the fourth view holds that they are instantaneous. Finally, it may be objected that every particular must be presented in one act of acquaintance. If so, then the perception of even a very short-lived thing would require an infinite number of mental acts. But the occurrence of such an infinite number of mental acts is an impossibility. Hence, the fourth view must be false. Against this objection it must be remarked that the fourth view does not imply that only one particular can be given in one act of acquaintance. But even if the assumption were true, it does not necessarily lead to an objection. For, if mental acts themselves are particulars, then it would follow from the fourth view that an infinite number of them could occur during a very small time interval.

While these objections are directed primarily against the notion of infinitely many particulars, others concern the notion of an instantaneous particular directly. It has been argued, for example, that we cannot be acquainted with instantaneous entities, because the sen-

---

[20] I say seem, because I do not think that these problems can only be solved in this way.
[21] I distinguish here between perceptual and physical objects. Compare G. Bergmann: "Physics and Ontology," *Philosophy of Science*, 28, 1961, 1-14.

sations produced on our sense organ are not strictly instantaneous.[22] One may add, I think, that no perceptual event is strictly instantaneous either. But this argument is not to the point. It is true, of course, that a very precise clock will measure the duration of even the most short-lived sensation or perceptual event. But what it measures is physical time, while we are merely concerned with perceptual time. The argument does not prove that a perceptual event which lasts, say, one-hundredth of a second, may not be perceived as instantaneous.

There remains, finally, the objection that no object of acquaintance is instantaneous. It is not denied, however, that we are in fact acquainted with perceptual objects. But if the fourth view is correct, then every acquaintance with a perceptual object constitutes an acquaintance with instantaneous particulars. In other words, an appeal to what we are in fact acquainted with, namely, phenomenal and perceptual objects, cannot possibly prove the fourth view wrong. This leads us to the last possibility. It may be claimed that in order to be acquainted with an entity, one must be acquainted with it in *isolation*. If it is also granted that all objects of acquaintance last for some phenomenal time, then it would follow that we are not acquainted with instantaneous particulars. But notice that the principle of acquaintance has been changed in a very important way. A philosopher who accepts this change, could no longer hold, for instance, that we are acquainted with any particulars, be they instantaneous or not, unless he is willing to concede that particulars can be presented which do not exemplify universals. If the particulars with which we are acquainted always exemplify universals, then they are never given in isolation; hence they are not given at all, if the modification of the principle of acquaintance is accepted. I think that few, if any, philosophers who accept the principle of acquaintance, would also accept the modification mentioned above.

---

[22] See Russell, *op. cit.*, p. 121

V. CONCEPTUALISM*

REINHARDT GROSSMANN

There can be no doubt that one is acquainted in perception with red things rather than redness alone. Nor can there be any doubt that one can name things with which one is acquainted. Each of these two facts forms the commonsensical background for an ontological criterion. According to the first criterion, what exists is what can be presented in perception independently of other things. Call this the *independence-criterion*.[1] According to the second, what exists is what can be named. Call this the *naming-criterion*.

Consider a visual field containing two red spots of the same shade of red. At least two sentences are true of it, namely, "this is red" and "that is red." Any satisfactory ontological analysis of this visual field must therefore do justice to the two facts that (a) there are two spots and not merely one; and (b), that these two spots nevertheless have something in common.

The realist gives the following description. He calls each of the two red spots a *fact*. Each fact is said to consist of two things, namely, an *individual* and a *property*. The individuals are named by "this" and "that," respectively. The property is named by "red." The two individuals are said to *exemplify* the same property. The realist thus counts three things altogether, namely, two individuals, which account for there being two spots, and one property, which accounts for the sameness in regard to color. This description forces the realist to repudiate the independence-criterion; for one cannot of course be acquainted either with a "bare" individual or with an unexemplified property. The realist accepts the naming-criterion instead. Upon his account, "this," "that," and "red" are names, and as such name existents. Notice, however, that in rejecting the independence-

---

* *The Review of Metaphysics*, 14, 1960, 243–254. Reprinted by permission.
[1] For an excellent analysis of the independence-criterion and its importance for the realism nomalism issue see Edwin B. Allaire, "Existence, Independence, and Universals," *The Philosophical Review*, 69, 1960, 485–496 and also pp. 3–13 of this book.

criterion, the realist has not denied the obvious *fact* that one is never presented either with individuals or with properties in isolation. This is as it should be.

The nominalist clings to the independence-criterion. He insists that the visual field contains only two existents, namely the two red spots; for they and only they are of a kind that can be presented independently. But this cannot be the whole of his account. To complete it, he must somehow also account for the two spots sharing the same property. There are three possible ways of doing that.

First. The nominalist may hold that "this" and "that" name the two red spots. Then he will also distinguish between so-called *proper names* and *common names.* "This" and "that" are (serve as) proper names; "red" is a common name. Hence, in "this is red" and "that is red," "this" and "that" name the two spots properly, while "red" names them both commonly. This analysis creates an insoluble problem. For, now the nominalist cannot account for the "is" in "this is red" and "that is red." Or, rather, the only plausible meaning he can assign to it is that of identity. And this will not do; for then it would follow from "this is red" and "that is red" that *this* and *that* are identical, that is, that there is only one spot and not two. Thus, upon the doctrine of common names, the nominalist may base his ontology on the independence-criterion, but only at the price of creating for himself a problem that seems to have no solution. The second possible version of nominalism is designed to avoid this impasse.

Second. A nominalist may conceive of the "is" as expressing a *part-whole relation.* He translates "this is red" and "that is red" into "this is part of red" and "that is part of red," respectively. In answer to the question what "red" refers to, he tells us that it refers to a *whole* composed of all the red things in the world.

This account, too, is unsatisfactory. As Quine has pointed out, it does not work for all properties.[2] Moreover, it provides no answer to the question as to what there is in or about the two spots that justifies our saying that both belong to the same whole. Spread out as this peculiar whole is through space and time, we obviously cannot first look at it in order to judge that *this* and *that* are among its parts.[3] It appears, then, that this analysis, far from yielding an ontology less populous than the realist's, actually adds to it. For, in addition to the

[2] Cf. Quine, *From a Logical Point of View* (Cambridge, 1953), pp. 72–73.
[3] Compare, for instance, I. M. Bochenski, "The Problem of Universals," in *The Problem of Universals* (Notre Dame, 1956), p. 47.

referents of "this" and "that" and whatever else there must be to justify our saying that both *this* and *that* belong to the same whole, there is now, as a fourth entity, the whole itself.

Be that as it may, it is worth noticing that a proponent of the second way will have to reinterpret the independence-criterion somehow. It is hard to imagine how this could be done. Red, conceived as the whole in question, is not and cannot be presented in perception. Hence, by the independence-criterion, it does not exist. Yet, all the "parts" of this "whole" exist. Hence, so does the whole. Or one would have to be prepared to use "exist," "part," and "whole" so that existent parts can jointly make up a nonexistent whole. Furthermore, if "red" is taken to be the proper name of an existent "whole," what distinguishes this kind of nominalism from realism? Why, in other words, should anyone think that this account is preferable to the realist's? The answer lies in a third important criterion of existence. According to this criterion, what exists is what is localized in space and time. Call it the *localization-criterion*. Conceived as a whole composed of all red things, red may reasonably be held to be so localized; conceived as a property, as the realist does, it cannot. This consideration suggests that the second way primarily appeals to those philosophers who reject properties (universals) because they are either explicitly or implicitly guided by the localization-criterion. However, we saw that this way, too, is unsatisfactory. This brings us to the third and last possibility.

Third. Conceiving of the "is" in "this is red" and "that is red" once more as expressing a part-whole relation, a nominalist could attempt to read the two sentences as "red is part of this" and "red is part of that," respectively. What, on this interpretation, is the referent of "red?"

If "red" is taken to be a (proper) name of a part of *this* and *that*, then it follows from the naming-criterion that red exists. In order to avoid this (to him) undesirable consequence, the nominalist who has taken the third way might try to fall back on the common-name doctrine, suggesting that "red" is a common rather than proper name. Unfortunately, in this context the suggestion makes absolutely no sense. For, if "red" is taken to be a common name, what would it be the common name of? Surely, it could not possibly be the common name of *this* and *that*, because then it would no longer make sense to say that red is "part of" *this* and *that*. Nor would it make sense to say that "red" is the common name of all red parts, because things that have common names also do or may have proper names. And what would be the proper name of this red part, i.e., the red part of *this*? Any possible answer to *this* question merely leads back to our *original* question, namely, as to how to account for the "sameness" in two numerically different things. Hence, there is upon the third way no possibility of taking "red" to be a common name. At this point the thoughtful nominalist can do one thing and one thing only. He must hold that "red" is a proper name, while at the same time rejecting the naming-criterion. "Red" can then be said to name properly without having to name an existent. Now, it seems, the nominalist can satisfactorily describe our paradigm of the two red spots without sacrificing the independence-criterion.

Thus we see that of the three ways only one, the third, is *prima facie* viable. In pursuing this way a bit further, we shall be able to uncover a serious shortcoming of the nominalist's position, and also prepare the ground for a discussion of conceptualism.

If "red," upon the nominalist's ontological analysis, turns out to be a name, then it must name something. In other words, though it be granted that "red" does not name an existent, it nevertheless must be the name of something. What, then, can the nominalist say about the ontological status of the thing named by "red"? Again, there is only one way out. The nominalist who has chosen the third way must admit that there are, ontologically speaking, things which do not exist. Or, in traditional terms, he must distinguish between *subsistents* and *existents*.

The realist, though for entirely different reasons, must make the same distinction. To understand why this is so, consider a visual field containing two spots as before, but assume that only one of the two is red, while the other is green. The realist can of course account for there being two spots; and he can also account for there being two properties. But he cannot as yet account for the fact that *this* rather than *that* is green, or, for that matter, for the fact that neither individual is both red and green. Somehow he must find the right individual together with the right property. Moreover, his finding them together must be grounded in what he sees, that is, in what is presented to him in the visual field. Consequently, the realist claims that he is not merely presented with two individuals and two properties, unconnected as it were, but also with this individual *exemplifying* red and that individual *exemplifying* green. In short, he asserts that he is also presented with the nexus of exemplification. This nexus, though, is not named. Or, rather, any attempt to name it is futile. Hence it follows upon the naming-criterion that the nexus of exemplification is not an existent. Yet, the realist will admit that he is presented with it. This leads him to say that the nexus of exemplification subsists.[4]

As far as the ontological dichotomy between existents and subsistents is concerned, we have found no difference between the nominalist on the one hand and the realist on the other. Both must make the distinction. However, each of them draws the line between these two ontological modes at a different place. The realist holds that properties exist, while the nexus of exemplification merely subsists; the nominalist asserts that properties merely subsist, while wholes (facts) exist. A shortcoming peculiar to the nominalistic analysis appears only when one asks whether or not the part-whole relation itself is somehow presented when one sees that, say, red is part of *this*. Usually and not surprisingly at all, the nominalist does not even raise this question. For, he obviously need not worry, as the realist must, as to how several *existents* stick together to form a whole. Yet, we saw, the nominalist does (or, at least, consistently must) talk about *subsistent* parts of wholes. This kind of talk eventually forces him to furnish an explication of the ontological status of the part-whole relation. His not facing the issue constitutes the shortcoming I just spoke of. In other words, as long as the nominalist does not secure some ontological status for the part-whole relation, the realist's analysis remains the only complete alternative.

It may be replied that only a small addition is needed to complete the nominalist's account. The nominalist could simply add that the part-whole relation subsists along with what he calls parts of wholes. This would not only complete his account, it would also be consistent with his insistence that universals, that is, properties and *relations*, merely subsist. Furthermore, he could consistently hold, with the realist, that the so-called partwhole "relation" is not really a relation in the ordinary sense, but, rather, a nexus, distinguished from "ordinary" relations by the circumstance that it cannot be named except at the price of futility. But notice, first, that this step does away with all the intuitive meaning we commonly attach to the terms "part," "whole," and "part-whole relation." Notice, secondly, that if the nominalist's account is completed in this way, properties (parts)

---

[4] Concerning the futility of naming exemplification and its connection with the famous Bradley paradox, see G. Bergmann, "Ineffability, Ontology, and Method," *The Philosophical Review*, 69, 1960, 19–40. As far as I know, Bergmann is the first in his tradition and, also, the only contemporary analyst who recognizes the need to "ontologize logic." See also what is said below about the status of being-part-of and falling-under.

belong to the same ontological mode as the nexus which binds them into wholes. This consequence is repugnant to those who insist on a distinction between the "descriptive" nature of "ordinary" relations and properties on the one hand and the "logical" nature of the nexus on the other.

These considerations notwithstanding, let us assume that, following the third way, the thoughtful nominalist gives ontological status to the part-whole relation by acknowledging that it subsists. A final comparison between his and the realist's view yields three similarities and three differences. (1) Both distinguish between subsistents and existents. (2) Both agree that a certain subsistent nexus is presented. (3) Both acknowledge that "red" names an instance of an ontological kind. (1') The realist recognizes two kinds of existent and one kind of subsistent, while the nominalist recognizes only one kind of existent and two kinds of subsistent.[5] (2') Accepting the naming-criterion, the realist asserts that properties exist, while the nominalist, guided by the independence-criterion, insists that they merely subsist. (3') The realist holds that bare individuals exist, although he agrees that they are never presented in isolation, while the nominalist does not accept them at all, either as existents or as subsistents. The basic difference, I submit, is (3'). For, (1') is merely a corollary of (2'); and (2') rests solely on what might be regarded the arbitrary decision of the nominalist to preserve the independence-criterion in face of the fact that properties must be named. But even (3'), it can be argued, is not really a decisive difference. For, as I shall not here show, the nominalist in his analysis of space and time eventually has to introduce some version or equivalent of the realist's bare individuals in the form of bare places in space and bare moments in time. And, surely, if bare individuals must be condemned as unintelligible, the same goes for bare places and bare moments. Be that as it may, the most important point to note is that the difference (2') flows essentially from the acceptance of two different kinds or modes of existence. Conceptualism, as I shall use the term, constitutes a radical attempt to widen the gap between these two modes i.e., between existing individuals on the one hand and subsisting properties on the other.

The conceptualist notes first that both realists and nominalists speak of being presented with things in perception. Then he asks: What does

---

[5] In respect to N. Goodman's nominalism of his *The Structure of Appearance*, it could be said that his two subsistents are the two (undefined) relations of *overlapping* and *being affiliated*.

it really mean to be so presented with, say, red? The nominalist, who asserts that "red" names a part of *this*, would undoubtedly also agree that there are other red things (of the same shade) and that "red" names parts of these things. Is it not then evident that in perceiving this red spot, I am only perceiving this (red) part and not all (red) parts named by "red"? If so, is it not also evident that what "red" names can never be completely presented in perception? The conceptualist is convinced by this argument. To the realist, he directs the following question. You say that "red" names a property of this individual, and you admit, of course, that other individuals have the same property. Now, while I am presented with this red spot, I am not also presented with all others. How then can the property be completely presented in this red spot? From these rhetorical questions my conceptualist draws the conclusion that whatever "red" may name, and he does agree that it names something, cannot be completely presented in the perception of one red thing. To speak traditionally, perception (*Anschauung*) can only present us with the "particular"; it is thought (*Denken*) that presents us with the "general."

The realist holds the conceptualist's conclusion to be unwarranted, pointing out that the latter fails to make a crucial distinction. Both individuals and properties are "wholly presented" in perception. Nor is there any difference in the way they are presented. The only difference is that while the (momentary) individual is also "wholly contained" in the perceptual field, the (timeless) property is not. This difference, my realist continues, is neither, epistemologically, one between ways of presentation nor, ontologically, one between modes of "existence." Rather, it is grounded in the way time, which roughly speaking is itself an existent, enters into the structure of the world. The conceptualist retorts to all this that he simply cannot understand any other sense of "being presented in perception" than that in which *this* (the red spot, the whole) is presented. In short, he denies that in perception one can be presented with anything but a particular *this*.[6]

Historically speaking, the conceptualist has much of the recent tradition on his side. According to this strand of the tradition, predication (*Urteilen*) rests on simple awareness (*Vorstellung* or *Anschauung*).

---

[6] The realist of this paragraph is Gustav Bergmann. See his essay on "Elementarism" (reprinted in *Meaning and Existence*, The University of Wisconsin Press, 1959). Nor is this the only way in which his defense of realism benefits from his analysis of time. In his review of Strawson's *Individuals* he explains the impact of another fundamental gambit. Upon one view we "know" what has been "presented" to us. Upon the other, we "know" it only if we can recognize it if it is presented to us again. We do so recognize properties but not of course, "bare" individuals. That shows the impact.

For example, the so-called judgment expressed by "this is red" is said to be based on the simple awareness (*Anschauung*) of *this*, or, perhaps, on the simple awareness that *this is* (*exists*). Notice how well this fits in with the conceptualist's fundamental contention. What one is directly aware of is always a *this*. What is directly presented in perception is an undifferentiated whole. Predication is therefore, according to this strand of the tradition, a function of thought, not of perception. To predicate a universal of something is to transcend whatever is presented in perception, letting the mind go to work on what is so presented. Or, to say the same thing more precisely, in predication the mind "subsumes" a *this* under a *concept*. This is the root of the conceptualist's view that *predication involves concepts rather than properties*.

Nor is this all. The conceptualist draws aid and comfort from another classical consideration. If perception presents merely a particular *this*, then it is hard to see how one could possibly communicate about it. Knowledge, however, is undoubtedly communicable. Knowledge can therefore not possibly reside in perception. Rather, it must be expressed in predication or judgment. And since predication is already presumed by the conceptualist to be a matter of concepts, so must be knowledge. Concepts, therefore, and not properties, accounts for the possibility of communication and knowledge.

So far I have emphasized the conceptualist's point of view as well as the traditional roads leading to it. Now I shall ask whether the realist can answer the criticism which is implicitly contained in conceptualism. Specifically, can the realist account for how in perception one is presented not with a *this*, but, rather, with an individual, a property, and exemplification? I think that he can. But the story is a long one and I shall only hint at it in this context. The gist is this. The realist argues that one is never in perception presented with a mere *this*; and against this mistaken view he asserts that *perception* (like all awareness) *is propositional*. He holds that one never perceives a mere *this*, but, rather, (that) *this is red*. If this is so, then there is no reason for inventing a "second eye"; the mind's eye, if I may so put it, *the mental eye of the conceptualist* with which to "see" (general) concepts independently of perception.

But let us assume, for the sake of the argument, that the conceptualist's point of view is well taken and ask him how he himself would describe our paradigm of the two red spots. He answers, first, that "this" and "that" name the two red spots. He holds, second, that "red" names a concept, that is, something that can only be grasped by the mental eye.[7] He continues, third, that "this is red" and "that is red" mean "this falls under the concept red" and "that falls under the concept red," respectively. Thus he agrees with the nominalist that "this" and "that" name the two red spots, i.e., in the realist's terminology, facts rather than individuals. He disagrees with both realist and nominalist in holding (a) that the referent of "red" is a concept, and (b) that the "is" must be explicated as "falls under." The last point is of crucial significance. We saw already that the nominalist has considerable difficulties in trying to secure ontological status for his part-whole relation. But whereas the nominalist's talk about this relation has at least a commonsensical ring to it, a fact that may help to conceal his difficulties, the conceptualist's falling-under nexus seems to be nothing but an invention of the metaphysician. Moreover, the conceptualist, no less than the nominalist, must somehow ground his nexus of falling-under ontologically; and it is hard to imagine how this could be done in a way that is not completely implausible. For what possible connection could there be between the *this* from the realm of perception and the concept from the realm of the mind. The falling-under nexus, therefore, proves to be a source of constant trouble to the conceptualist. Small wonder, then, that he should try to eliminate it completely, as Frege did.[8]

Let us ask, finally, what, if anything, the conceptualist has committed himself to with regard to the "existence" of concepts. It seems that he still has a number of alternatives.

First. The conceptualist could adopt the naming-criterion. Since concepts are named, they would then be said to exist along with the referents of "this" and "that."

Second. He could reject the naming-criterion and instead accept the independence-criterion. From the fact that concepts are named, it would then not follow that they exist. But notice that the independence-criterion was originally tailored to perception alone, not to thought. This shows that there is a third possibility.

Third. The conceptualist could introduce a new criterion of existence which replaces the old independence-criterion for perception. According to this new criterion, *what exists is what can be presented either in perception or in thought independently of other things*. To grasp that this

---

[7] This is so on either one of two further possibilities, namely, first, that concepts are taken to subsist solely "in the mind," or, second, that they are assigned to an "objective realm."

[8] Frege's way out consists in saying that concepts are "unsaturated," so that they can "stick" to objects without requiring a special nexus. Compare my "Frege's Ontology," *The Philosophical Review*, 70, 1961, 23–40 and also pp. 106–120 of this book.

is a real alternative, consider that according to many philosophers, although one cannot perceive red (or redness) in isolation, one can so think (of) it. If this be true, then upon the new criterion, concepts exist – not because they are named, but because they can be thought (of) independently.

In the history of philosophy, conceptualism is closely linked with nominalism. More often than not, conceptualists held that concepts subsist rather than exist. Nor is this surprising. Remember the so-called localization-criterion: what exists is what is localized in space and time. This criterion and the conceptualist doctrine that one can in perception be presented only with a particular *this* are just two sides of the same coin. More precisely, the things that are localized upon the one criterion are often held to be exactly those with which one can be presented upon the other. (Time and space have been called *"Formen der Anschauung."*) This makes it plausible, to say the least, that the conceptualist, however unwittingly, may also be guided by the localization-criterion. If so, he will deny that concepts exist.

Comparing all three, realist, nominalist, and conceptualist, we note these similarities. All three admit that there are two ontological modes, namely, existents and subsistents. All three are forced to make this distinction because they accept one of several criteria, naming, independence, or localization, as the most significant criterion of existence. The conceptualist, however, stands with the nominalist when it comes to separating existents from subsistents. To one who explicates different ontological uses of "exist" rather than adopting one himself, this is of little consequence. The deepest issue, I submit, is not whether universals are called "properties," or "concepts"; whether, perhaps, they are "parts" of something else; or whether, finally, they should be said to exist rather than merely being called subsistents. What then is this deepest issue? To state it, I avail myself of a metaphor I used a while ago. According to the conceptualist we have, as it were, two eyes; the eye of perception and the eye of the mind. With the latter we "see" the universal. This fundamental dualism both realist and nominalist reject.

VI. SENSORY INTUITION AND THE
DOGMA OF LOCALIZATION *

REINHARDT GROSSMANN

Conceptualism, like any other philosophical doctrine of comparable scope, has both ontological and epistemological aspects. Ontologically, however, conceptualism does not differ significantly from certain forms of nominalism.[1] At its root lies an epistemological thesis: *All objects of sensory intuition are localized in space and time.*[2] In this paper, I wish to explore some of the consequences of this thesis.

I

According to the thesis of localization, all objects of sensory intuition are localized in space and time. If one adds to this the further premise that universals are not localized, then it follows apparently that universals cannot be objects of sensory intuition. A philosopher who accepts this argument has two alternatives. He may hold that there are no universals at all, but only objects of sensory intuition. Or he could assert that there are both universals and objects of sensory intuition, but that one is acquainted with universals through a different kind of mental act. As I shall try to show, the first alternative fails. There remains only the second, namely conceptualism. Put differently, the argument from localization leads inevitably to conceptualism.

Upon the first alternative, a philosopher starts usually from two distinctions. He distinguishes, firstly, between *wholes* and their *parts.* He distinguishes, secondly, between *separable* and *inseparable* parts.[3]

* Inquiry, 5, 1962, 238–251. Reprinted by permission.
[1] I have discussed the ontological ramifications and possibilities of conceptualism elsewhere. See "Conceptualism," *The Review of Metaphysics*, 14, 1960, 243–54 and also pp. 40–49 of this book.

[2] I shall distinguish between *sensory intuition* and *presentation* as two distinct ways in which one might be acquainted with particular things and universals, respectively.

[3] This distinction goes back at least to Berkeley. It was revived by Stumpf and accepted by most of Brentano's students. See C. Stumpf: *Über den psychologischen Ursprung der Raumvorstellung* (Leipzig, 1873), pp. 108ff. Also E. Husserl: *Logische Untersuchungen*, Vol. 2, pp. 230ff.

Consider, for instance, a large square composed of several smaller squares. Assume that one of the latter is of a certain shade of green. This small square is called a separable part of the larger one. On the other hand, the shade of green is called an inseparable part of the small square. This gives the general idea. It ties in with a number of traditional views. For example, a separable part is considered to be an independent existent, because it can exist independently of its whole. An inseparable part, however, cannot exist alone or in isolation. This shows a connection with the classical notions of *independent* and *dependent* existents.[4] Furthermore, what exists dependently does not really exist at all. It merely *subsists*. Only independent existents *exist*. This shows how the distinction between separable and inseparable parts ties in with certain forms of nominalism.

According to the part-whole analysis, a whole consists of a number of connected parts. The notation '$W = f(p_1, p_2)$' depicts this idea: W is the whole, p_1 and p_2 are its parts, and f is the nexus that connects the parts.[5] Let W be of a certain shade of green. It then contains this shade as a dependent part. Call this part $green_1$. What kind of entity is $green_1$? $green_1$ cannot be a universal, that is, a color shared by several wholes; for we are told that another thing of the same color would contain not $green_1$ but, rather, $green_2$. Nor is $green_1$ a bare particular; for it does not merely indicate a numerical difference between this whole and another one. Hence $green_1$ is neither a universal nor a bare particular. It is a special kind of ultimate entity, traditionally known as a *perfect particular*.

Perfect particulars, whether so called or not, have played a major role in philosophy.[6] Their attraction can be easily understood. They do fulfill the condition of being localized and can therefore serve as

In Brentano's later philosophy, the doctrine of inseparable parts finds its expression in his views on so-called synsemantic phrases. See especially his *Kategorienlehre* (Leipzig ,1933).

It should also be noted that this distinction throws some light on Frege's distinction between saturated and unsaturated things. See especially a remark in "On the Foundations of Geometry," *The Philosophical Review*, 69, 1960, p. 13.

[4] For a detailed analysis of the dependent-independent dichotomy and its significance for ontology see E. Allaire: "Existence, Independence, and Universals," *The Philosophical Review*, 69, 1960, 485–96 and also pp. 3–13 of this book.

[5] Compare K. Twardowski: *Zur Lehre vom Inhalt und Gegenstand der Vorstellungen* (Wien, 1894), pp. 55–58.

[6] Compare, to mention just a few, Husserl: *op. cit.*, Vol. 2. Further, A Meinong: *Über die Erfahrungsgrundlagen unseres Wissens* (Berlin, 1906), p. 27; and G. E. Moore: *Principia Ethica* (Cambridge, reprinted 1954), p. 41.

H. Hochberg has recently offered an interesting explication of Moore's notion of a non-natural property in terms of Moore's ontology of perfect particulars. See his "Moore's Ontology and Non-natural Properties," *The Review of Metaphysics*, 15, 1962, 365–395 and also pp. 121–147 of this book.

objects of sensory intuition. But this is not all. They also seem to offer a way out of the dualism between fact- and thing-ontologies; for they are facts of a sort, rather than either bare particulars or universals, and yet they are supposed to be *simple* things.[7] Furthermore, they also seem to offer a way out of the realism-nominalism controversy; for they are supposed to be localized in space and time like bare particulars, and yet they also seem to function as universals. In short, perfect particulars seem to represent a satisfactory solution from any ontological point of view.

How does the proponent of perfect particulars propose to analyze the perception, say, of a green spot?[8] He might say that perceiving a green spot consists in being acquainted through sensory intuition with a whole composed of $green_1$ and other perfect particulars. But this analysis will not do. For assume that there are two green spots of the same shade of green. Then at least two sentences are true, namely, (1) 'This is green,' and (2) 'That is green.' Any satisfactory ontological analysis must therefore do justice to these two facts: (a) that there are two spots rather than one, and (b) that these two spots have the same color. The proponent of perfect particulars could attempt to translate(1) and(2) into (3) '$Green_1$ is part of this whole' and (4) '$Green_2$ is part of that whole,' respectively. But now we must remember that $green_1$ and $green_2$ are supposed to be simple rather than complex, as well as different rather than the same. Hence, we have in $green_1$ and $green_2$ two simple, different things. What then accounts for the sameness in regard to color? In terms of perfect particulars alone, there is no satisfactory answer to this question.[9]

It might be objected that the sameness in regard to color needs no

---

[7] For a confrontation of thing- and fact-ontologies in a contemporary context see G. Bergmann's review of P. Strawson's *Individuals*: "Strawson's Ontology," *The Journal of Philosophy*, 57, 1960, 601–22.

[8] The following description is somewhat simplified for two reasons. First, even though I speak here of perception, the problem can equally well be formulated in terms of *sensing*. Philosophers who prefer a sense-data analysis of perception may say that sensa are perfect particulars. (Compare, for instance, H. Bergmann: *Untersuchungen zum Problem der inneren Wahrnehmung*, Halle, 1908). Others speak of perfect particulars as rudimentary perceptual objects rather than sensa. (Compare Husserl's *Logische Untersuchungen;* also Hoefler's *Psychologie*, Prague and Leipzig, 1897, p. 18; and Pfänder's *Einführung in die Psychologie*, Leipzig, 1904, pp. 278 ff.)

Second, the proponent of perfect particulars could hold that perception involves more than mere sensory intuition. He might hold, for instance, that it involves a judgment of the form "This (whole) exists"; or, perhaps, of the form "$Green_1$ is part of this whole." But as long as no universals are used in the analysis, these variations do not matter to the following considerations.

[9] For this and the following point see E. Allaire: "Bare Particulars," *Philosophical Studies*, 14, 1963, 1–8 and also pp. 14–21 of this book.

ontological basis. Rather, let it be grounded, if at all, in the fact that we call both spots green (or, rather, by whatever name this particular shade of green is known). Consider, for instance, two spots of different shades of green. Here, too, we might say that this is green and that is green, using 'green' twice. But must we therefore conclude that there is a further entity shared by the two shades of green? This consideration seems to show how absurd or dangerous it is to require ontological grounding for our first case.

However, this kind of argument is not sound. It merely shows that the requirement is absurd in certain cases. It is absurd in the case of the two different shades of green. Of course, that one sees two shades of green rather than, say, a shade of green and a shade of red, is by no stretch of the imagination a "linguistic" matter. But that one calls two shades of green both green, while calling two other shades green and red, is a "linguistic" matter.

We conclude then that the analysis in terms of perfect particulars alone will not do. As long as perfect particulars are held to be both simple and different in every different whole, nothing will account for the sameness among wholes. The proponent of perfect particulars, therefore, is forced to acknowledge that there are universals in addition to perfect particulars.[10] If he also accepts the argument from localization mentioned above, he will be forced to accept the second alternative; namely, that in addition to objects of sensory intuition there are universals with which one is acquainted in a different way. This is what I meant when I said that the argument from localization leads inevitably to conceptualism.

II

The proponent of perfect particulars must hold that there are universals in addition to perfect particulars. With this addition, his analysis of perceiving two green spots succeeds. Each spot is considered to be a whole composed of perfect particulars. Perfect particulars are supposed to exemplify universals. For instance, the two perfect particulars $green_1$ and $green_2$ are supposed to exemplify the same universal, namely, a certain shade of green. The two spots are numerically different because they contain numerically different perfect particulars. Yet they have the same color because $green_1$ and $green_2$

---

[10] These universals could be relations of similarity among perfect particulars, even though I shall assume in the following discussions that they are nonrelational universals like green.

exemplify the same universal. Furthermore, based on the thesis of localization, the conceptualist holds that the perfect particulars $green_1$ and $green_2$, together with other perfect particulars, are given in sensory intuition, while the universal green is given in a different act. Call this act *presentation*. Thus while perfect particulars are *intuited*, universals are *presented*. Expressed in a well-known metaphor, there are two eyes: the eye of the senses which acquaints us with the particular and the eye of the mind which contemplates universals.

Contrast this view with what I shall call realism. According to the realist, one is acquainted in one and the same act of sensory intuition with both a bare particular and a universal.[11] More accurately, when perceiving, say, a green spot, one is acquainted with a bare particular, referred to by 'this', a universal, referred to by 'green', and the *nexus of exemplification*, represented by 'is', which connects the particular with the universal. In short, according to the realist, all acts of sensory intuition are *propositional*. Or, in terms of the metaphor, there is only one eye which sees that a particular exemplifies a universal.[12]

There are thus two basic differences between realism and conceptualism. First, as a consequence of the thesis of localization, the conceptualist holds that two different acts are involved in the perception of a green spot – namely, intuition and presentation – while the realist holds that one and the same act presents us with both a particular and a universal. Put differently, for the conceptualist each entity is given in *isolation*, while the realist holds that they are given together. Second, as a consequence of accepting perfect particulars the conceptualist must hold that there are two basic connections among entities. Perfect particulars are connected through the part-whole nexus. But they are also connected with universals through the nexus of exemplification. The realist, it is obvious, needs only the nexus of exemplification. Hence the conceptualist has to defend a richer ontology than the realist.[13]

These two differences are closely related. The thesis of localization leads to the conceptualist's notion that objects of sensory intuition and universals must each be given in isolation. But if objects of sensory in-

---

[11] Here again it would not matter whether one thinks of sensory intuition as an act of sensing (sensa) or as an act of perceiving (perceptual objects).

[12] For a more detailed account of the realist's view see G. Bergmann: *Meaning and Existence* (Madison, Wisconsin, 1960), pp. 3–38; and also his "Acts," *The Indian Journal of Philosophy*, 2, 1960, 1–30 and 96–117.

[13] Needless to say, it has often been overlooked that these connections must have some ontological status. Compare G. Bergmann: "The Ontology of Edmund Husserl," *Methodos*, 12, 1960, 359–92.

tuition are given in isolation, they could not possibly be bare particulars; for what sense could it make to say that mere numerical difference is given in isolation? The thesis of localization explains the conceptualist's aversion to bare particulars.[14] Further, because of this aversion, the conceptualist invents perfect particulars as objects of sensory intuition. But these entities necessitate the introduction of two basic ties, the part-whole nexus and the nexus of exemplification.

The notion of a perfect particular and the thesis of localization are the two cornerstones of conceptualism. Neither survives a careful analysis.

In regard to perfect particulars, I referred to them by such expressions as 'green$_1$'. Now it is obvious that this expression consists of two parts. It consists, firstly, of a word for a certain shade of green, and it contains, secondly, an index. Moreover, both parts are essential. For a mere index would indicate, not a perfect particular but a bare particular, and if we left out the index, one could no longer distinguish between two perfect particulars which exemplify the same shade of green. A similar consideration holds for expressions like 'this-green' and 'that-green' which are sometimes used to refer to perfect particulars. The realist could therefore argue that perfect particulars are not really simple, as claimed by the conceptualist. Each one of them really consists of a bare particular, as indicated by the index, and a universal, as indicated by the respective word or phrase.

The conceptualist could answer that perfect particulars are indeed simple; they are mere "thises." But since we cannot communicate in terms like 'this' or 'that', we must first subsume objects of sensory intuition under universals, speaking then, say, of this-green.[15] In other words, objects of sensory intuition are completely simple, but communication requires that we speak about them by using complex expressions.[16] The occurrence of 'green' in 'green$_1$' or 'this-green' therefore does not indicate that a perfect particular contains green as a

---

[14] This aversion has been pointed out repeatedly by G. Bergmann. Compare, for instance, his "Russell on Particulars," *The Philosophical Review*, 56, 1947, 59–72; and also his "The Ontology of Edmund Husserl," *loc. cit.*

[15] The view that one cannot communicate about objects of sensory intuition is a very common one, based on the idea that "intuitions without concepts are blind." Compare, for instance, B. Bolzano: *Wissenschaftslehre* (Leipzig, 1929), Vol. 1, p. 327; Vol. 3, p. 95. Also H. Bergmann, *op. cit.*, pp. 3, 7 and 8. A. Messer: *Empfindung und Denken* (Leipzig, 1908), p. 35. And A .Marty: *Untersuchungen zur Grundlegung der allgemeinen Grammatik und Sprachphilosophie* (Halle, 1908), Vol. 1, pp. 433ff.

[16] It is sometimes held that one cannot communicate about objects of sensory intuition directly because such objects are "private." Compare, for instance, A. Messer, *op. cit.*, p. 35.

part. Now this seems to mean that the objects of sensory intuition are not at all perfect particulars, but bare particulars instead. For, obviously, if such an object is in every case a mere "this," then it is precisely the kind of thing commonly called a bare particular. Moreover it is precisely because the *realist* holds that particulars are bare that he will insist that one cannot communicate about them directly.[17] Hence, if the conceptualist really means what he says, then the objects of intuition must be bare. But then the conceptualist is once more faced with the problem as to how one can be acquainted with mere numerical difference in *isolation*. Remembering this difficulty the conceptualist retreats to his original position: he asserts that the addition of such words as 'green' does not really add anything to what is already contained in the mere *this*.[18] But now he faces the problem that perfect particulars cannot be simple.

The realist's criticism may pull the conceptualist in the opposite direction. Instead of saying that the 'green' in 'this-green' is merely added for communication, he could say that the index or 'this' is superfluous. Upon this view, he can still distinguish between objects of intuition and universals by distinguishing between a universal and its "instances." He then introduces the classical distinction between *characters* and *attributes*.[19] Perfect particulars are now attributes; wholes are composed of such attributes; and individuation is achieved through special spatial and temporal attributes. However, aside from certain well-known difficulties, this analysis cannot be accepted by the conceptualist. For attributes, even though they can be simple, are not localized in space and time. They still function as universals; for two different wholes can contain, according to this analysis, the *same* non-spatial and non-temporal attributes.

The assertion that all objects of sensory intuition are simple is thus at odds with the assertion that they are perfect particulars. For if they are simple, then there seem to be only two possibilities. Either they are bare particulars or they are attributes. In the first case, the conceptualist would have to say that bare particulars can be given in isolation. In the secone case, he could no longer hold the thesis of localization. Perfect particulars are supposed to be simple; and yet

---

[17] Compare, for instance, G. Bergmann's review of Strawson's *Individuals, loc. cit.*

[18] See B. Bolzano, *op. cit.*, Vol. 1, p. 258. Bolzano calls such intuitions "*überfüllt.* "See Vol. 1, pp. 309–15, Vol. 3, p. 408. Compare also H. Bergmann, *op. cit.*, p. 5.

[19] Compare G. Bergmann's section on G. E. Moore in "Meaning and Ontology," *Inquiry*, 5, 1962, 129ff.

they must be complex. This is the basic contradiction in the conceptualist's notion of a perfect particular.[20]

Turning to the thesis of localization, the second cornerstone of conceptualism, we note that realism must be false if universals cannot be given in sensory intuition. Equally clearly, conceptualism loses its motivation if one can be acquainted with universals together with particulars in one and the same act of sensory intuition. The dispute between realist and conceptualist therefore comes down to whether or not universals cannot be given in sensory intuition. There are two defenses of this assertion; one direct, one indirect, as it were.

The indirect defense rests on the argument from localization. As previously mentioned, this argument has the form: (1) All and only objects of sensory intuition are localized; (2) Universals are not localized; (3) Therefore, universals cannot be given in sensory intuition. Now it seems that this argument allows for several different interpretations, depending on what is meant by 'localized'. [21] An entity may be said to be localized (localized$_1$) if and only if it exemplifies spatial and/or temporal relations. Most philosophers will agree that in this sense only particulars are localized. On the other hand, an entity may be said to be localized (localized$_2$) if and only if it is exemplified by a particular, that is, an entity which is itself localized$_1$. Again, most philosophers will agree that only universals can be localized$_2$.[22]

The claim that all objects of sensory intuition are localized is certainly true, if what is meant is that there are no objects of sensory intuition which are not either particulars or exemplified by particulars. As the conceptualist correctly points out, one never sees, say, green in isolation, but rather green at this particular place and this particular moment. Hence, the first premise of the argument from localization is true, if we interpret it to mean that all objects of intuition are either localized$_1$ or localized$_2$. But upon this interpretation, the second premise turns out to be false. For universals, as we just saw, are certainly localized$_2$. On the other hand, the second premise is certainly true, if what is meant is that universals are not localized$_1$;

[20] The same problem arises for some substance philosophies. It is asserted that a substance consists of a bare substance and an attribute. But it is also asserted that nothing is really added by the attribute to the bare substance. Compare F. Brentano: *Psychologie vom empirischen Standpunkt* (Leipzig, 1925), Vol. 2, p. 214; Vol. 3, p. 189. And his *Kategorienlehre* (Leipzig, 1933), pp. 11, 53-54, and 222.

[21] Compare for the following my "Frege's Ontology," *The Philosophical Review*, 70, 1961, 23-40 and also pp. 106-120 of this book.

[22] I confine the argument to universals of the first level, leaving out universals which are exemplified by universals.

for universals do not exemplify spatial and temporal relations. But upon this interpretation, it is no longer obvious that the first premise is true. Or else, the conceptualist must insist that the first premise states, in terms of localization₁, that universals cannot be objects of sensory intuition. In this case, rather than proving that universals cannot be objects of sensory intuition, the conceptualist simply asserts this by saying that they must be particulars. If so, then he must argue on independent grounds for his assertion. And this leads us to what I called a moment ago the direct argument.

The direct argument rests on the assertion that one is always acquainted (in sensory intuition) with this particular green here and that particular green there, but never with the universal green. Nor does one mean the universal green when one speaks of this green here or that green there.[23] Moreover, it is often held that this green here or that green there can come into being and disappear, while it makes no sense to say of the universal green that it could come into being or disappear.[24] Now, as to the first point, there seems no denying that one can mean this particular *shade* of green here, as opposed to another shade over there. What one has in mind, though, would be still a particular shade as it can also occur at other places, that is, a universal rather than a particular. But could one not also mean not just this particular shade of green, as contrasted with other shades, but rather this shade as it appears here and now? And does one not always see any color as it appears at this particular place and moment? The answers are obvious. Yet the realist would insist that one means or sees in each case a universal rather than a perfect particular. More accurately, he would insist that what one sees or means is a universal *as exemplified by a particular*, that is, this particular rather than another one. To say, then, that one always sees (or intuits) a color at a particular place and moment, is to say merely that one never sees a color which is not exemplified by a particular. In regard to the second point, namely, that "particular pieces of green" can come into being and disappear, the realist argues in a similar fashion. What happens in these instances is that a particular exemplifies or "no longer" exemplifies a universal.[25] The realist simply rejects the distinction between "individual pieces of green" and the universal green. We see, then, that the direct defense

---

[23] See A. Messer, *op. cit.*, p. 124, and the footnote on p. 127.

[24] Compare A. Meinong: *Hume Studien* (Wien, 1877), Vol. 1, p. 24. However, Meinong talks there about attributes rather than perfect particulars.

[25] Of course, the realist may hold that particulars are "momentary" entities which cannot undergo any change. Compare G. Bergmann: *Meaning and Existence*, pp. 182–5, 225–63.

of the assertion that universals cannot be given in sensory intuition fails. And this means that we have eliminated the most powerful motivation for the whole conceptualistic enterprise.

III

The conceptualist needs two eyes: one for the particular, one for the universal. But this is not all. The thoughtful conceptualist will have to acknowledge the existence of a third eye for *predication*.

Let us assume that the conceptualist is right: we are acquainted with particulars in sensory intuition and with universals through acts of presentation. How does predication arise? The problem confronting the conceptualist can be illustrated by the following example. Assume that there are two spots, one of a certain shade of green, the other a certain shade of red. According to the conceptualist one is acquainted with two perfect particulars; and one is also acquainted, though through acts of a different kind, with two universals. But how does one know that *this* spot rather than *that* one is green or that *that* spot rather than *this* one is red? The realist has no problem. He claims, as we remember that one is acquainted in one and the same act with a particular, a universal, and the nexus of exemplification holding between them. Thus he would say that each of the two particulars is given together with its universal, since one is acquainted with the nexus of exemplification as holding between each particular and its universal.

The conceptualist can solve the problem only if he acknowledges that one is acquainted with exemplification. But how is one acquainted with the nexus? Is there perhaps a third eye which presents us with exemplification in isolation? Or does the eye which presents us with "ordinary" universals also acquaint us with the nexus of exemplification? Finally, is there perhaps a third eye that acquaints us with perfect particulars and universals as connected?

The first two alternatives are unsatisfactory. In either case, one would need a further eye. According to the first alternative, one would be acquainted with a particular, a universal, and exemplification, but with each in isolation. Surely this will not do; for how would one know that this particular rather than the other one is green? The second alternative leads to the same question. As long as one sees each entity in isolation, even seeing two of them through the same eye, there is no answer. If it should be held that one is presented with the universal together with exemplification in one and the same act, the problem still is not solved; for even though a universal comes together with the nexus, nothing as yet tells us which particular goes with which "unsaturated" universal.[26] There is only one way out for the conceptualist. He must assume that there is a third eye, judgment or predication, different both from sensory intuition and from presentation, through which one is acquainted with particular and universal as connected.

But this alternative runs counter to the whole conceptualistic view. For one thing, it could mean that there is at least one constituent, exemplification, which is not given in isolation. While both perfect particular and universal appear first in isolation, exemplification occurs only together with particular and universal – unless, of course, the eye of presentation is assumed to see exemplification in isolation first, before predication can take place. More importantly, predication would have to present us with both the localized and the unlocalized, if I may so put it, in one plane. Hence predication would have to achieve what neither sensory intuition nor presentation could achieve. But why should one insist, as the conceptualist does, that neither sensory intuition nor presentation can acquaint us with both particulars and universals, if one is forced to introduce an act which does achieve this feat?

However, all these difficulties seem to disappear, if the conceptualist claims that exemplification is not at all "passively" given, but rather established by the mind. This view raises the question as to how the mind succeeds in connecting particulars with universals. Only two answers have even a shadow of plausibility.

First, it may be said that if a particular is given in sensory intuition the mind grasps what universal it exemplifies, because the particular affords some kind of cue as to how the mind must connect it. It is obvious that this proposal will not work, if the objects of sensory intuition are either bare or perfect particulars. For, if they are bare, then they could not possibly afford any cue; and if they are perfect particulars, then they are supposed to be simple, and again they could not provide any cue.[27]

The second answer is somewhat more elaborate. Starting from the

---

[26] By taking concepts to be unsaturated, Frege avoids Bradley's infinite regress, as I have shown in my Frege paper, but he does not get around the problem discussed in this paragraph.

[27] This is one reason why I did not consider the view that universals are "created" by abstraction from perfect particulars. It is clear that this view will not work; for simple perfect particulars will not give any cue as to what to abstract from them.

assumption that there are two eyes, one for the particular, the other for universals, the conceptualist claims that there is a third eye, *judgment*, which acquaints us with a connection between acts of sensory intuition and acts of presentation. In doing so, judgment indirectly establishes a connection between the objects of these two acts, that is, between particular and universal.[28]

This account has certain advantages. For instance, if we assume that acts themselves are perfect particulars, then judgment would deal with two perfect particulars rather than with a particular and a universal. Hence it would concern two localized things rather than a localized and an unlocalized entity.[29] Also, in some sense, the nexus of exemplification could be said to be reducible to the part-whole nexus. To speak of exemplification would really mean to speak of the part-whole nexus between acts. Hence it might be claimed that this analysis does away with the nexus of exemplification altogether in favour of the part-whole nexus. As against these advantages, however, the following difficulties arise. Judgment, the third eye, must acquaint us with two acts *as connected*. This means that it must acquaint us with perfect particulars as well as the part-whole nexus. This nexus can hardly be viewed as anything but a universal. Hence the conceptualist is forced to hold that there is, in addition to intuition and presentation, a third act which (a) does not present us with things in isolation and (b) acquaints us with what is localized (perfect particulars) together with what is not localized (the part-whole nexus).

To sum up. The problem of predication forces the conceptualist to part with the dogma of isolation and the dogma of localization. It forces him to admit that there is at least one way in which one is acquainted with things in connection rather than in isolation. And it forces him also to admit that there is at least one way in which one is acquainted with the localized together with the unlocalized. Being aware of these consequences, the conceptualist could retreat to a simplified form of conceptualism.

IV

He may offer the following view. Sensory intuition acquaints us with perfect particulars and perfect particulars only.[30] In addition to

[28] Compare, for instance, Husserl's view in his *Logische Untersuchungen* and Bergmann's article on Husserl.

[29] Localization must be understood here in the narrower sense of localization in time only.

[30] At this point, the conceptualist may even admit that the objects of sensory intuition are bare rather than perfect particulars.

sensory intuition, though, there is predication. Through this mental act one is presented with a perfect particular as connected with its universal. Hence, particulars are given in isolation, while universals are presented together with other entities. Upon this view, there are only two eyes – namely, sensory intuition and predication.

Perceiving a green spot is analyzed in the following way. Through an act of sensory intuition one is acquainted with a sensation or *sense datum*. This sense datum is a perfect particular. In addition, there occurs an act of predication. This act is propositional; its "object" is the circumstance that this particular falls under the concept green. Perception involves, then, sensory intuition and predication.[31] It involves the eye of the senses as well as the eye of the mind.

Contrast this with what a realist might say. Perception, he agrees, involves sensation (sense-data). In addition, it involves an act of perception.[32] However, while the conceptualist holds that sense-data are given in isolation, the realist holds that acts of sensing are no less propositional than acts of perceiving. The realist insists that on the level of sensing, particular and universal are also given as connected.

It is quite clear from this comparison that the conceptualist has come a long way in modifying his original position. What remains of his original view is the dogma that objects of sensory intuition must be localized and given in isolation. But notice also that the metaphor of the two eyes has changed its meaning. As it applied to the original form of conceptualism, it had its root in the ontological distinction between particulars and universals. There was one eye for particulars and one for universals. Each eye presented its object in isolation. As the metaphor applies to the modified conceptualism of this section, and even more clearly to the position of the realist, it has its root in the distinction between sensing and perceiving. According to the realist, there is the eye of the senses and the eye of the mind. The former consists in acts of sensing; the latter, in such acts as perceiving, believing, thinking, etc. In perception, both eyes work together, that is, there are sensations and there are also acts which are neither sensations nor acts of sensing. However, these two eyes do not see their

---

[31] One must not object that this view is untenable because perfect particulars give no cue as to how they are connected with universals. As long as the conceptualist admits that there is one act in which particulars and universals are given as connected, this kind of criticism will not apply to his position.

[32] This act of perception is similar to predication in that both acts are propositional. One important difference, however, is this. The particular with which an act of perception acquaints us is "a perceptual" particular, while the particular of predication is assumed to be a sense-datum.

objects in isolation. Nor do they see ontologically different kinds of entities.[33] The controversy between realist and conceptualist, then, does not concern the question as to whether or not two eyes are involved *in perception*. Rather, it is about what the two eyes see.

[33] Different ontological kinds in the sense in which particulars are ontologically different from universals. In some other sense, sensa are of course ontologically different from perceptual objects.

VII. COMMON NAMES

REINHARDT GROSSMANN

The doctrine of common names has a long history. It always finds proponents who think that it is a way out of the classical nominalistic difficulties. I wish to show that this doctrine does not even make sense when considered apart from the nominalism which it supposedly vindicates, and that it could be of no help to the nominalist, even if it made sense.

I

Consider the following three sentences: (1) 'Socrates is a man'; (2) 'Every man is mortal'; and (3) 'Man is a species'. A philosophical realist holds that 'man' names (refers to, stands for, signifies) a common nature or *universal*. But he will have to face a difficulty in connection with sentence (2); for it is clear that (2) does not express that the universal man is mortal. Rather, it asserts that every *individual man* is mortal. There are two well-known ways out of this difficulty. First, the realist may simply agree that 'man' does not name a universal in (2), but many individual men. This leads him to the view that a general term may name different entities, *depending on the context in which it occurs*. For instance, 'man' may name either a universal, as in contexts like (1) and (3), or it may name individual men, as in contexts like (2). This view is known as supposition theory and plays a dominant role in medieval logic. Second, the realist may take (2) to mean: "For all x, if x is a man, then x is mortal." Upon this analysis, his difficulty disappears; for 'man' functions then in (2) just as it does in (1). This type of analysis plays a dominant role in modern logic. We see that it makes supposition theory superfluous for the realist.[1] More specifically, it does away with the notion that a general term may refer to several individual things.

[1] Provided, of course, that the distinction between use and mention is made.

A nominalist denies that there is a common nature or universal which could be named by 'man'. He holds that 'man', if it names anything in the outside world, must name individual men. That leads to certain difficulties in connection with sentences (1) and (3). To start with (3), it is obvious that in this sentence 'man' cannot possibly name individual men. The nominalist may claim that it names a *concept in the mind*. Nor is there anything else he could plausibly say.[2] For (1) the nominalist has two possibilities. First, he may hold that in (1), just as in (3), 'man' names a concept in the mind. If so, then he arrives at the following view. Depending on the context, the term 'man' names either individual men, as in (2), or a concept in the mind, as in (1) and (3). If he also accepts the modern analysis of (2), then he may hold that a general term always names a concept in the mind. Again, supposition theory becomes superfluous and with it the doctrine that a general term may name several individual things.

The second possible way of dealing with (1) consists in saying that 'man' occurs in it as a *common name* for individual men, just as in (2). This analysis rests on the notion that 'man' names *commonly* what 'Socrates' names *properly*. It is this notion which I shall discuss more thoroughly in the next section. However, several things are clear already from what has been said so far.

Since we accept the modern treatment of sentences like (2), it is clear that the notion of a common name must be discussed in terms of examples like (1). It is also obvious that we may postpone the discussion of contexts like (3); for if the doctrine of common names makes sense at all, then it must at the very least be applicable to sentences like (1). Further, we may discuss the doctrine without first deciding whether individual things consist of particulars and universals, or of matter and forms, or of substances and accidents. For, the doctrine of common names does not rest on a particular ontological analysis of individual things such as men or green spots. It merely claims that certain expressions can name them commonly. However, this is not to say that the discussion will have no bearing on the realism-nominalism controversy. Quite to the contrary. If the doctrine of common names must be rejected, then so must be every version of nominalism which depends on it.

---

[2] He may analyze 'Man is a species' into "'Man' is a species." However, in this case, 'man' cannot be treated as a mere sign, but must be viewed as a sign with meaning. The meaning would be a mental concept. Compare also Turnbull's article in this volume.

II

Lesniewski is one of the most recent proponents of the common name doctrine. His view has been explained and defended by Sinisi.[3] According to this view, there are both proper and common names of individual things, but no (proper) names of universals (properties, qualities, common natures, etc.). A proper name refers to exactly one individual thing, while a common name refers to several individual things. For instance, in 'a is green', 'a' is said to name a particular green thing, say, a green spot, while 'green' is said to name commonly this spot as well as other green things.

Now this analysis of 'a is green' is certainly not complete and therefore as yet not satisfactory. Two further things are required. First, one must explicate what it means for a term to be a common name or, in other words, one must make sense of the notion that a word may refer to things *commonly*. Second, one must explain what connection the copula 'is' expresses when it occurs between a proper and a common name; for, say, 'a is green' is a sentence and not a mere list of names. These two requirements are not independent of each other. To see this clearly, consider the following four attempts at completing the common name analysis of 'a is green'.

(1) The copula may be thought to express that the thing *a* has the quality or property of being green. In this case, however, 'green' would have to name a quality or property; it could not possibly name *a* as well as other green things. Hence the attempt to interpret the copula as expressing exemplification clashes with the assertion that 'green' functions as a common name of several individual things. (2) The copula could perhaps express class membership. If it does, then 'green' must refer to the class of green things. The common name 'green' does not refer to this class. Rather, it is said to name each member of this class commonly, without naming the class as such. Hence the copula cannot express class membership. (3) The copula may stand for class inclusion. In this case, though, both 'a' as well as 'green' would have to name classes, while, according to the common name analysis, 'a' names one individual thing and 'green' names several individual things. (4) Finally, the copula may be taken to express identity. This seems to be the most plausible interpretation. Yet, even a brief reflection shows that this interpretation does not agree with the common name doctrine.

3 See V. F. Sinisi: "Nominalism and Common Names," *The Philosophtical Review,* 71, 1962, 230–35.

between two names which name one and only one thing each, be that thing an individual, a property, a class, or a relation. A common name, however, is supposed to refer to more than one thing. Hence the copula cannot possibly express identity.

This fact seems to have been overlooked by some proponents of the common name doctrine; or else, they must have meant something radically different by 'common name'. According to supposition theory, 'green' stands for several green things in '*a* is green'. However, some proponents of this view also held that '*a* is green' means '*a* is this green thing here' or, for short, '*a* is this'. [4] Now if 'green' is a common name, then '*a* is green' cannot possibly mean '*a* is this'. On the other hand, if it means '*a* is this', then 'green' cannot be a common name. Put in terms of identity, if 'green' is a common name, then the copula cannot possibly express identity; and if it does express identity, then 'green' cannot be a common name. What type or version of the common name doctrine would be compatible with the notion that the copula stands for identity?

It may be held that 'green' is a common name only in so far as it may occur in different contexts; as it occurs in a definite context, it would always be a proper name. For example, 'green' may be said to be a common name, because it can occur in both '*a* is green' and '*b* is green', where *a* and *b* are two different things. However, in each one of these two sentences, it would function as a proper name. But upon this view, there could be no proper names at all; for even, say, '*a*' can occur in different contexts, namely, in '*a* is green' and '*a* is round'. Hence, if the distinction between proper and common names is accepted, something must be added to the view under consideration. Obviously, what must be added to safeguard the distinction between proper and common names is that a common name can, while a proper name cannot refer to different things in different contexts. But then we must ask which one of the many possible things 'green' names, depending on the context. I can think of several answers. (1) It may be said that 'green' functions always as another proper name of the subject of the context. For instance, in '*a* is green' and '*b* is green', 'green' would function as another proper name of *a* in the first sentence and as another proper name of *b* in the second sentence. However, this would mean that every sentence of the form '*a* is green', be it true or false, would reduce to '*a* is *a*'. This answer will therefore not do. (2) It may be held that we must distinguish between 'green' as it occurs in isolation and as

---

[4] Compare Boehner: *Medieval Logic* (Chicago, 1952), p. 38.

it occurs in such contexts as '*a* is green'. In isolation, 'green' names all and only those things which are green. In a specific context, though, it names one and only one of these green things. This raises the question as to which green thing is named by 'green' when it occurs in a definite context. It is clear that 'green' could not name one and the same thing in all contexts; for if it named, say *b*, then '*a* is green' would be false, even if *a* is green. This leaves us with only one possible alternative Someone may hold that 'green' names the subject of the context, say, *a*, if and only if *a* is green. Otherwise, it names an arbitrary member of the class of green things. But this would have the consequence that every true sentence of the form '*a* is green' would be analytic. Moreover, in order to know what 'green' names in a given context, we would have to know first whether or not that context is true. And surely in order to know whether or not, say, '*a* is green' is true, we must already know what 'green' names in this sentence. Hence this last alternative, too, fails.

We conclude that the copula between a proper and a common name cannot express identity. This puts us in a better position to understand the basic difficulty of the common name doctrine. Since a common name must name several things without naming a class of things, the copula must express a connection between a particular thing and a "group of things," if I may so put it, yet not express a connection between a particular thing and a class of things. What could this connection be? The impossibility of an answer is the deepest reason why the common name doctrine makes no sense.

Sinisi agrees that the copula cannot express exemplification, class membership, class inclusion, or identity. Yet he thinks that its meaning can be elucidated. To this end, he cites a certain axiom of Lesniewski's ontology.[5] This axiom contains the primitive sign 'ϵ' expressing the copula between a proper and a common name. Sinisi claims, first, that Lesniewski's axiom *determines the meaning* of 'ϵ', and, second, that this explication enables us to understand what it means for a word to be a common name.

In what sense does the axiom determine the meaning of 'ϵ'? Lesniewski's axiom is of course not a *definition* of 'ϵ'. Hence it cannot be claimed that the meaning of 'ϵ' is defined by the axiom. Sinisi agrees with this point. He may however think of the axiom as an *implicit definition* of 'ϵ'. If so, then there would be no reason for citing Les-

---

[5] The axiom reads: $(x)\ (y)\ (x \in y \equiv ((Ec)\ (c \in x).(c)\ (d)\ ((c \in x.d \in x) \supset c \in d).(c)\ (c \in x \supset \in y)))$.

niewski's axiom in order to determine the meaning of the copula between a proper and a common name. Since we all know how to use such sentences as 'a is green', we may be said to possess all the implicit definitions we could possibly need in order to explicate the copula.[6] I take it therefore that Sinisi does not think of the axiom as an implicit definition of 'ϵ'.

The sign 'ϵ' must therefore get its meaning through an *interpretation* of the axiom. Indeed, this seems to be what Sinisi has in mind; for he offers us five interpretations of the axiom in order to illuminate the meaning of 'ϵ'; one of his own, three by Lesniewski, one by Kotarbinski.

According to his own interpretation, the axiom states that to say x is y *is to say* that: (1) there exists at least one x, and (2) there exists at most one x, and (3) whatever is x is y. Several things should be noted. First, the axiom does not say, as Sinisi claims, that to say x is y *is to say* etc.; it merely states that x is y *if and only if* etc. Second, the more accurate reading of conditions (1) and (2) would be: "there exists at least one thing which *is* x and there exists at most one thing which *is* x," where instead of the 'is' we have in the axiom of course 'ϵ'. Now keeping in mind that the variable 'x' ranges over individual things rather than properties, what are we to make of these two conditions? The only plausible interpretation I can think of construes the 'is' as a sign of identity. Upon this interpretation, conditions (1) and (2) read: "there exists at least one thing which is *identical* with x and there exists at most one thing which is *identical* with x." According to Sinisi, however, 'ϵ' does not express identity. If so, what could conditions (1) and (2) possibly mean? It turns out that Sinisi's formulations of conditions (1) and (2), and hence part of the interpretation of the axiom, presupposes an understanding of the common–name copula.

Consider next condition (3). How are we to understand the phrase 'whatever *is* x *is* y'? Since 'x' ranges over individual things, what else could the first 'is' express but identity? The second 'is' stands presumably between a proper and a common name. Again, to understand this 'is' is to understand the copula between a proper and a common name.

The three interpretations by Lesniewski do not help us either. According to the first, the sign 'ϵ' in '$A \ \epsilon \ b$' is used in the same sense as

[6] Compare also Frege's criticism of the notion of an implicit definition in his "On the Fundations of Geometry," *The Philosophical Review*, 69, 1960, 3–17.

the 'is' in such propositions as '*a* is green'. Obviously, what Lesniewski must have in mind is that the sign 'ϵ' is to be interpreted as the 'is' in '*a* is green', when 'green' is treated as a common name. Equally obviously, this interpretation will not help us to understand the common-name copula in '*a* is green'. According to the second, '*A* ϵ *b*' is equivalent to a proposition of the type 'every *A* is *b*, and at most one object is *A*'; according to the third, it is equivalent to '*A* is one of the objects *b*' so understood that it remains valid in the case when *A* is the only object which is *b*.

So far we have seen that neither Sinisi's nor Lesniewski's interpretations help us to understand the copula between a proper and a common name. The shoe is on the other foot, as it were: in order to understand their interpretations, we must already be able to make sense of the copula. Kotarbinski's interpretation, however, is different; it adds a new twist.

According to him, the axiom reads: "Whatever names are taken for *A* and *B*, the sentence '*A* is *B*' is equivalent to the logical product of the following sentences: (1) whatever name is taken for *X*, it is true that if its designatum *falls under A*, then it falls under *B*; (2) it is possible to choose a name for *X* such that its designatum *falls under A*: (3) whatever names are taken for *X* and *Y*, it is true that if the designatum of the second *falls under A*, then the designatum of the first *is* the designatum of the second." Kotarbinski thus translates the sign 'ϵ' generally as 'falls under'. However, in condition (3), he also reads it once as 'is'. Nor can there be any doubt that the 'is' in (3) must express identity. This fact alone suffices to reject his interpretation; for it seems hardly possible that one and the same sign has two different meanings in a clarified language, meaning once the same as 'falls under' and once 'is identical with'. If it is claimed that 'falls under' and 'is' are after all only two different ways of expressing the same thing in English, one would like to know how the phrase 'if the designatum of the first falls under *A*' could be expressed in terms of the 'is' as it occurs in the expression 'the designatum of the first is the designatum of the second'.

On the whole, though, Kotarbinski translates the sign 'ϵ' into 'falls under', where it is assumed that more than one thing may fall under a name. This is the new twist which I mentioned. For, upon his interpretation, the problem as to how to make sense of the common-name copula and the problem as to how to make sense of the notion of a common name are one and the same. If the 'is' of '*a* is green' is expressed by 'ϵ', and if the latter is to be read 'falls under', then '*a* is green' must become 'a falls under 'green''. Hence the copula expresses precisely the connection which presumably obtains between a common name and the things it names commonly. Thus, if we can make sense of the notion of a common name, we will also have explicated the copula. Upon Kotarbinski's interpretation, the process of elucidation does not proceed as outlined by Sinisi: we must not first be made to understand the copula and then, in terms of the copula, the notion of a common name. Rather, if we come to see how a name can name commonly, then we shall understand what the copula expresses.

This suggests a fresh start: instead of concentrating on the meaning of the copula, we shall investigate the notion of a common name. We know that a common name does not refer to a single entity, be it an individual thing, a property, or a class. Yet, its referent is not some strange entity. The difficulties connected with the notion of a common name do therefore not arise from the kind of entity named, but rather from the manner in which it is supposed to name ordinary individual things. Let 'green' be a common name and a, b, and c three things named by it. The general idea seems to be this. 'Green' is supposedly connected with each one of these three things by a separate "string," but there is no "string" that connects 'green' with all three things (the class). To say that 'green' names commonly, is to draw attention to all three strings. If it named properly, then there would be just one string connecting the name with just one entity. In order to distinguish between these two different kinds of connections, we shall say that an individual thing is *named* by a proper name, while several individual things *fall under* a common name.

Can we make sense, in a nonmetaphorical way, of the connection called 'falling under'? There seem to be only two possible ways in which we may try. First, we may take a cue from a different philosophical context in which 'falls under' is frequently used. One says in that connection that a thing falls under a concept, where it is understood that more than one thing may fall under a concept.[7] In this respect there is thus an analogy between saying that a thing falls under a common name and saying that a thing falls under a concept. However, the latter use of 'falls under' is based on a distinction between individual things (objects) and concepts (universals). The nexus of falling under is conceived of as obtaining between a thing and any of its properties.

[7] This terminology is of course Frege's. One should therefore also note his criticism of the common-name doctrine in the review of Husserl's "Philosophie der Arithmetik," *Zeitschrift für Philosophie und philosophische Kritik*, 103, 1894, 313–332, and at other places.

In brief, it is expressed by the 'is' of exemplification. This shows that the expression 'falls under' as used by Kotarbinski must mean something entirely different from what it means in connection with concepts. Hence we cannot hope to elucidate the notion of a common name in terms of the nexus between individual and universal.

Second, the things which fall under a common name constitute a class. We may say that this class is *associated* with the common name, though not *named* by it. Consider now the expression 'cos $n\alpha = 1$'. It contains the variable 'n'. This variable does not name any particular thing (number). Nor does it refer to a class of things (numbers). Rather, we say that it is associated with such a class, namely, its range. In this respect, there is a complete analogy between common names and variables. Yet, it is clear that we cannot explicate the notion of a common name in terms of a variable. If 'green' were a variable, then 'a is green' could not be said to express a proposition. The occurrence of 'green' would merely indicate that one can substitute for 'green' the proper name of one of the things from the range of the common name. Moreover, if one replaces the common name 'green' by such a proper name, then one would get an expression of the form 'a is b'; and what else but identity could be expressed by the copula in this type of expression?

The notion of a common name remains obscure. Sinisi's attempts to clarify it in terms of the copula fail, because they presuppose that we already understand the connection expressed by the copula between a proper and a common name. Nor do we have a direct explanation of the notion of a common name. We only know negatively that the connection between a common name and the things it names is neither that between a proper name and the entity it names, nor that between a concept and the things which fall under it, nor, finally, that between a variable and the things which constitute its range.

III

Having shown that the common name doctrine is unacceptable, we may return to its nominalistic source. According to one view, 'a is green' is to be analyzed into 'a falls under 'green''. Hence the sentence 'a is green' expresses a connection between the individual thing a and the word 'green'. Compare this with the realist's analysis. He claims that the sentence expresses a connection between the thing a and another thing, namely, green. According to him, it does not mention words at all. To put it succinctly, for the realist it is a statement about the world, while for the nominalist it is a statement about a connection between world and language.

Attaching proper names to things is in an obvious sense a quite arbitrary procedure. It is merely a matter of "convention." Does this also hold for common names? Assume that it does. In this case, the sentence 'a is green' would express a quite arbitrary and conventional connection between a thing and a word. Obviously, the realist would demur. 'A is green', he insists, expresses a connection between things in the world. This connection may or may not hold; but whether or not it does, is completely independent of all linguistic practices. Furthermore, the realist justifiedly claims that we do not really have a choice in this matter. If the connection between a thing and a common name, say, 'green' were arbitrary and a matter of convention, then we would not be able to say whether or not a thing before us is green, unless we knew that this particular thing is conventionally called green. But clearly we can and do say with complete confidence that a thing before our very eyes is green, even if no one has ever told us that it is called green. This proves conclusively that a common name cannot be arbitrarily attached to things. In this respect, there must be an important difference between proper and common names.

If we assume that there is such a difference, i.e., that common names are not arbitrarily attached to things, then we must raise the question as to what there is in or about things that determines their common names. The obvious answer is of course that certain things are all, say, green. But to say that a and b and c are green, cannot mean that a and b and c *fall under* 'green'. For we asked what there is in or about these things that makes them all fall under 'green', and to answer that they all fall under 'green' is no answer at all. The nominalistic proponent of common names cannot rest his case by analyzing 'a is green' to mean 'a falls under 'green''. He must also explain what there is in or about a that is expressed by 'a is green'.

The same objection applies to one version of conceptualism.[8] Assume that 'a is green' is analyzed into 'a falls under the mental concept green'. Assume further that it is completely arbitrary and a matter of convention under which mental concept a thing falls. Upon these assumptions, we cannot explain why only certain things are said

---

[8] This version is different from the one I discuss in two papers in this volume. In this version, concepts are mental entities. According to the conceptualism discussed in the other two articles, concepts are objective non-mental entities.

to be green and how we know that they are green, without having been told that they are. If we assume that the connection between things and mental concepts is not arbitrary, then we must explain what there is in or about, say, *a* that is expressed by '*a* is green'.

In the tradition, we find one standard explanation. It rests on a distinction between common names or concepts on the one hand and particularized essences (perfect particulars) on the other. '*A* is green' is analyzed either into '*a* falls under 'green'' or into '*a* falls under the mental concept green'. However, the connection between *a* and 'green' or the mental concept green is said to be based on something in *a*. Thus it is not arbitrary. Specifically, *a* is said to contain a particularized essence. Let us call this entity 'green$_1$'. Now green$_1$ must be distinguished from the word 'green' and the mental concept green. The former is an individual entity, while the latter may properly be called universals. This means of course that *a* does not contain a universal; for it does not contain either words or concepts. The process by which the mind forms a concept or arrives at a common name is called *abstraction*.

It can easily be shown that this view will not do.[9] A particularized essence, being an individual entity, must be numerically different from, say, one individual green thing to another. Now there are two possibilities. Either two particularized essences are merely *numerically* distinct or they also show either *qualitative* sameness or difference. In the first case, one could not explain why the concept (common name) green should be abstracted from two green things rather than a green and a red thing; for particularized essences would be merely numerically distinct. If, on the other hand, we assume that particularized essences may or may not qualitatively differ from each other, then the question arises as to what there is in or about these essences that accounts for their being qualitatively the same or different. But this very same question, formulated for ordinary things, was to be answered in terms of particularized essences. The nominalist tried to explain how ordinary things can be qualitatively the same, though numerically distinct. According to his explanation, particularized essences account for qualitative sameness. As it turns out, though, this merely shifts the problem from ordinary things to particularized essences; for he must now explain how particularized essences can be qualitatively the same, though numerically distinct.

To sum up. Even if the common name doctrine were acceptable, it

[9] Compare Essays I and VI of this book.

could be of no help to a nominalist. For, even if he could explain what it means for a word to name commonly, he cannot explain what there is in or about individual things that collects them under one common name. It is indeed one of the most curious facts in the history of philosophy that a certain type of nominalism should derive from the doctrine of common names. Perhaps the only explanation is that the spurious doctrine of particularized essences and the spurious doctrine of common names tended to reinforce each other.

SYSTEMS

VIII. OCKHAM'S NOMINALISTIC LOGIC:
SOME TWENTIETH CENTURY REFLECTIONS *

ROBERT G. TURNBULL

The logic of William of Ockham is commonly – and, I believe, rightly – thought to be nominalistic. It is also commonly – and, I believe, wrongly – thought to be helpful in the solution of those philosophical problems which cluster about the issue of the "one and the many." The allegedly helpful features of his logic are the theories of signification and supposition. I intend to show that these theories, far from being helpful, lead to certain intolerable results, in particular, (1) construing singular propositions, like "Socrates is a man," either as analytic or as no propositions at all (i.e., neither true nor false) and (2) construing all general propositions as either analytic or contradictory. These results follow from taking Ockham as offering object language analyses of object language propositions. Taking him as offering metalanguage analyses of object language propositions is to start off with attributing an intolerable "result" to his logic. It will be helpful, at the end, briefly to compare his logic with that of a contemporary nominalist, Nelson Goodman, for neither of the intolerable results follows from Goodman's logic. Whether the latter is, therefore, acceptable is another issue.

My strategy is as follows. In Part I, I wish to show that a rather straightforward interpretation of Ockham does have him offering metalinguistic analyses of object language propositions and also to show how certain contemporary interpreters and Ockham himself have managed to blind themselves to this fact. In Part II, I wish to show that the so-called "descent to singulars" affords a possibility of construing Ockham as offering object language analyses of object language propositions and to show how, given the doctrines discussed in Part I, he is led to adopt the 'is' of identity, the latter in such a way as to lead into the "intolerable results" mentioned above. In Part III, I wish to make the brief comparison with Goodman's logic.

* The New Scholasticism 36, 1962, 313–329. Reprinted by permission.

No detailed descriptions of the Ockhamite theories of signification and supposition will be attempted. Ockham states them quite clearly, and there exist excellent contemporary accounts of both, especially those of Fr. Boehner and Prof. Moody.[1] I shall discuss just what is necessary to make good the several claims listed above. The discussion will, furthermore, be limited to Ockham's doctrine of categorical propositions of present time. This is quite enough, for his doctrines of past, future, and modal propositions are directly dependent upon his doctrine of present-time categoricals.

PART I

Suppose a certain incautious realist claims that a proposition of the form "x is ϕ" means that a certain individual is characterized by a certain universal. He may then claim

(1) "x_1 is f" = def. "x_1 is characterized by f."

The danger of claiming (1) is by now patent, for the pattern is familiar. Bradley lies in wait for our incautious realist. So, interestingly enough, does William of Ockham, though he does not draw Bradley's moral. As Moody notes,[2] Ockham's moral is rather like the moral of Carnap's "fallacy" of the "material mode of speech." Ockham writes:

...'Socrates is a man,' 'Socrates is an animal,' do not denote that Socrates has humanity or animality.... They rather denote... that he is something that the predicate 'man' and the predicate 'animal' stand for or represent; for each of these predicates stands for Socrates. ... all of the following propositions are false in their *literal* meaning: 'Man belongs to the quiddity of Socrates,' 'Man is the essence of Socrates,' 'Humanity is in Socrates,' 'Socrates has humanity,' 'Socrates is a man by his humanity.' [3]

The passage suggests that Ockham would adopt, instead of (1), either

(2) "x_1 is f" = def. " 'f' stands for x_1"

or

(2a) "x_1 is f" = def. "There is something which 'f' stands for and it is identical with x_1."

(As to the difference, if any, between (2) and (2a) I shall reserve

[1] Cf. P. Boehner, *Collected Articles on Ockham*, ed. E. Buytaert (St. Bonaventure, N. Y., 1958); E. Moody, *The Logic of William of Ockham* (New York, 1935); E. Moody, *Truth and Consequence in Medieval Logic* (Amsterdam, 1953).

[2] *Truth and Consequence in Medieval Logic*, p. 37.

[3] Ockham, *Summa Totius Logicae*, II, Ch. 2 (Boehner's translation).

comment until Part II.) Though much will be said concerning (2), what is of present interest is Ockham's claim (in effect) that the right side of (1) is not (indeed, could not) be true in its "literal meaning."

Suppose that f is a species. Ockham would render this as the supposition that 'f' is a species. This, by the reasoning which produced (2), gives us

(3) " 'f' is a species" = def. " 'species' stands for 'f.' "

The right side of (1), taken *literally*, according to Ockham, yields

"x_1 is characterized by f" = def. " 'characterized by f' stands for x_1."

But 'f,' *not* 'characterized by f,' stands for x_1, so the right side of the above is, taken *literally*, false. What 'x_1 is characterized by f' becomes, taken *non-literally* and on Ockham's grounds, is the conjunction of the right sides of (2) and (3). But (3) is a proposition of the *second intention*. Thus the right side of (1), taken *non-literally*, combines a proposition of the first intention (object language) with one of the second intention (metalanguage). If one takes it *literally*, he will be tempted to take it as a simple proposition of the first intention. Our incautious realist, so tempted, succumbs and thus, according to Ockham, unjustifiably crowds his ontology with *abstracta*.

Our realist was indeed incautious. Were he more cautious (or better informed), he would insist that the right side (1) is literally false, but that certain *philosophical* propositions are true, namely, "There are individuals," "There are universals," and "Individuals are characterized by universals." The right side of (1), he will add, is a *fusion* of a common sense and a philosophical proposition. (This contrasts interestingly with the Ockhamite insistence that it is a *confusion* of propositions of different "levels.") As far as a *cautious* realist would go in the direction of (1) is to accept the trivially true proposition,

(4) "x_1 is f" means x_1 is f.

The acceptance of (4), however, patently gives no aid and comfort to realism or, for that matter, to any philosophical doctrine.

Let us now reconsider (2). Trivially Ockham must agree with (4). If the right side of (2) is taken as a sentence, then

(4a) " 'f' stands for x_1" *means* 'f' stands for x_1

is also trivially true. This explains what I meant when I said that (4) gives no aid and comfort to realism. (2), however, goes well beyond (4) and (4a). The *prima facie* trouble with it is that it contains a quoted expression on the right side, "*f*." One might complain that (2) attempts to equate a metalinguistic proposition with an object language proposition. If so, Ockham himself has confused levels of language (or intentions). I think that, as a matter of fact, he has. The rest of this part of the paper will be devoted to an attempt to explain how Ockham and his friendly interpreters have managed to conceal the confusion from themselves. Part II, however, will consider a possibility of construing Ockham as *not* confusing levels of language.

Ockham would no doubt object to the charge of confusion levelled above that, though (3) is metalinguistic (second-intentional), the right side of (2) is not. He would claim that the expression to the right of 'stands for' is properly quoted in a metalinguistic expression, but the hallmark of the object language (first intention) is that such an expression is not in quotes. And the expression to the right of 'stand for' is not quoted in (2). Such is the hold of the (Aristotelian) doctrine of "common names."

What seems to have led Ockham to think that " '*f*' stands for x_1" is of the first intention is his doctrine of truth. I can best develop what I have in mind here by adverting to the account of "truth conditions" in Prof. Moody's *Truth and Consequence in Medieval Logic*. Moody intends his account as an explanation in contemporary terms of Ockham (as well as Jean Buridan and Albert of Saxony). The account is put in terms of "truth conditions" for *general* propositions. I shall, in what follows, amend it slightly so as not to complicate the issue.

Consider

(5) "x_1 is *f*" is true if and only if x_1 is *f*.

This is both familiar and trivially true. Moody, interpreting Ockham, seems to assign the same status (trivially true) to

(6) "x_1 is *f*" is true if and only if '*f*' stands for x_1.

The expression to the right of 'if and only if' in (6) is identical with the expression to the right of '= def.' in (2). Moody takes (6) as a specification of what he calls a "metatheorem." [4] Now (6) is not entailed by (5), any more than (2) is entailed by (4) *and for the same reason*. (5) *may* be appropriately called a "metatheorem" (or a specification of one), for it is trivially true. (6) could be properly called a "metatheorem" (or specification of one) only if (2) were trivially true. But it

---

[4] *Truth and Consequence*, etc., p. 35. Following are samples of what Moody, on that page, calls "metatheorems": "T 'Some F exists.' ⊃. (∃x). 'F' $_s x$" and "T 'Some *F* is a *G*.' ⊃. (∃x). 'F' $_s x$. 'G' $_s x$."

is (4), not (2), which is trivially true. If one could persuade himself that (2) is true, he may be tempted to call (6) a "metatheorem" (or specification of one). And, of course, *vice versa*.

But things are not quite so simple. Fr. Boehner congratulates Ockham on having provided a clear interpretation of the dictum, *"Veritas est adequatio rei et intellectus,"* by taking *'adequatio'* to mean the standing for the same of the subject and predicate of a proposition.[5] Now there is a sense in which both expressions connected by 'if any only if' in (5) stand for the same. *But* (5) *does not require that 'f' and 'x₁' stand for the same.*[6] Boehner, however, understands Ockham as finding (5) inexplicit, i.e., not saying "all that can and should be said in order to make the connotation of "true" and "false" explicit."[7] Making it explicit, as Boehner understands Ockham, would require transforming it into (6)! Thus Boehner (and, presumably, Ockham, though I know of no text which simply says this) takes (6) as following from (5) as the more explicit follows from the less explicit.

There is a sense, of course, in which an analysis makes more explicit that of which it is the analysis. (2), assuming it acceptable (which, I should say, it is not), would be a rendering explicit of this sort. But (2) is not trivially true, as (4) is. As Prof. Tarski has pointed out, propositions like (5), though trivially true, are, in a sense, means of rendering explicit the scholastic dictum (i.e., *"Veritas est, etc."*).[8] Assume for the moment that the scholastic dictum *is* trivially true. (5), Tarski's way of making it explicit, is (or is also) trivially true. (6), Ockham's way of making it explicit, is *not* trivially true (unless we assume that (2) is trivially true, which it is not). The difference makes a difference. If, nevertheless, one assumes that (6) is merely a rendering explicit of a trivially true but inexplicit dictum, he may easily think that it, like (5), is also trivially true. If the temptation to think matters thusly is

[5] Boehner, *op. cit.*, essay entitled "Ockham's Theory of Truth," pp. 174–200. Cf. p. 175, where Boehner writes: "We only intend to present Ockham's theory of truth as a most convenient means for a clearer understanding of the scholastic concept of truth." In another essay, p. 261, he writes: "Ockham leads us a step further when he says that a true proposition signifies a state of affairs as it is, and a false proposition signifies a state of affairs as it is not. When does a proposition signify or not signify a state of affairs as it is or as it is not? The answer constantly given by Ockham is: If subject and predicate supposit for the same or do not supposit for the same. If and only if there is the coincidence of the supposition of subject and predicate will a proposition be true."

[6] Nor, incidentally, would (5) require that subject and predicate stand for the same even if the proposition involved were a general one, as, e.g., "Some *f* is *g*" is true if and only if some *f* is *g*. So far as this trivially true proposition goes, '*f*' and '*g*' could stand for two quite different *abstracta*.

[7] *Ibid.*, p. 261.

[8] A. Tarski, "The Semantic Conception of Truth," *Philosophy and Phenomenological Research*, 4, 1944, 341–375.

helped along by the verbal bridge of "standing for the same," he may very well take (6) as a specification of a "metatheorem." Moody exhibits well the nature of this temptation by commenting that we may (following his modernization of Ockham) replace "the expressions "'F' s x" ["'F' stands for x"] and "'G' s x" ["'G' stands for x,"] occurring in the methatheoretical descriptions of truth conditions, by the corresponding propositional functions '$F\,x$' and '$G\,x$.'" [9] I need not comment. Moody simply does not grasp the difference which, I insist, makes a difference.

I conclude this section by pointing out that the right side of (5) is an object language (first-intentional) proposition. If one is tempted to think of (6) as having the status of (5), he will be equally tempted to think of the right side of *it* as being an object language proposition. This is what I meant when I said that what seems to have led Ockham to think that "'f' stands for x_1" is of the first intention is his doctrine of truth.

PART II

If this were all, we could rather easily dismiss Ockham on these issues. He appears, however, to escape from his own metalinguistic account of object language propositions in the so-called "descent to singulars." What I wish to show in this section is that, though the descent to singulars affords a picture of Ockham offering object language analyses of object language propositions, the price he pays is a large one. He keeps a vestige (and an important one!) of the meta-linguistic analysis in the form of the '*is*' of identity.

Consider the forms for general (positive) propositions which we should expect from Ockham on the basis of Part I:

(7) "Every f is a g" =
    def. "(x) (If 'f' stands for x, then 'g' stands for x)."

(8) "Some f is a g" =
    def. "$(\exists x)$ ('f' stands for x and 'g' stands for x)."

(7) and (8) are completely analogous to (2). They are, of course, open to the objection that they offer metalinguistic analyses of object language propositions. I state them partly to complete the picture drawn in Part I, partly because I wish to show a little later that, to

[9] Moody, *Truth and Consequence*, etc.,p. 52.

maintain a semblance of intelligibility, Ockham must return to them.[10] They will, moreover, help in explaining the doctrine of the descent to singulars. To explain that doctrine, I must say something about the theories of signification and supposition.

Ockham distinguished *categorematic* and *syncategorematic* terms, the former being (roughly) what we call "descriptive," the latter, "logical." Categorematic terms are thought to have meaning independently of propositional contexts, namely "signification." Signification is an individual or set of individuals. Syncategorematic terms have no significations. They do, nevertheless, determine the "suppositions" of categorematic terms in propositions. Suppositions are, as it were, specifications of significations, the possibility for such specification arising from the ambiguity of "set of individuals" (disjunctive or conjunctive?) and the possibilities for combining such sets where two categorematic terms are involved.

In the proposition, "Every f is a g," 'f' has "confused and distributed supposition" and 'g' has "merely confused supposition." [11] Confused and distributed supposition is a conjunctive set, as f_1 and f_2 and f_3 and etc. The syncategorematic term 'every' determines this supposition. Merely confused supposition is determined by the syncategorematics 'every,' 'is,' and 'a.' It is a disjunctive set *qua* coupled by "identity" with the supposition of the subject term. This suggests:

(9) "Every f is a g" = def. "$(f_1 = g_1 \text{ or } f_1 = g_2 \text{ or } f_1 = g_3 \text{ or } \text{etc.})$ and $(f_2 = g_1 \text{ or } f_2 = g_2 \text{ or } f_2 = g_3 \text{ or } \text{etc.})$ *and* etc."

In the proposition, "Some f is a g," 'f' and 'g' both have "determinate supposition." Omitting (as irrelevant for the present purpose) the characterization of this supposition, the proposition seems to yield

(10) "Some f is a g" = def. "$(f_1 = g_1 \text{ or } f_1 = g_2 \text{ or } f_1 = g_3 \text{ or } \text{etc.})$ *or* $(f_2 = g_1 \text{ or } f_2 = g_2 \text{ or } f_2 = g_3 \text{ or } \text{etc.})$ *or* etc." [12]

(9) and (10) give an idea of the Ockhamite "descent to singulars." Ockham, however, would not approve of either (9) or (10), for it suggests that, in stating a general proposition, what one actually states is a vast number of singular propositions. Not having the machinery of

[10] (7) and (8), interestingly enough, are analyses presupposed in the statement of Moody's "methatheorems." Cf. Moody, *Truth and Consequence*, etc., pp. 35–6, also p. 51.

[11] The relevant texts in Ockham are to be found in *Summa Totius Logicae*, I, Chapters 62–70.

[12] I have followed Moody in formulating the right sides of (9) and (10). Cf. *Truth and Consequence*, etc., pp. 48–49. He explicitly rejects, however, (9) and (10) as the Ockhamite rendering of general propositions. So do I (as we shall see immediately), but I do not agree with Moody concerning the correct rendering (as we shall see later).

operators, Ockham puts the "descent to singulars" in such a way as to *suggest* (9) and (10). It is to be noticed, nevertheless, that the right sides of (9) and (10) appear to be object language propositions; they contain no quoted expressions.

If we were to put what Ockham seems to have in mind in analyzing general propositions in contemporary terms, i.e., in a symbolism, we would have to resort to a rather unusual mode of expression. Trying to do so, however, will shed light on Ockham's adoption of the 'is' of identity. In the following two formulae, *the variables are to be construed as ranging over, as it were, the subscripts.*

(11) "Every f is a g" = *def.* "$(m) (\exists n) (f_m = g_n)$."

(12) "Some f is a g" = def. "$(\exists m) (\exists n) (f_m = g_n)$."

Several things become clear when one reflects upon these formulae.

First, if one takes the universal operator as a "conjunctive operator" and the existential operator as a "disjunctive operator," systematic substitution for the "subscript variables" in (11) and (12) would yield (9) and (10). They are general formulae for the "descent to singulars." *Second*, (11) and (12) explain Ockham's adoption of the 'is' of identity. If one embraces "common names" — as Ockham did – and wishes to give object language analyses of object language general propositions, there is no other alternative. Consider that (a) there must be two operators (otherwise no "descent to singulars" in the Ockhamite pattern), (b) to have the variables range over individuals thought to be characterized by f and g is to fall into the realist's clutches, (c) there is no proposition if 'f' and 'g' are taken as variables. *Third*, note that " 'f_1' stands for x" (i.e., "x_1 is an f_1") makes no sense, though " 'f' stands for x_1" (i.e., "x_1 is an f") does and so does " 'f' stands for f_1" (i.e., "f_1 is an f.") It turns out, therefore, that "$x_1 = f_1$." *Fourth*, if, on Ockham's grounds, I wish to say that this f (namely f_1) is a g, I cannot say that 'g' stands for f_1; for, of course, it does not. 'f' does. What I have to say is rather that 'g' stands for, say, g_1 and that f_1 is identical with g_1.

I may now, at long last, comment on the difference (if any) between (2) and (2a). Consider (2). In the light of (12), we might construe it (getting away from the metalinguistic formulation) as:

(13) "x_1 is (an) f" = def. "$(\exists m) (f_m = x_1)$."

(2a) becomes, by parity of reasoning,

(14) "x_1 is (an) f" = def. "$(\exists m) (f_m = x_1$ and $f_m = x_1)$."

It is clear from (13) and (14) that, if we take Ockham as giving an object language analysis of object language propositions, there is no difference between (2) and (2a).

Note carefully that in (13) 'x_1' is *not* a value of 'm.' At this point an interesting question arises. Suppose that f_1 is the "valued f" which is identical with x_1. Does '$=$' mean the same in "$f_1 = f_1$" (or "$x_1 = x_1$") and also in "$f_1 = x_1$"? *If it does mean the same*, then true singular propositions are either analytic or not propositions at all. To show this more clearly let me use "Socrates is a man" as an example. This becomes, according to (13), "$(\exists m)$ (Man_m = Socrates)." Suppose, further that the sentence is true, then, say, Man_1 may be the "valued Man" and Man_1 = Socrates. (Note: If 'Socrates' really is a name, some sentence of the form, "Socrates is a —" must be true; and some value of the assigned "predicate" in the true sentence will be identical with Socrates.) So we get "$(\exists m)$ (Man_m = Man_1.)" But this either means that man$_1$ (this man) is a man (and is thus analytic) or merely means Man_1 (and is thus not a proposition at all). (Compare, respectively, "$(\exists x)$ (Man $x \supset$ Man a)" and "$(\exists x)$ ($x = a$).") *If, on the other hand,* '$=$' *does not mean the same*, then Ockham's ontology is queerly enriched. We have, as it were, not only Socrates but also man$_1$, even though Socrates = man$_1$. They are "identical" only in the sense that Frege's Evening Star and Morning Star are identical. (Compare a "realist" expression containing, say "$x = y$" as a part. No substitution of two *different* constants for those respective variables can be true. For example, '$a = b$' cannot be true. Russell's description sentence is *a propos*: "$(\exists x) [(fx) \cdot (y) (fy \equiv y = x) \cdot (g\,x)]$.") What may be more relevant, they are "identical" in the sense that a certain (Scotist) *haecceitas* might be identical with *this quidditas*. The difficulties here are notorious. Fortunately (for the present purpose) Ockham makes it quite clear that he will have nothing to do with this alternative.

It is interesting to note that the quotation from Ockham's *Summa* which is cited immediately preceeding the statement of (2) makes use of *two* singular propositions, namely, "Socrates is a man" and "Socrates is an animal." Suppose that Socrates is (identical with) man$_1$. "Man_1 is an animal" may, of course be a synthetic proposition, for, as it were, the "subscripting possibilities" for 'animal' may be narrower than those for 'man'. "$(\exists m)$ (Animal_m = Man_1)" might be false. (It is thus unlike "$(\exists m)$ (Man_m = Man_1).") So, too, "$(\exists_m)$ (man_m = Animal_1)" might be false. That Ockham uses *two* singular propositions to make his claim is a symptom of the underlying trouble, and it masks the absurdity of his doctrine of singular propositions.

We must now return to (11) and (12). Consider 'f_m.' We may, with appropriate reservations, call it a "non-propositional function." We may, in the same spirit, even say that it determines a "class" whose members are, of course, f_1, f_2, etc. We may even think of it as being what Ockham calls a "common or confused intellection" (i.e., not a mere shape or sound). Of this Ockham writes

For instance, to say that we have a confused intellection of man, means that we have a cognition by which we do not understand one man rather than another, but that by such a cognition we have a cognition of a man rather than a donkey .... And so it could be said that one and the same cognition refers to an infinite number of singulars without being a cognition proper to any one of them.[13]

Now consider '(m) f_m.' This "unconfuses" us a bit, for it, presumably, determines a conjunctive "class." '$(\exists m)$ g_m,' by the same token, determines a disjunctive "class." The relevance of these considerations to the doctrines of signification and supposition is obvious. It is important to keep in mind that none of these three expressions is a proposition, for none is true or false.

In (11) we have patently the conjoining of such a disjunctive "class" with a conjunctive one. Suppose that (11) is true. Then, assuming (as Ockham does) that universal propositions have "existential import," some such propositions as "$f_1 = g_1$" must be true. Unless at least one such proposition is true, (11) cannot be true. But how does '$=$' in that singular proposition differ from '$=$' in "$f_1 = f_1$" or "$g_1 = g_1$?" If it does not differ in meaning, then any universal proposition which is true is necessarily true. Mutatis mutandis, any universal proposition which is false is necessarily false. We may even go farther. If 'f_1' and 'g_1' are (logically) proper names, then "$f_1 = g_1$" is necessarily false. On the present supposition (and without resorting to the metalinguistic interpretation of object language propositions), the only true universal propositions have the logical form "(m) $(\exists n)$ $(f_m = f_n)$." Ockham escapes this impossible conclusion by returning to the metalinguistic construction of object language general propositions. This brings us back to (7). After all 'f' and 'g' are two different "common names"! The same issues obviously arise concerning (12) and lead us back to (8). If '$=$' does differ in meaning, then we are back, as we noted before, with Frege and Scotus, an alternative which Ockham rejected.[14]

[13] Expositio super librum Perihermenias (Boehner's translation).
[14] I think it arguable that the positions of Scotus and Frege are properly construable as attempts to escape the intolerable conclusions of the above paragraph while staying in the general ambience of nominalism. Cf., in this connection, G. Bergmann, "Frege's Hidden Nominalism," Philosophical Review, 67, 1958, 437–59 (reprinted in Bergmann's Meaning and Existence (Madison, 1960), 205–224).

It remains to consider briefly an objection which Moody would make to (11) and (12).

It must be emphasized that the general proposition represented by the formula 'Some F is a G' does not make the singular statements represented by '$F_1 = G_1$,' '$F_1 = G_2$,' etc., in disjunction .... What the general proposition asserts is that there is at least one case in which ostensive use of the general terms 'F' and 'G' for individuals for which they stand, would yield a true singular statement of the form $x = y$, where 'x' is replaced by one of the ostensive uses of 'F' and 'y' by one of the ostensive uses of 'G.' [15]

I have, of course, noted earlier that Ockham would not approve of (9) or (10) and thus agree with Moody that the general proposition does not "make the singular statements." What is of present interest is Moody's talk of "ostensive uses" of "general terms." He interprets "Some F is a G" as saying "There is at least one ostensive use of 'F' and at least one ostensive use of 'G' such that the two uses are related to each other by identity." Moody's objection would then presumably be that "ostensive uses" (whatever they are) are different from names.

Now I can see how, depending upon interpretation, a value for an Ockhamite variable might be either a name of an individual or an individual. But neither Socrates nor 'Socrates' is, by any stretch of my imagination, an ostensive use. (Nor are this man and 'this man' ostensive uses.) Moody seems to have chosen a rather odd way to return to the metalinguistic interpretation of Ockham. What his interpretation amounts to is that "Some F is a G" means that there is at least one instance in which 'F' and 'G' stand for one and the same individual, i.e., (8) is the correct interpretation of Ockham.

It is just possible that Moody is influenced by the current (Wittgensteinian) dictum that the meaning is the use and thus construes Ockham as a 14th Century Gilbert Ryle or Peter Strawson. He may even think of the "formula" (sic) "Every man is an animal" as the statement of an "inference ticket" which authorizes "logical transportation" from saying 'Man' (in "ostensive" situations) to saying 'Animal.' [16] That this is an impossible alternative is clear from the fact that 'Man' (or saying 'Man' in "ostensive" conditions – whatever these may be) is an incomplexum and is thus neither true nor false.

---

[15] *Truth and Consequence*, etc., p. 49.
[16] Cf. G. Ryle, " 'If,' 'So' and 'Because,' " in *Philosophical Analysis* ed. Max Black (Ithaca, 1950). Cf. also N. Colburn, "Logic and Prof. Ryle," *Philosophy of Science*, 21, 1954, 132–140.

PART III

I think it may now be fairly claimed that Ockham's logic has the intolerable consequences mentioned in the introduction. The theories of signification and supposition lead to (a) construing singular propositions either as analytic or as no propositions at all *and* (b) construing all general propositions as either necessarily true (analytic) or necessarily false (contradictory). The only alternative requires us to construe all ostensibly object-language propositions as metalinguistic, and this is equally intolerable.

It remains only to draw the promised contrast with the logic of Nelson Goodman. The logic used as the framework for Goodman's construction of the world out of "qualia" is the so-called "calculus of individuals." [17] As he uses it, there are two undefined "predicates," namely, 'overlapping' and 'being affiliated.' Both are relational, indeed, even symmetrical. *Prima facie*, therefore, Goodman has predication in a realist's sense (nor does he ever attempt analysis of object language propositions by means of metalinguistic propositions). 'Is identical with' is, in the "calculus of individuals," a *defined* term.[18] What Goodman will not allow, however, are "predicate" variables. Taking the slogan of himself and Prof. Quine, "To be is to be a value of a (bound) variable," he can insist that all "there is" are individuals and thus qualify as a nominalist. Since he has "predicates," Goodman can (and does) avoid the intolerable consequences of Ockham's nominalistic logic.

The reason I have put 'predicate' in double inverted commas in the preceding paragraph is that it is questionable whether, in any usual sense, either of the two terms involved is a predicate. Professor Gustav Bergmann, taking careful note of the fact that these are *all* of Goodman's "predicates" and that both are symmetrical, has pointed out that 'overlapping' and 'being affiliated' could easily be construed as "two modes of combining terms into simple clauses. To emphasize this interpretation one could, if one wished, write '(x, y)' and '$[x, y]$' " [11] instead of 'overlaps (x, y)' and 'affiliated with (x, y).' Even on this radically "syntactical" interpretation, Goodman's logic provides for

---

[17] First published by Lesniewski. See fn. on p. 42 of N. Goodman's *The Structure of Appearance* (Cambridge, 1951), for a listing of various publications of it. My statements concerning Goodman are drawn from *The Structure of Appearance*.

[18] *Ibid.*, p. 45.

[19] G. Bergmann, "Particularity and the New Nominalism," *Methodos*, 6, 1954, 131–147. The quotation is from p, 147.

the possibility of quantification and does not have the intolerable consequences of Ockham's logic. It may be worth noting, in passing, that the examples which Ockham is prone to use ("Socrates is a man") would be, in Goodman's system, exceedingly complex constructions from simple "relational" propositions.

My chief reason for making this highly abbreviated reference to Goodman is to point out that in *his* nominalistic system there is no vestige of the hoary doctrine of "common names." This, at bottom, is the chief reason why his nominalistic logic does not have the intolerable consequences of Ockham's. This is, of course, not the place to attempt criticism of Goodman. I merely wish to emphasize that, whatever his shortcomings, they do not include that question-begging defense of nominalism which is the doctrine of "common names." With this in mind, I think it tolerably clear that the present essay has shown, via discussion of Ockham, that the doctrine of "common names" *is* a question-begging defense of nominalism.

IX. BERKELEY'S IDEALISM *

Edwin B. Allaire

Berkeley's idealism may be expressed as follows. (1) There are only two kinds of existents, minds and sensible objects. (2) The kinds are inseparable: the *esse* of a mind is *percipere*, the *esse* of a sensible object is *percipi*. More precisely, Berkeley's idealism is the latter part of (2) together with (1). Though many philosophers accept (1), few accept (2). Whereas the former seems commonsensical, the latter does not. That chairs, tables, mountains and so on *must be* perceived seems beyond understanding, let alone conviction. Yet, Berkeley was convinced of it. Why? What fed his conviction? In this paper I propose to show that Berkeley drew considerable energy from a rather simple mistake which pervades his dialectic.

The claim that *esse est percipi* consists of three claims: first, minds are the only substances; second, sensible objects are merely collections of qualities; third, qualities must inhere in a substance. Since the only substances are minds, the three claims may be compressed: sensible objects must inhere in a mind. Further, since sensible objects inhere in a mind in the sense that they are perceived by it, 'inhere in' may be replaced by 'be perceived by'. Thus, sensible objects must be perceived (by a mind); i.e., *esse est percipi*.

The point of so unfolding Berkeley's idealism is to call attention to the role played by the dictum that qualities must inhere in a substance. Contrasting Berkeley's use of it with Aristotle's will provide an insight into the former's mistake. In Berkeley's ontology the dictum has no ground. Hence, his use of it is a mistake.

According to Aristotle, a physical object consists of a substance and its qualities (accidents). The latter are said to be incapable of existing apart from the former. In other words, qualities are *dependent* upon

* *Theoria*, 1963. Reprinted by permission.
 In the preparation of this paper I have benefited greatly from discussions with my colleague, Professor Harry M. Bracken.

substances. Now Aristotle correctly thinks of qualities as relative to that of which they are predicated, a substance upon his analysis. Thus, for him to assert that qualities must inhere in a substance is, if not true, at least intelligible. For qualities are predicated of substances.

According to Berkeley, a sensible object consists only of its qualities. He fails to realize however that qualities are such only relative to that of which they are predicated, a collection of them upon his analysis. Failing to realize that, he does not correctly and consistently say that qualities are incapable of existing apart from a collection. Instead, he mistakenly says that qualities must inhere in a substance. He is thus driven to idealism, claiming that sensible objects are mind dependent. For his ontology includes only mental substances, i.e., minds.

Ignoring for the moment whether or not Berkeley is in fact guilty of the mistake of which I have accused him, let me try to make the mistake itself clear. An entity is a quality relative to something. That is, a quality is a quality *of something*; namely, that of which it is predicated. To say the same thing differently, the required correlative of the category of quality must be the kind of which qualities are predicated. That kind is either a substance or a collection of qualities, depending on how one analyses such entities as chairs, tables, and so on. To maintain that a quality is incapable of existing apart from entities of the kind it is predicated of is one thing. To maintain that a quality is incapable of existing apart from an entity of the kind that it is not predicated of is quite another. The former is intelligible, the latter is not.

For Aristotle, qualities are predicated of substances; for Berkeley, of collections of qualities. That is, for the former, 'the die' in 'the die is hard' refers to an entity wholly distinct and different in kind from what 'hard' refers to. For the latter, it refers to an entity which is not wholly distinct from what 'hard' refers to and which in fact is merely a collection of such entities as hard. To repeat, though it is intelligible for Aristotle to maintain that qualities must inhere in a substance, it is not for Berkeley. For the latter, qualities are not predicated of substances.

Of course, if Berkeley were to maintain what he emphatically and sensibly denies, viz., that, say, hard is predicable of the mind when the mind perceives a hard die, then his adoption of Aristotle's dictum would be intelligible. Berkeley's mistake, therefore, is that he persists in claiming that qualities must inhere in a substance even though he insists that they are not predicated of a substance.

Before trying to show that Berkeley is guilty of the above mistake, it will be helpful to distinguish two possible meanings of 'esse est percipi'. Some Berkeley interpreters argue that the principle is used as a meaning criterion or, perhaps better, a principle of acquaintance. According to them, the principle explicates one meaning of 'exist': an entity *exists* if it can be spoken of, and what can be spoken of is what is perceived or what is *like* what is perceived. So used the principle secures the nonexistence of material substance: neither it nor what is like it is perceived.

I, for one, do not believe that Berkeley ever uses 'esse est percipi' in that way. Whether or not he does is irrelevant, however. For he does use it in the idealistic way to assert that sensible objects *must be* perceived or, more accurately, sensed. Moreover, even if Berkeley does use the principle as a meaning criterion, so used it does not entail idealism. From the claim that only what is perceivable exists it does not follow that what is perceivable must be perceived. Of course, if one were to claim that Berkeley's alleged meaning-criterion restricts speech to what is perceived by the speaker while speaking, idealism would follow. But so, too, would solipsism. Such an interpretation of Berkeley's philosophy is patently misguided. Berkeley too often insists that though a sensible object must be perceived, it need not be perceived by the mind that is perceiving it.

It is only the idealistic sense – if there be another – of 'esse est percipi' that is supported by what I have called Berkeley's mistake. The idealistic sense is a conclusion to an argument, one premiss of which is that qualities must inhere in a substance. As it happens, another premiss is that matter does not exist, a premiss which does rest on what could plausibly be called a meaning criterion. Be that as it may, given the distinction between the two possible uses of 'esse est percipi' the dialectical pattern of Berkeley's idealism is remarkably simple. First, by using a meaning criterion (or Principle of Acquaintance) he secures the existence of minds and sensible objects as well as the nonexistence of matter. Second, again drawing on the meaning criterion, he argues that sensible objects consist only of qualities. Third, subscribing to Aristotle's dictum, he concludes that sensible objects are incapable of existing apart from minds; their *esse est percipi*.

In what follows I hope to show three things: (I) that Berkeley made the mistake (of subscribing to Aristotle's dictum); (II) why he failed to notice it; (III) how he allowed it to determine his "problem of notions."

I

In the following passage [1] Philonous, in order to secure the non-existence of matter, invokes what may reasonably be called a Principle of Acquaintance.

HYLAS. Since .... you have no idea of the mind of God, how can you conceive it possible, that things should exist in his mind? Or, if you can conceive the mind of God without having an idea of it, why may not I be allowed to conceive the existence of matter, notwithstanding that I have no idea of it?

PHILONOUS. As to your first question; I own I have properly no idea, either of God or any other spirit; for these being active, cannot be represented by things perfectly inert, as our ideas are. I do nevertheless know, that I who am a spirit or thinking substance, exist as certainly, as I know my ideas exist. Farther, I know what I mean by the terms I and myself; and I know this immediately, or in-tuitively, though I do not perceive it as I perceive a triangle, a colour, or a sound. The mind, spirit or soul, is that indivisible unextended thing, which thinks, acts and perceives .... Ideas are things inactive, and perceived: and spirits a sort of beings altogether different from them. I do not therefore say my soul is an idea or like an idea. However, taking the word idea in a large sense, my soul may be said to furnish me with an idea, that is, an image or likeness of God, though indeed extremely inadequate .... My own mind and my ideas I have an immediate knowledge of; and by the help of these, do mediately apprehend the possibility of the existence of other spirits and ideas. .... For the second: I suppose by this time you can answer it your self. For you neither perceive matter objectively, as you do an inactive being or idea, nor know it as you do your self by a reflex act neither do you mediately apprehend it by similitude of the one or the other: nor yet collect it by reasoning from that which you know immediately.

The quoted passage offers an argument for the nonexistence of matter, an argument which rests squarely on the claim that neither it nor what is like it is presented, either in sense or reflection. That is, since matter is not presented it *does not* exist and since it is not *like* what is presented it *can not* exist.

Whether or not one chooses to explicate this argument as suggested above is unimportant. What is important is that even though it may establish that matter does not exist, it does not establish idealism. Nor does the argument of Section 3 establish that.

I think an intuitive knowledge may be obtained of this [i.e., esse est percipi], by any one that shall attend to what is meant by the term exist when applied to sensible things. That table I write on, I say, exists, that is, I see and feel it; and if I were out of my study I should say it existed, meaning thereby that if I was in my study I might perceive it, or that some other spirit actually does perceive it.

This passage, I submit, does not establish what Berkeley thinks,

[1] The Works of George Berkeley, ed. by A. A. Luce and T. E. Jessop (9 vols., London, 1948–57), Vol. II, pp. 231–32. (All references to Berkeley will be to this edition, hereafter abbreviated 'Works'.)

viz., *esse est percipi*. The use of 'exist' it calls attention to establishes at most that matter does not exist. The last phrase of the passage, the one embodying idealism, is clearly unwarranted. To put the point otherwise, though Sec. 3 may establish that to be is to be perceivable it does not establish that what is perceived must be perceivable. And the latter is what must be established if Berkeley is to support what he asserts in Sec. 6:

All those bodies which compose the mighty frame of the world, have not any subsistence without a mind, that their being is to be perceived or known; that consequently so long as they are not actually perceived by me, or do not exist in my mind or that of any other created spirit, they must either have no existence at all, or else subsist in the mind of some eternal spirit: it being perfectly unintelligible .... to attribute to any single part of them existence independent of a spirit.

Berkeley's idealism, then, is not established simply by calling attention to the use of 'exist' exhibited in Sec. 3, nor by claiming on the basis of that use, that matter does not exist. The latter is merely the first step in the march to idealism. The second step concerns the analysis of sensible objects.

.... to me a die seems to be nothing distinct from those things which are termed its modes or accidents. And to say a die is hard, extended, and square, is not to attribute those qualities to a subject distinct from and supporting them, but only an explication of the word die.[2]

In this passage Berkeley, drawing again on what he claims one is acquainted with, denies that a sensible object consists of a substance and its qualities. Accordingly, he maintains that when one predicates a quality of a "thing" one is not, as Aristotle would have us believe, saying that it inheres in a distinct substance. Rather, one is saying that it is a member of the collection of qualities which is the die. By calling the constituents sensible qualities, Berkeley can thus support his next and final step.

It was a mistake to think, that what is here said derogates in the least from the reality of things. It is acknowledged on the received principles, that extension, motion, and in a word all sensible qualities, have need of a support, as not being able to subsist by themselves. But the objects perceived by sense, are allowed to be nothing but combinations of those qualities, and consequently cannot subsist by themselves ..... According to us the unthinking beings perceived by sense have no existence distinct from being perceived, and cannot therefore exist in any other substance, than those unextended, indivisible substances, or *spirits*, which act and think, and perceive them.[3]

This passage marks Berkeley's arrival at idealism. Qualities need

---

[2] Sec. 49.
[3] Sec. 91.

a support, a substance in which to exist. But the only substances available are minds. Hence, qualities must be supported by minds, they must be in minds. That is, sensible objects must be perceived for 'in the mind' and 'perceived by' are used synonomously by Berkeley. (Sec 6: ".... so long as [bodies] are not actually perceived by me, or do not exist in my mind....")

Berkeley's steps to idealism are firm and definite. Only minds (in reflection) and sensible objects (in sense) exist, for they are the only *kinds* immediately known. Moreover, sensible objects are merely collections of qualities, and qualities need a substantial support. Since minds are the only substances, sensible objects must be *supported by* minds, they must be *in* minds, they must be *perceived by* minds: their *esse est percipi*.

I am, of course, not claiming that Berkeley himself unfolded idealism as described above; nor am I claiming that he was aware that it could be so unfolded. The *Principles* is clearly not developed in strict conformity to that pattern. Nevertheless, the pattern has an extraordinary hold on him. Much of what he says feeds upon it. Sec. 7 is a case in point.

From what has been said, it follows, there is not any other substance than *spirit*, or that which perceives. But for the fuller proof of this point, let it be considered, the sensible qualities are colour, figure, motion, smell, taste, and such like, that is, the ideas perceived by sense. Now for an idea to exist in an unperceiving thing, is a manifest contradiction; for to have an idea is all one as to perceive: that therefore wherein colour, figure, and like qualities exist, must perceive them; hence it is clear there can be no unthinking substance or substratum of those ideas.

"What has been said" (Sec. 6) is that sensible objects must be sensed. Thus, in this passage Berkeley is arguing that one who denies that embraces a contradiction; namely, that ideas exist in an unperceiving substance. The passage is therefore designed to prove that *esse est percipi* as well as that matter does not exist. Both proofs rest on the implicit premiss that qualities must be *in* a substance. For, Berkeley argues that if the sensible qualities are not *in* a mind they must be *in* matter. That is so only if one subscribes to the Aristotelian dictum. In other words, the denial that sensible objects are sensed results in a contradiction only if one believes, first, that qualities must inhere in a substance, and, second, that the qualities with which one is directly acquainted are *ideas*.

Notice that if Berkeley were to dispense with the Aristotelian dictum his argument would rest entirely on calling the sensed qualities ideas. Such an argument, though it would offer some support to the *esse* conclusion, would in itself offer none to the conclusion that matter does not exist. Moreover, Berkeley himself is not content to rest his entire case on 'idea' and its mentalistic connotations.

I own the word *idea* not being commonly used for *thing* sounds out of the way. My reason for using it was, because a necessary relation to the mind is understood to be implied by that term . . . .

It would be foolish to deny that Berkeley's use of 'idea' paves a convenient path to idealism. Indeed, Berkeley often takes advantage of the term and its question-begging connotations. It would also be foolish to deny that, given the historical context, there is some justification for his using it as he does. Nevertheless, he is aware that 'idea' merely implies what wants proof; namely, idealism – which he believes can be proved. His belief stems, I submit, in large measure from his almost unexamined acceptance of the dictum that qualities must inhere in a substance. I say "almost" because there is a passage in the *Dialogues* [4] in which Berkeley seems to indicate that he is aware of the great burden the dictum bears.

HYLAS. It is just come into my head, that the ground of all our mistakes lies in your treating of each quality by itself. Now I grant that each quality cannot singly subsist without the mind. Colour cannot without extension, neither can figure without some other sensible quality. But as the several qualities united or blended together form entire sensible things, nothing hinders why such things may not be supposed to exist without the mind.
PHILONOUS. Either, Hylas, you are jesting, or have a very bad memory. Though indeed we went through all the qualities by name one after another; yet my arguments, or rather your concessions nowhere tend to prove, that the secondary qualities did not subsist each alone by itself; but that they were not at all without the mind. Indeed in treating of figure and motion, we concluded they could not exist without the mind, because it was impossible even in thought to separate them from all secondary qualities, so as to conceive them existing by themselves . . . .

Hylas's suggestion that a *collection* of qualities may "subsist without the mind" is merely another way of questioning the claim that qualities must be *in* a substance. It is thus another way of questioning that *esse est percipi*. Ignoring for the moment Hylas's significant limitation – that single qualities cannot so subsist – Philonous's answer is confused, even circular. He merely appeals again to his original arguments against the primary-secondary quality distinction. Regardless of the soundness of those arguments, they all rest on the very principle in question. If the secondary qualities are not *in* the object it does not follow that they

---

[4] *Works*, Vol. II, pp. 235–36.

are in the mind, *unless* one believes that qualities must be in a substance. Berkeley's failure to appreciate that merely points up his mistake. The context – the primary-secondary distinction – makes the mistake understandable, though. Those who originally drew the distinction made the same mistake. In other words, they did not realize that the distinction required a more radical break with the Aristotelian frame of reference than they were prepared to make. Once it is admitted that, say, red, does not stand in the inherence relation to that of which it is predicated, it no longer makes sense to maintain that red must inhere in a substance. The latter, of course, is the basis for the traditional arguments that secondary qualities are subjective in the sense that they are "modifications" of the mind.

I want now to examine Sec. 49. There Berkeley argues that though, say, red is in the mind (when the mind senses red) it is not a quality of the mind. The argument appears to undermine all that has thus far been said. By analysing that argument I shall try not only to dispel the appearance but also to shed further light on Berkeley's mistake.

.... it may perhaps be objected, that if extension and figure exist only in the mind, it follows that the mind is extended and figured; since extension is a mode or attribute, which (to speak with the Schools) is predicated of the subject in which it exists. I answer, those qualities are in the mind only as they are perceived by it, that is, not by way of *mode* or *attribute*, but only by way of *idea;* and it no more follows, that the soul or mind is extended because extension exists in it alone, than it does that it is red or blue, because those colours are on all hands acknowledged to exist in it, and no where else. As to what philosophers say of subject and mode, that seems very groundless and unintelligible. For instance, in this proposition, a die is hard, extended and square, they will have it that the word *die* denotes a subject or substance, distinct from the hardness, extension and figure, which are predicated of it, and in which they exist. This I cannot comprehend: to me a die seems to be nothing distinct from those things which are termed its modes or accidents. And to say that a die is hard, extended and square, is not to attribute those qualities to a subject distinct from and supporting them, but only an explication of the meaning of the word *die*.

Though extension and figure are *in* minds, minds are not extended or figured. That is Berkeley's point. He secures it by subtly distinguishing between two senses of 'in'. Consider the sentences (a) 'John sees a red die' and (b) 'The die is red'. Both can be rephrased: (a') Red is *in* John's mind; (b') Red is *in* the die. What is the difference between the two meanings of 'in'? According to Berkeley, 'in' in (b') means "part of." That is, 'the die' stands for a collection of entities one of which 'red' stands for. 'In' in (a') means that 'red' stands for an entity which inheres in the mind and is thus distinct from it, i.e., not a *part of* it. The mind is a substance and not a collection of the items sensed by

it. By explicating 'quality' such that an entity is a quality of another
only if it is a *part of* the other, Berkeley can say that red is not a quality
of the mind. Furthermore, by explicating 'is' such that it can only be
used in sentences where a quality is attributed to an object, Berkeley
can maintain that though red is *in* the mind, the mind cannot be said
to be red. For, to repeat, red is not a part of the mind.

Sec. 49 does not prohibit one from saying that red is in the mind
in the sense in which for Aristotle red is in the die. For him a quality
is not a part of the object. Berkeley himself is also willing to say
precisely that at other places, in particular, where he is intent upon
establishing that *esse est percipi*. In fact, he wants to maintain that
red is a quality of both what it is predicated of and what it is not
predicated of. Given the two meanings of 'quality,' that is unex-
ceptionable. What is exceptionable is that Berkeley applies to the
non-predication context what belongs to the predication one; viz., that
qualities must inhere in a substance. At this point it is worth calling
attention to how easy it is for Berkeley to confuse matters. Given the
ambiguity of 'quality' and the fact that he fails to see that qualities
which must inhere are such only relative to what they are predicated of,
it is not surprising that Berkeley mistakenly believed that Aristotle's
dictum applied to sensible objects in their relation to the mind.

Before exploring more fully why Berkeley made the mistake he
did, I want to examine the connection, or lack of such, between his
mistake and his attack on representative realism or, what for him
amounts to the same thing, scepticism.[5] The representative realists
maintain that the objects which are immediately presented and, thus,
of which we have indubitable knowledge are not the *real* objects.
Rather the latter are represented by the former. Knowledge of the real
objects (i.e., the existents) is therefore uncertain. Berkeley, holding
implicitly that knowledge must be both "infallibile and of the real,"
saw correctly that representative realism engendered scepticism. His
gambit, as one says, was to collapse the idea-thing dichotomy. In
other words, he argued that the real objects are the ones with which we
are directly acquainted and of which we have indubitable knowledge.
Now all of Berkeley's arguments for the collapse of the idea-thing
dichotomy reduce to the claim that what is immediately perceived (in
sense or reflection) is real. Concisely stated, he rests his case against the
representative realists on a principle of acquaintance. The principle

---

[5] For a discussion of Berkeley's involvement with scepticism, see R. H. Popkin, "Berkeley
and Pyrrhonism," *Review of Metaphysics*, 5, 1951, 223–246.

does not entail idealism; unless, of course, one refers to those entities as "ideas." As shown above, 'idea', though an obvious bridge to idealisn cannot bear the entire burden. Nor does Berkeley wish it to. Indeed, given his sensitivity to the term, it appears to bear less weight than usually thought. The burden is actually borne by 'quality', a term which Berkeley also uses in characterizing the entities of sense. Be that as it may, the point at hand is that the attack on representative realism must be distinguished from the defense of idealism. The rejection of the former does not entail the latter. To say the same thing differently, the difference between "what is sensible exists" and "what is sensible must be sensed" can not be ignored.

II

Having shown how Berkeley's mistake supports his idealism, it needs to be shown why he made it. The simplest cause is that he failed to realize that a quality is such only relative to the kind of which it is predicated. In other words, Berkeley had an inadequate grasp of the meaning of 'quality'. Perhaps that is the only cause of the mistake. However, since he is sometimes – e.g., in Sec. 49 – conspicuously aware of the blurs surrounding the meaning of 'quality', other prominent features of his dialectic must support, if not cause, the mistake. These other features, two of which will be discussed, may themselves issue from the mistake. They nevertheless support it, for they are either strikingly commonsensical or deeply engrained linguistic habits. One feature of the former kind is Berkeley's anti-Platonism.

Aristotle's dictum is sometimes expressed as follows: qualities cannot exist independently of substances. Its purpose is to undermine Platonism which, given the present discussion, is the doctrine that qualities can and do so exist. In other words, the Platonist holds that qualities are independent existents. According to the Aristotelians that is objectionable: it obliterates the difference between substances and qualities.

Berkeley also wages war on Platonism, which, given the "way of ideas," carries the label "abstract ideas." Since material substance is unavailable to Berkeley, Aristotle's weapon is also unavailable. A new though similar one must be fashioned. Berkeley does just that, claiming that qualities cannot exist independently of (individuated) collections of them. The claim is in fact embodied in Hylas's suggestion that though collections of qualities can exist independently of the mind, single

qualities cannot. More significantly, in Sec. 7 of the Introduction
to the *Principles*, Berkeley makes the claim his own.

It is agreed on all hands, that qualities or *modes* of things do never really exist
each of them apart by itself separated from all others, but are mixed as it were in
the same object.

In Berkeley's ontology this principle serves the same purpose as
Aristotle's does in his. It bars the existence of independent qualities.
It "assures" us that we will never perceive an unembodied quality.
The principle is used in attacking the doctrine of abstract ideas which,
given Berkeley's identification of possible with imaginable, is tantamount to Platonism, since it allows the possibility of perceiving
unembodied qualities.

Berkeley, then, sometimes appreciates the fact that within his
ontology the attack on Platonism calls for a weapon other than, though
similar to, Aristotle's. Unhappily, he does not always appreciate that.
In Sec. 91 he says, "the objects perceived by sense, are allowed to be
nothing but combinations of those qualities, and consequently cannot
subsist by themselves . . . ." At this point Berkeley appeals to Aristotle's attack on Platonism, for he overlooks the fact that according to
him, some collections of qualities are not merely composite qualities
but individuals and thus need not inhere either in substances or in
further collections. Though it may be the case that this lapse is engendered by his feeble hold on the meaning of 'quality', it may also be
the case that his rigid anti-Platonism makes him overlook the fact
that in his ontology some collections of qualities are individuals and,
thus, independent. Be that as it may, Berkeley fails to grasp what
Hylas seems to: even without material substance, one can oppose
Platonism without defending idealism. For, some collections, those
which are individuated, are individuals and need no further support.
Thus, they need not be *in* minds. In this connection it is worth noting
that Berkeley, by dispensing with matter, dispenses with the traditional principle of individuation. Yet he never comes to grips with
the problem of individuation. Perhaps that explains why he sometimes
neglects to distinguish a collection as an individual from a collection as
a composite quality.

The phrases 'without the mind' and 'in the mind' are two of Berkeley's favorites. The connotations of both provide subtle bridges to
idealism. They are so used that it is difficult if not impossible to resist
thinking of sensible objects as qualities (in the Aristotelian sense) of
the mind. Indeed, together with Berkeley's use of 'idea', their uses

overcome any such resistance. Once sensible objects are so construed, idealism – the denial that sensible objects are independent of the mind – follows. In order to appreciate Berkeley's use of the phrases consider the following passages.[6]

I shall further add, that after the same manner, as modern philosophers prove certain sensible qualities to have no existence in matter, or without the mind, the same thing may be likewise proved of all other sensible qualities whatsoever. . . . . heat and cold are affections of the mind . . . .

. . . . if we had a new sense, it could only furnish us with new ideas or sensations, and then we should have the same reason against their existing in an unperceiving substance that has already been offered with relation to colour, and the like. Qualities . . . . are nothing else but *sensations* or *ideas*, which exist only in a *mind* perceiving them.

. . . . *spirits* and *ideas*. The former are *active, indivisible* substances: the latter are *inert, fleeting, dependent beings*, which subsist not by themselves, but are supported by, or exist in minds or spiritual substances.

These passages show clearly that Berkeley frequently categorizes minds as substances, independent entities, and sensible objects as entities which are *supported by* or *in* those substances. Thus, the latter are thought of as dependent and in turn as qualities. To express the point differently, Berkeley thinks of sensible objects as qualities of the mind in the same sense that Aristotle thinks of accidents as qualities of material substances. Berkeley is mislead by, as one says, the grammar of 'in the mind'. He therefore says of minds and sensible objects what Aristotle says of substances and accidents. It is not surprising therefore to find Berkeley relating his categories in the same way that Aristotle relates his. As accidents cannot exist independently of substances, so too sensible objects cannot exist independently of minds.

In summary, Berkeley's path to idealism is a network of closely related mistakes which tempt him to believe that the categories of sensible objects (which are *merely* collections of qualities) and minds are correlative in the same sense as the categories of accidents and substances. Thus, not only does Berkeley term his categories "mind" and "idea," he also and most significantly terms them "substance" and "quality." Accordingly, *'esse est percipi'* as used in Berkeley's ontology derives from and has a meaning analogous to *'to be is to inhere'* as used in Aristotle's ontology.

Berkeley's mistake is not his alone however. His predecessors, at least those who defended the primary-secondary quality distinction, made a similar one. Claiming as they did that since, say, colors are not *in* matter, they must be *in* mind, they mistakenly retained a feature of Aristotle's analysis of qualities. Their mistake, less disastrous since it only made part of the world mind-dependent, provided a bridge from realism to idealism, a bridge which carried us still farther from common sense.

III

One question remains: How does Berkeley's mistake determine his problem of notions?

Berkeley's principal aim is to destroy scepticism which he correctly sees as a parasite on representative realism. Unlike Descartes, Berkeley attempts to destroy the guest by destroying the host. Now the only thing that keeps the parasite alive is the host's distinction between representing and represented entities. The former, sometimes called ideas, are known with certainty; the latter, sometimes called things, are not so known. Berkeley collapses the distinction, arguing that only what can be known with certainty, either in sense or reflection, is *real*. Moreover and more disastrously, what can be known with certainty is what is *in the mind*.

'In the mind' misleads Berkeley into thinking of the entities known as qualities of the mind. In the case of sensible objects, there is a logic to that: they are called variously "ideas" and "qualities." However, if only what is in the mind can be known with certainty and if what is in the mind is a quality of it, how can minds be known? Being substances, they cannot be qualities of the mind. Yet, they exist according to Berkeley. Thus they must be immediately presented and in some sense in the mind. If they were not, the parasite would live again, for what is without the mind must, when known, be represented by something in the mind. At least that is the pattern of Berkeley's dialectic. Therefore, once Berkeley identifies, on the one hand, "being known" with "in the mind" and, on the other, "in the mind" with "quality of the mind," knowledge of mind constitutes an insoluble problem.

Berkeley, of course, realizes the problem. He argues that minds are known notionally rather than by way of ideas. That is no solution, however. It amounts in fact to repeating the difference between minds and ideas while implying that things of different kinds are known differently. He also argues that "one knows the meaning of the terms *I* and *myself*." That too is no solution. It fails to say how the mind is known; how the mind is in the mind when the mind is aware of itself. In other words, Berkeley claims but does not explain that the mind is known. He never tells us what sort of thing a notion is. The reason is that, on the one hand, when identifying a notion with a mind he cannot say how mind is in itself and thus known, and, on the other, when distinguishing a notion from a mind he realizes that scepticism is thus pardoned.

X. FREGE'S ONTOLOGY *

Reinhardt Grossmann

Frege's system has two rather puzzling parts: (1) he insists on the sense-denotation distinction for names but makes no such distinction for concept words; (2) he describes concepts and concept words as being unsaturated. (1) raises the problem whether concept words either denote or express concepts. This problem has been discussed by W. Marshall and M. Dummet.[1] (2) raises a number of different problems, for it led Frege to introduce so-called value ranges and concept correlates. These problems have been discussed by Peter Geach, R. S. Wells, and Gustav Bergmann.[2] Since both kinds of problems arise from Frege's notion of concept, it is plausible, as Bergmann tries to show, that they have their roots in a hidden nominalism. E. D. Klemke, however, has recently argued against Bergmann that Frege was clearly not a nominalist.[3]

In this paper I shall first suggest the structural reasons for Frege's insistence on (1) and (2). Then I shall make some comments about the issue whether or not Frege was a nominalist. But of course a complete discussion of Frege's philosophy must not be expected in this paper.

I

I begin by describing some features of Bolzano's *Wissenschaftslehre*, for much of what I shall have to say about Frege can best be understood

---

* *The Philosophical Review*, 70, 1961, 23–40. Reprinted by permission.
[1] W. Marshall, "Frege's Theory of Functions and Objects," *Philosophical Review*, 62, 1953, 374–390; and M. Dummet, "Frege on Functions, a Reply," *ibid.*, 64, 1955, 96–107.
[2] P. T. Geach, "Class and Concept," *Philosophical Review*, 64, 1955, 561–570; R. S. Wells, "Frege's Ontology," *Review of Metaphysics*, 4, 1951, 537–573; and G. Bergmann, "Frege's Hidden Nominalism," *Philosophical Review*, 67, 1958, 437–459 (reprinted in Bergmann's *Meaning and Existence*, Madison, Wis., 1960).
[3] E. D. Klemke, "Professor Bergmann and Frege's Hidden Nominalism," *Philosophical Review*, 68, 1959, 507–514.

against the background of Bolzano's view.[4] According to Bolzano, all
things are of one of three kinds:

First, there are different kinds of *mental states* (*subjective Vorstellungen*), namely, (a) individual ideas (*subjective Einzelvorstellungen*),
(b) general ideas (*subjective Allgemeinvorstellungen*), and (c) thoughts
(*gedachte Sätze*). Things of these three kinds are supposed to exist in
individual minds: in this respect they are "subjective" rather than
"objective." [5]

Second, there are so-called *objects₁* (*Gegenstände*), namely, (a) *indi-*
vidual things and (b) properties (*Beschaffenheiten* and *Relationen*).
These things are not in any individual mind, but exist independently
of minds and are therefore "objective" rather than "subjective." [6]

Third, there are *senses* (*objective Vorstellungen*), namely, (a) individual
concepts (*objective Einzelvorstellungen*), (b) general concepts (*objective
Allgemeinvorstellungen*), and (c) propositions (*Sätze an sich*). These
things differ from mental states in that they are as "objective" as
objects₁. But they also differ from the latter. One important difference
is that they are more closely connected with mental states than are
objects₁. Assume, for instance, that I think that this tree is green.
According to Bolzano, there occurs then a thought in my mind. This
thought is a mental (subjective) state. By means of it, I am said to
think *of* the proposition that this tree is green. In brief, *in* thinking a
thought, one is said to think *of* a proposition. Similarly, in thinking
(having) an idea, one "connects" directly with a concept (individual or
general) and only indirectly, through the concept, with an object₁.[7]

The general reason for the introduction of senses is a "logical" one
and can be stated as follows. The things properly studied by logic are
agreed to be concepts and propositions. But they could not possibly be
mental states; for "subjective" mental states are studied by psychology, and logic must be sharply separated from psychology. While
the things studied by logic must be very much like ideas and thoughts,
they cannot be "subjective." Rather, they are the "objective" counter-
parts of ideas and thoughts. In short, they are "objective" senses.[8]

One specific reason for the introduction of senses consists in the

[4] B. Bolzano, *Wissenschaftslehre* (new ed., 4 vols.; Leipzig, 1929). Compare also Y. Bar-
Hillel, "Bolzano's Definition of Analytic Propositions," *Methodos*, 2, 1950, 32–55; and H. R.
Smart, "Bolzano's Logic," *Philosophical Review*, 53, 1944, 513–533.

[5] *Wissenschaftslehre*, I, 77, 99, 219.

[6] *Ibid.*, pp. 219–222, 331, 378–387.

[7] *Ibid.*, pp. 216–218.

[8] *Ibid.*, pp. 61–67.

following consideration. Assume that two persons think, as one says, of the same mathematical theorem. This presumably raises the question whether or not the two thoughts are the "same." Some philosophers hold that there are in this case most certainly two thoughts, but they do not explain what is expressed by saying that the two thoughts are of the same theorem. Other philosophers, impressed by the latter fact, are tempted to say that the two thoughts are the "same." But this is equally unsatisfactory; for there are obviously two thoughts and not just one. According to Bolzano, the correct analysis of our example has two steps. He holds, first, that there are indeed two thoughts, that is, two "subjective" mental states and not just one. He claims, second, that these two thoughts are of one and the same objective thing, namely, of the mathematical proposition. This analysis, it is evident, introduces senses as objective entities.[9]

According to Bolzano, mental states and objects$_1$ on the one hand and senses on the other exist in different ways. In one sense of the term, what exists exists at a certain place and for a certain length of time. Mental states and objects$_1$ are existents in this sense. Senses, however, do not exist in this way or manner. Yet they are not nothing; they are there. What in this manner is there can fall under a concept or, in other words, can be the object$_2$ of a concept.[10] This distinction explains my use of the subscripts attached to the word "object." By means of these subscripts, I wish to distinguish between two meanings of the word "object." The use of "object$_1$" signifies an ontological kind. Objects$_1$ must be distinguished from senses; for only the former exist in the sense just explained. However, "object" may also be used to refer to whatever may fall under a concept. In particular, a sense itself may fall under a concept. I indicate this use by writing "object$_2$." According to this distinction, every object$_1$ is an object$_2$, but not every object$_2$ is an object$_1$.[11]

I mentioned that there are two kinds of senses, namely, propositions on the one hand and concepts (individual or general) on the other. Now in regard to these two kinds, we must note the following important points.

Propositions. (1) Bolzano distinguishes between judgments (*Urteile*) and propositions (*Sätze an sich*). Every judgment contains a propo-

---

[9] *Ibid.,* pp. 84, 113–114, 216–218, 428–429.
[10] *Ibid.,* pp. 78, 112, 144–145, 154–155, 216–218, 426–427; II, 52–54.
[11] This distinction applies also to Frege's ontology. However, in regard to Frege, one must note the further distinction between objects$_2$ (proper) and concepts. See below.

sition, but the mere thought of a proposition is not a judgment.[12] More-over, judgments are said to exist in the minds of persons that make them, while propositions, as we just saw, do not exist in this way.[13] (2) A sentence, that is, a string of spoken or written words, is said to *express* a proposition.[14] (3) Every proposition consists of a number of concepts in the manner in which a whole consists of its parts. A singular proposition, for instance, consists of an individual concept (*Subjectvorstellung*), the concept expressed by "has" ("is"), and the concept expressed by the predicate (*Prädicatvorstellung*).[15] (4) The *sum* of these concepts is called the *content* of a proposition. All that matters for the determination of a content are the respective con-cepts but not the manner in which they are conjoined.[16] For instance, the two propositions expressed by "John loves Mary" and "Mary is loved by John" have the same content.[17] However, Bolzano also insists that they are not the same proposition; these two sentences express different senses although they have the same content.[18]

Concepts. (1) Bolzano distinguishes between the content (*Inhalt*) and the extension (*Umfang*) of a concept.[19] The content of a "complex" concept, individual or general, consists of the sum of its "simple" constituents.[20] The content of a simple concept is the concept itself. The extension of a concept consists of the objects$_2$ that fall under it.[21] An individual concept, for instance, has as its extension one and only one object$_2$. A general concept, on the other hand, can either be empty or have more than one thing as its extension. (2) Concepts are never identical, although they may have either the same content (in which case neither one can be simple) or the same extension, or both.[22] This means that two different expressions always express different con-cepts.[23]

---

[12] *Wissenschaftslehre*, I, 154–155.

[13] *Ibid.*, pp. 154–155.

[14] *Ibid.*, p. 121.

[15] *Ibid.*, pp. 99, 216–218; II, 8–10, 16, 18.

[16] *Ibid.*, pp. 113–114, 243–244, 353–354, 434.

[17] I think Bolzano would also say that the propositions expressed by "John loves Mary" and "Mary loves John" have the same content. See *Wissenschaftslehre*, I, 243–244.

[18] *Ibid.*, pp. 428–429, 434, 436–438, 445–447.

[19] *Ibid.*, pp. 297–300, 353–354.

[20] *Ibid.*, pp. 243–244.

[21] *Ibid.*, pp. 297–300.

[22] *Ibid.*, pp. 428–429, 434, 436–437.

[23] *Ibid.*, p. 434. Compare also Frege's point of view: *Translations from the Philosophical Writings*, trans. by P. Geach and M. Black (Oxford, 1952), p. 29 and the footnote on p. 46. For a recent discussion of this view see, for instance, N. Goodman, "On Likeness of Meaning," *Analysis*, 10, 1950, 1–7; "On Some Differences about Meaning," *ibid.*, 13, 1953, 90-96;

This concludes my description of Bolzano's system. I turn now to Frege.

II

Frege, in his *Begriffsschrift*, does not outline a comprehensive semantical or philosophical system.[24] Keeping this point in mind, let us review some of his ideas in the light of Bolzano's distinctions.

First, Frege tells us that the most important single notion for what he is about is that of a *conceptual content* (*begrifflicher Inhalt*).[25] In his explanation of this notion he makes the following three points. (1) He distinguishes between contents that can and contents that cannot be judged about.[26] This corresponds to Bolzano's distinction between contents of concepts (individual or general) and contents of propositions. (2) He distinguishes between judgments and mere conjunctions of concepts, the latter being conceived as possible contents of judgments.[27] This corresponds to Bolzano's distinction between judgments and mere contents of propositions. (3) Frege claims that two sentences may have the same conceptual content and yet differ in sense.[28] On this view, for instance, "John loves Mary" and "Mary is loved by John" express different senses but have the same conceptual content. This corresponds to Bolzano's view that two propositions cannot be identical, although they may have the same content.

This comparison between Frege's notion of a conceptual content and Bolzano's notion of the content of a proposition shows that there is no significant difference between the two. And this seems to suggest that Frege was well aware of a general sense-denotation distinction at the time when he wrote the *Begriffsschrift*, though, of course, not necessarily of the specific one described in "On Sense and Denotation." [29] For it seems extraordinary to assume that he should not have distinguished between senses (concepts and conceptual contents) and objects$_1$.[30] But the best way to show that this assumption is unreason-

Wienpahl, "More about Denial of Sameness of Meaning," *ibid.*, 12, 1951, 19–23; R. Rudner, "On Sinn as a Combination of Physical Properties," *Mind*, 51, 1952, 82–84; and my "Propositional Attitudes," *Philosophical Quarterly*, 10, 1960, 301–12.

[24] G. Frege, *Begriffsschrift* (Halle, 1879).

[25] *Ibid.*, p. iv.

[26] *Ibid.*, p. 2.

[27] *Ibid.*, p. 2.

[28] *Ibid.*, p. 3.

[29] His "Über Sinn und Bedeutung," *Zeitschrift für Philosophie und philosophische Kritik*, 100 (1892), 25–50 (*Translations*, pp. 56–78).

[30] This does not mean, however, that Frege held in the *Begriffsschrift* that sentences are names denoting the True or the False. I think that he took this specific step much later (at the time of "Über Sinn und Bedeutung").

able consists in explaining why Frege, though aware of it, did not explicitly mention a sense-denotation distinction in the *Begriffsschrift*.

I think he had at least three reasons. First, and perhaps of greatest importance, the system of the *Begriffsschrift* centers around the notion of a conceptual content of a sentence. Conceptual contents consist of concepts rather than objects$_1$. Hence there was no necessity for the purposes of the *Begriffsschrift* to talk about anything but what is expressed rather than denoted by expressions. Second, as far as whole sentences are concerned, there are no objects$_1$ corresponding to thoughts and propositions, in Bolzano's ontology. To conceive of sentences as names that denote as well as express something, as Frege does in "On Sense and Denotation," required a radically new step, namely, the introduction of the True and the False as denotations of sentences. If one therefore assumes that this step was not yet taken by Frege when he wrote the *Begriffsschrift*, it becomes obvious that he could not possibly have talked about the denotation (in addition to the sense) of a sentence. Third, upon Frege's analysis of identity (equality) as outlined in the *Begriffsschrift*, identity statements assert that two expressions have the same conceptual content rather than the same denotation, as he later holds. I shall not explain his earlier view, but remind the reader that it involves Frege's intention to account for the "synthetic nature" of some identity statements.[31]

Second, if Frege's *Begriffsschrift*, as I have tried to show, resembles Bolzano's system in several important respects – if, in particular, Frege should have been fully aware of a sense-denotation distinction before he wrote "On Sense and Denotation" – then it must also not be overlooked that there are at least two important differences between Frege's and Bolzano's treatment of senses. First, Frege introduced so-called second-level concepts.[32] Second, he replaced Bolzano's subject-predicate analysis by a function-argument analysis.[33] This step is obviously suggested to him by the logistic treatment of mathematics. But it is also in direct accord with his (and Bolzano's) notion of a conceptual content. To see this clearly one must remember that conceptual contents are conceived of as sums of concepts. This means that as far as conceptual contents are concerned, the subject and predicate places of sentences are of no importance whatsoever. All parts of a proposition are of equal status, irrespective of their po-

---

[31] *Begriffsschrift*, pp. 13–15, and "Über Sinn und Bedeutung" (*Translations*, pp. 56–57).
[32] *Begriffsschrift*, p. 17.
[33] *Ibid.*, p. vii.

sitions in a proposition. However, Frege seems to have noticed, soon after the appearance of the *Begriffsschrift*, that the very notion of a proposition requires a distinction between concepts and objects$_2$.

III

He mentions this matter briefly in the *Grundlagen*.[34] A full account is given in Frege's answer to some remarks by B. Kerry.[35] Kerry had pointed out, basing his statements on Bolzano's view, that a concept itself is an object$_2$. Consider, for example, the sentence "The concept 'horse' is a concept easily attained." Kerry claims that this sentence says that the concept "horse" falls under the concept "a concept easily attained," and is thus an object$_2$ of the latter. Frege, on the other hand, defends the view that the phrase "the concept 'horse' " does not refer to a concept but rather to an object$_2$ as distinguished from a concept.[36] He holds that a concept is always predicative in character and that it can never occur as the subject of a sentence. So much for the two opposing views. I wish to show that Frege's treatment of concepts can be considered a direct consequence of his earlier and also of Bolzano's view.

Bolzano and the Frege of the *Begriffsschrift* hold that all propositions consist of concepts in analogy to a whole's consisting of parts. Frege now seems to have raised the following question: how can three concepts, taken as things of the same kind and standing side by side, yield the kind of unity a proposition is supposed to have?[37] In other words, how can an individual concept, a general concept, and the relational concept of falling under a concept, when taken as things of the same kind, yield a proposition rather than a conceptual content, that is, a sum of concepts? Frege, I think, discovered here a very genuine problem. How important it is can perhaps best be seen if we look at it from a different point of view.

According to some philosophers, "this tree is green" (if true) describes the fact that a certain individual exemplifies a certain property. In order to speak about facts, they must therefore speak about the

---

[34] *Die Grundlagen der Arithmetik* (Breslau, 1884); *The Foundations of Arithmetic*, trans. by J. L. Austin (New York, 1950), p. x.

[35] B. Kerry, "Über Anschauung und ihre psychische Verarbeitung," *Vierteljahrsschrift für wissenschaftliche Philosophie*, 9, 1885, 433–493; 10, 1886, 419–467; 11, 1887, 53–116, 249–307; 13, 1889, 71–124, 392–419; 14, 1890, 317–353; 15, 1891, 127–167.

[36] Frege's "Über Begriff und Gegenstand," *Vierteljahrsschrift für wissenschaftliche Philosophie*, 16, 1892, 192–205 (*Translations*, pp. 42–55).

[37] See, for instance, *Translations*, pp. 54–55.

relation of exemplification. One can now formulate Frege's question in terms of exemplification: how can three things – an individual, a property, and the relation of exemplification, standing side by side – yield a fact? Facts just do not consist of three things standing side by side like chairs. The problem in usually solved by a distinction between two kinds of "things": things like individuals and properties on the one hand and the "thing" exemplification on the other. One adds that the relation of exemplification is a very special "thing," unlike all other things including ordinary relations.[38] Notice, though, that in saying this one introduces a new kind of thing, an "unsaturated" thing if you wish. But this, as we know, is precisely Frege's own solution. However, while some philosophers make the nexus of exemplification into a special unsaturated thing and hence introduce a new kind of entity in addition to individuals and properties, Frege solves the problem on a different level by making concepts themselves into unsaturated things.[39] This allows him to dispense with the relational concept of falling under (a concept). He needs therefore no "tie" at all between objects$_2$ and concepts. In this respect his solution is extremely ingenious.[40] One wonders why later students thought it false at worst and curious at best.[41]

The point I wish to make, however, has nothing to do with whether one accepts or rejects Frege's solution. It is that Frege's object-concept distinction must be regarded as "syntactical" rather than "ontological." It must be viewed as a distinction between objects$_2$ and concepts rather than between objects$_1$ and concepts. At least two considerations speak for this interpretation.

First, Frege's distinction can be made in a purely "syntactical" way,

---

[38] See, for instance, G. Bergmann, *Meaning and Existence*, pp. 208 and 210.

[39] See, for instance, Frege's "Über Begriff und Gegenstand" and his "On the Foundations of Geometry," *Philosophical Review*, 69, 1960, 3–17.

[40] It should be noted, though, that Frege's solution requires one further distinction and one more explanation. The distinction is this. According to Frege, concepts can fall under higher concepts. In this case, since concepts are unsaturated, we have as it were two unsaturated things standing side by side. Frege consistently holds that two concepts "hold together" in a different way from a concept and an object$_2$. Thus he solves a problem which I think is peculiar to his system. His solution can be expressed either by saying that an object$_2$ falls *under* a concept, while a concept falls *within* a concept of higher level; or by saying that a concept of second level is a radically different thing from a concept of first level in that they can "hold together," although they are both unsaturated. (See "Über Begriff und Gegenstand," p. 201; *Translations*, p. 51.) The explanation concerns such sentences as "green is a color." As far as I know, Frege does not explain how he would analyze such sentences. One might suggest, however, that they be rewritten in the form "the concept green is a color-concept." Upon this kind of analysis, they would say that a certain concept correlate (an object$_2$) falls under a certain concept.

[41] Compare, however, M. Black, "Language and Reality," *Proceedings and Addresses of The American Philosophical Association*, 32, 1959, 5–17.

that is, without reference to criteria of existence. So formulated it reads as follows. There are expressions that can appear only in the subject places of well-formed (singular) sentences; there are also expressions that can occur only in the predicate places of sentences; no expression can occur in both the subject and the predicate places of sentences. Expressions that occur in subject places denote objects; expressions that occur in predicate places denote concepts.[42]

Second, one can easily show that senses other than concepts are objects$_2$, though of course not objects$_1$. In the sentence "John believes that the earth is round," the phrase "the earth is round" appears, according to Frege, as a name.[43] This name, when standing alone, denotes the True and expresses a sense. Let us call its denotation (the True) its ordinary denotation; its sense, the ordinary sense. In belief contexts, Frege holds, this sentence no longer denotes its ordinary denotation, but rather its ordinary sense. The subordinate clause in "John believes that the earth is round" thus denotes the sense of "the earth is round." In other words, in belief contexts, "the earth is round" is a *name* of the ordinary sense of this sentence. What is denoted by a name, according to Frege's object$_2$-concept distinction, must be an object$_2$. Hence senses (other than concepts) must be objects$_2$.

To sum up: so far I have tried to show that something like the sense-denotation distinction, namely, a sense-object$_1$ distinction, must have been known to Frege before he introduced it (in a specific form) in his paper "On Sense and Denotation." I emphasized that this distinction was ontological in kind. Then I explained how the two notions of a proposition and a conceptual content led to Frege's distinction between concepts and objects$_2$. I stressed that this further distinction was a syntactical rather than ontological one. If this account is correct, it follows that the ontological status of concepts will be determined by the sense-object$_1$ rather than the concept-object$_2$ dichotomy. It would follow, at any rate, that the two must be sharply distinguished in a discussion of the question whether or not Frege was a nominalist. Before we can enter into this discussion, however, we must clear up one more point, namely, Frege's use of the terms "concept" and "property."

IV

Bolzano distinguishes between (general) concepts and properties. This is an ontological distinction; for only properties, not concepts,

---

[42] I assume here that concept words *denote* concepts; see below.
[43] Über Sinn und Bedeutung," p. 39 (*Translations*, p. 68).

are objects₁. Frege, on the other hand, makes no such distintion. He holds that to say that F is a property of x means the same as to say that x falls under the concept F.[44] "Property" and "concept" are used by him interchangeably. Usually he speaks of concepts; occasionally, though, when German grammar makes the use of "concept" rather clumsy, he also uses the word "property." In most accounts of Frege's view, no significance is attached to this fact. Frege's interchangeable use of "property" and "concept" is apparently thought to be merely a terminological matter.[45] I shall show that it is more than that, that it signifies an important feature of Frege's philosophy.

It must first be observed that Frege assimilates properties to concepts and not conversely. He explains his notion of concept and states then that the word "property" may be used to refer to concepts. Assume now that Frege's concepts and hence his properties are senses in Bolzano's use of the term. It follows, of course, that they could not possibly be Bolzano's properties. Nor, I think, could they possibly be the things one ordinarily calls properties. And this means that Frege does not speak about "ordinary" properties when he uses the words "concept" and "property." [46] This is indeed the conclusion we must draw if we take the similarity between Frege's and Bolzano's systems seriously. But has Frege really banished "ordinary" properties? I think that he has. However, my view may appear so extraordinary that I shall have to prove it independently of the contention that Frege's concepts are senses rather than objects₁ in Bolzano's sense.

Frege explains that *concepts belong to the realm of logic; they are not sensible.* A concept word may be accompanied by mental states, that is, for instance, by sense impressions, *but these sense impressions are not the referent of a concept word.*[47] A concept, I take it, is thus not the kind of thing that "comes through the senses," but rather something that is "grasped by the mental eye." [48] It is clear that this use of "concept" and hence "property" does not agree with what one ordinarily means when talking about properties.

At another place Frege tells us that *there are no concepts in the outside world.*[49] Taking "concept" to be synonymous with "property," he asserts here that there are no properties in the outside world. Surely

[44] Über Begriff und Gegenstand," p. 201 (*Translations*, p. 51).

[45] See, for instance, Klemke, *op. cit.*

[46] I realize, of course, that the phrase "ordinary property" needs explanation. But I think that it will become sufficiently clear from the following paragraphs.

[47] *Foundations*, p. 37, footnote.

[48] Frege's *Grundgesetze der Arithmetik*, I (Jena, 1893), xxiv.

[49] *Foundations*, p. 99.

this use of "property" differs considerably from the ordinary use of the word. At still another place Frege asserts that concepts are objective but not *real* (*wirklich*). He denies that they are real because they do not act, mediately or immediately, on our senses.[50]

These and other contexts show that Frege's concepts are not properties in the ordinary sense. Still, someone may refuse to accept the conclusion that Frege omitted properties from his ontology. The only thing I can do at this point is to explain how the omission fits well into the wider frame of his philosophy, that it makes sense, and that it is therefore not unreasonable to attribute it to Frege.

Now according to Frege, there are so-called "*subjective Vorstellungen*" (mental states). In particular, all sense impressions are such mental states. Hence, if one sees a blue spot, then one has a "*subjective Vorstellung*." This sense impression, however, is not the referent of the concept word "blue." Moreover, whatever one can communicate about the blue spot is not of the same kind as a sense impression but is rather a conceptual kind. "*Subjective Vorstellungen*" in general are not communicable.[51] Hence there is no room for words referring to them in the clarified language proposed by Frege. What then do we mean by the concept word "blue"? We always mean, according to Frege, an objective concept, something that does not come through the senses but is grasped by the mind. Of course, sense impressions may in some sense be necessary for our intellectual life; without them, as Frege puts it, we might be as dumb as a board.[52] But this must by no means obscure the truth that concept words refer to things that have nothing whatsoever to do with our senses.

Upon this explication of "concept" and "property" what can be said about the question whether concept words denote or express concepts? Frege says that concept words denote (*bedeuten*) concepts. I take it, therefore, that he thinks of them as denoting rather than expressing concepts. I take it for granted also that he does not make the sense-denotation distinction for concept words, at least not explicitly. These two things seem reasonably certain. What is so puzzling about them is the fact that one sees no obstacle to extending the sense-denotation distinction to cover concept words in addition to names. What is puzzling, in other words, is that one has no answer to the question why Frege did not make the distinction for concept words

[50] *Grundgesetze*, p. xviii.
[51] *Foundations*, p. 35.
[52] *Ibid.*, p. 115, footnote.

after he had introduced it for names. I think that his reasons can now be easily seen. Consider two of the most obvious proposals to extend the distinction to concept words.

First, a concept word could not possibly denote a property (an object$_1$) as distinguished from a concept; for there are no such properties in Frege's system. He could therefore not possibly hold that concept words denote properties and express concepts.

Second, a concept word could not possibly denote a class (value range), and this for at least two reasons. First, classes are objects$_2$ for Frege.[53] Hence if a class were the denotation of a concept word in a sentence, we would have the case where two objects$_2$, the object$_2$ denoted by the subject expression and the object$_2$ (the class) denoted by the predicate expression, stand side by side without yielding a whole. Second, a concept could not be the sense of the name of the corresponding class, because the denotation of, say, "green" must be different from the denotation of "the sense of 'the class of green things.'" That it must be different follows directly from Frege's (and Bolzano's) view; for when one thinks the subjective idea "green," one thinks of a different thing from what one thinks of when one thinks the idea "the class of green things." This means that Frege could not hold that concept words denote classes and express concepts.

But although it is now clear that concept words could not denote anything but concepts, in accordance with Frege's use there is the possibility that they could express so-called concept correlates. Frege could have said that "green," for instance, denotes a concept and expresses the concept correlate denoted by "the concept green"; for even though he insists that "the concept green" denotes an object$_2$ (rather than a concept), he does not claim that it denotes an object$_1$ rather than a sense. In other words, although he holds that it denotes a saturated rather than an unsaturated thing, he does not hold that it denotes something other than a sense. Assuming that it does denote a sense, one could complete Frege's system in such a fashion that concept words are said to denote concepts and to express concept correlates. This, I think, is the only possibility within Frege's system of introducing the sense-denotation dichotomy for concept words.[54]

---

[53] See "Function and Concept," *Translations*, p. 32. I note in passing that this view eventually leads to the Russell paradox; see W. V. Quine, "On Frege's Way Out," *Mind*, 64, 1955, 145–159.

[54] Compare in this respect Frege's system with the one outlined by A. Church in his "A Formulation of the Logic of Sense and Denotation," in *Structure, Method and Meaning: Essays in Honor of Henry M. Sheffer* (New York, 1951), 3–24.

V

The question whether or not Frege was a nominalist makes little sense if one does not specify what one means by "nominalism," or, alternatively, what one's criterion for existence is. I shall consider three possible specifications.

First, Frege himself distinguishes between two meanings of "there is." Let me call them exist$_1$ and exist$_2$. He says that one must keep apart two wholly different cases in which one speaks of existence. In the one case the question is whether a proper name denotes something; in the other it is whether a concept comprehends objects under itself.[55] Frege argues in this context against the following view. Construing the thing denoted by a proper name as the extension of this name, and holding that a concept word refers to its extension, one may mistakenly think that since a proper name without denotation is illegitimate, a concept word without extension must be equally illegitimate. Against this view Frege asserts that a concept word does not denote an extension but a concept. A concept word may well have a denotation, that is, it may denote a concept, even though nothing falls under the concept. For instance, the concept word "round square" denotes, according to Frege, a concept. It has therefore a denotation. But since nothing is a round square, nothing falls under the concept. It is implied here, I think, that a certain concept exists even if nothing falls under it as long as there is a concept word that refers to it. One must therefore distinguish between the following two kinds of existence statements: (1) "α exists." This I write "α exists$_1$" and take to mean " 'α' denotes something." Eisenhower exists$_1$. Clearly, every object$_2$ exists$_1$. Moreover, if concept words do name concepts, then (1) is true in case either "tree" or "round square" is substituted for "α," irrespective of the fact that while there are trees, there are no round squares. (2) "An F exists." This I write "F exists$_2$" and take to mean "There is an F." Trees exist$_2$; round squares do not.

It is clear, of course, that in Frege's ontology objects$_2$ exist$_1$. But it is also obvious that concepts exist$_1$ in the same way; for concept words denote concepts. Hence there is no distinction between the manner in which objects$_2$ and the manner in which concepts exist. Klemke seems to take Frege's exist$_1$ as his criterion.[56] He concludes therefore that Frege is not a nominalist. Upon his criterion this is undoubtedly so.

---

[55] *Translations*, pp. 104–105.

[56] Klemke, *op. cit.*

But to accept it as the only relevant one means to overlook some important features of Frege's ontology.

Second, according to Bolzano, concepts do not exist like objects$_1$. Since objects$_1$ comprise properties, one must conclude that concepts do not exist like properties. This suggests the following consideration. One may hold that properties do not exist in space and time. They do not exemplify spatial and temporal relations; only individuals do. In a schema like that of *Principia Mathematica*, this is brought out by the fact that properties and spatial and temporal relations are of the same type-level.[57] In this sense, then, properties are not in space and time. They are not, as I shall say for short, localized$_1$. However, Bolzano asserts that properties are in space and time while concepts are not and this leads him to say that the latter do not exist like the former. What he seems to have in mind is this. Although agreeing that properties are not localized$_1$, he wishes to say that they are nevertheless localized (localized$_2$) in the sense that they are exemplified by individuals which are localized$_1$. For example, the property blue may be said to be localized$_2$ here and now by being exemplified here and now by a certain individual. Another way of saying the same thing is to insist that although properties do not exemplify spatial and temporal relations, their being exemplified by individuals takes place in space and time. Upon this distinction between what is localized$_1$ and what is localized$_2$, it is easily seen that concepts do not exist like properties. For properties, though not localized$_1$, are at least localized$_2$; concepts, on the other hand, are neither localized$_1$ not localized$_2$. This is to say, we are never acquainted with an individual's exemplifying a concept but only with its exemplifying a property.

Consider in the light of this Frege's view of concepts. We remember that he does not distinguish between concepts and properties. In his philosophy there are only concepts. We also remember that concepts are not got through the senses but grasped by the mind. It would seem that what can only be so grasped must be unlocalized$_2$. Frege's concepts, I therefore think, not only do not exemplify spatial and temporal relations; they are not even exemplified in space and time. There are no concepts, as he says, in the outside world, in the totality of space.[58]

If, therefore, one understands by "nominalism" the view that properties are not even localized$_2$ in space and time, then Frege was

---

[57] See, for instance, G. Bergmann, *Meaning and Existence*, pp. 124–131.
[58] *Foundations*, p. 99.

most certainly a nominalist. This conclusion agrees well with some of
the things a realist may say to defend his position that properties
exist. For though he admits that properties are not localized$_1$ in space
and time, he also insists that they are localized$_2$. In other words, even
though the realist acknowledges that properties do not exemplify
spatial and temporal relations, he nevertheless asserts that they are
exemplified in space and time by individuals. That they are in this
manner exemplified, and that he can therefore be acquainted with
them by being acquainted with individuals, is the realist's reason for
holding that properties exist. From this point of view a nominalist is
one who denies that he is ever acquainted with properties in this way.
From this point of view Frege is a nominalist. But notice that his is a
very peculiar kind of nominalism. For though he denies that properties
(concepts) are localized$_2$, he steadfastly asserts that they exist. In what
further sense may concepts be held to exist?

Third, Frege's answer, I submit, would take the following form.
There are things which are localized$_1$ in space and time. There are also
things which are not so localized. All senses in general and all concepts
in particular are of the latter kind. That these things exist, even though
they are not localized in any sense, is shown by the fact that they can
be apprehended by minds. What exists in this sense is what can
interact with minds.[59] We may reasonable infer from this criterion (1)
that Frege could agree that concepts do not exist in terms of being
localized (in any sense) and that he could be considered a nominalist
for this reason; and (2) that he holds concepts to be real because they
can be apprehended by minds and that he must therefore be called a
realist.

---

[59] Frege's "The Thought: A Logical Inquiry," *Mind*, 65, 1956, 309–311.

XI. MOORE'S ONTOLOGY AND
NON-NATURAL PROPERTIES*

HERBERT HOCHBERG

Moore's distinction between natural and non-natural properties has never been clearly and cogently made. In this paper I will attempt to show that this distinction stems from an ontology that Moore adhered to at the time *Principia Ethica* was written. While such an attempt may not clarify the distinction, it will, I believe, at least show why that distinction is not clear. For, as we shall see, Moore's ontology, at the turn of the century, was both complicated and confused.

First, we shall consider the distinction a set forth in *Principia*. Next, on the basis of what Moore says there, a view as to the nature of universals will be attributed to him. This view will provide the ground for a radical distinction between natural and non-natural properties. But it will not quite jibe with other things he says at a slightly later period. Nor will it be clear why he holds to such a view of universals. Finally we shall consider a very early paper of Moore's, written just prior to *Principia*. An analysis of this paper will reveal a rather strange and complex ontology implicit in it. This, in turn, will show (a) the source of the ontology of *Principia*; (b) why the ontology attributed to him in *Principia* does not jibe with other things he says; and (c) the origin of the notion of non-natural properties.

The problem arises in a remarkable passage in *Principia*. There Moore writes:

Can we imagine 'good' as existing *by itself* in time, and not merely as a property of some natural object? For myself, I cannot so imagine it, whereas with the greater number of properties of objects – those which I call the natural properties – their existence does seem to me to be independent of the existence of those objects. They are, in fact, rather parts of which the object is made up than mere predicates which attach to it. If they were all taken away, no object would be left, not even a bare substance: for they are in themselves substantial and give to the object all the substance that it has. But this is not so with good.[1]

* *The Review of Metaphysics* 15, 1962, 365–395. Reprinted by permission.
[1] G. E. Moore, *Principia Ethica* (Cambridge University Press: Cambridge, reprinted 1954), p. 41.

In a criticism of this passage Broad argued:

Now it seems to me that *every* characteristic of a natural object answers to Moore's criterion of non-naturalness, and that *no* characteristic could possibly be natural in his sense. I do not believe for a moment that a penny is a whole of which brownness and roundness are parts, nor do I believe that the brownness or roundness of a penny could exist in time all by itself. Hence if I accepted Moore's account , I should have to reckon brownness, roundness, pleasantness, etc., as *non-natural* characteristics.[2]

In a reply, written almost forty years after the publication of *Principia Ethica*, Moore accepted Broad's criticism and acknowledged that his earlier account was "utterly silly and preposterous." [3] But Moore did not attempt to explain why he had made the distinction the way he did in *Principia*. Rather, by calling his earlier view "silly and preposterous," he seems to suggest that it was just a wild and spontaneous notion he once had. But it goes deeper than that. We will now see why it does.

(A) MOORE'S NOMINALISM

Natural qualities, Moore tells us, exist in time, are substantial, and are parts of natural objects. He further tells us that it is easy to say what sorts of things are natural objects. Minds, thoughts, and, for that matter, anything which may be said to exist is a natural object. Sometimes he uses the term "object" to include both qualities and what we might call particulars. At other times qualities are spoken of as properties of natural objects rather than as objects themselves. All this might suggest that at this stage of his thought Moore, explicitly or implicitly, considered the property yellow in a particular yellow patch as something like an Aristotelian *this yellowness*. This would fit with its being considered as substantial, existing in time, and being *a part* of the yellow patch. (Hereafter, I will refer to such things as a *this yellowness*, a *this redness*, etc., as "simple particulars" or "simple objects.") In short, natural properties are, for Moore, construed nominalistically as simple particulars. An "ordinary" particular, like a yellow patch, would then be thought to be a composite substance containing simple substances, like this yellowness, as parts. Such simple particulars are not composed, in turn, of, say, a bare *this* and the property yellow. They do not, on such a view, seem to be composed of

---

[2] C. D. Broad, "Certain Features in Moore's Ethical Doctrines," in *The Philosophy of G. E. Moore*, edited by P. A. Schilpp (Northwestern University: Evanston, 1942), p. 59.

[3] G. E. Moore, "A Reply to My Critics," in *The Philosophy of G. E. Moore*, p. 582.

anything at all. In fact Moore tells us that there are no bare *thises*.[4] A composite particular, like a yellow patch, is then made up only of simple particulars without any bare substantial element. As Moore says, these simple particulars would "give the object all the substance that it has." [5] To say of a composite particular, say, a yellow square named "Paul," that it is yellow would be to say either that Paul contains a particular yellowness or that a particular yellowness is a part of Paul. "Contains" or, alternatively, "is a part of" would then signify a relation that holds between two particulars – one composite and one simple. *Contains* holding between two particulars would then replace *exemplification* holding between a particular and a universal in the analysis of assertions like "Paul is yellow."

At this point it will be necessary to specify some further terminology that will be used in the ensuing analysis. One basic division will be between ontological *entities*, on the one hand, and ontological *ties*, or structural relations, on the other. Such ontological ties hold between entities. *Exemplification* and *contains* are examples of ontological ties. The term "entity" will apply to existents and non-existents. Thus an entity will have some ontological "status" even though it is not an existent object or thing. "Object" and "thing" will be reserved to indicate existents, and the former will be used to refer only to particulars, and not to universals. Simple particulars, as well as universals, will sometimes be called properties, but such simple particulars will not be referred to as universals. With this in mind we may return to Moore.

We are not here concerned with all the difficulties of the view I attributed to Moore, but only with the possibility that Moore might have held such a view, albeit implicitly, in *Principia*. We can see why he might have been attracted to such a position. On the one hand he does not wish to accept bare substances, or bare particulars, in his ontology. One who holds to the existence of universals is naturally led into acknowledging bare particulars as well. For, holding to the existence of universals, one might feel required to acknowledge such bare particulars to exemplify the universals and provide the basis for individuation. A yellow square would be "composed" (in some sense) of the universal yellow, the universal square, and a bare particular. Thus the rejection of bare particulars may lead one to reject universals. On the other hand, Moore is apparently bothered by universals in their own right. This is made clear by what he says of natural properties

---

4 See note 1 above.
5 See note 1 above.

in the passage cited above, as well as by what he later says in *Some Main Problems of Philosophy*. In this latter work he is trying to decide whether or not there are any universals like redness, whiteness, etc. In the course of his discussion he writes:

And it *is* very natural to think this; it is very natural, for instance, to think of the universal 'pure red' as resembling particular patches of pure red in precisely the respect in which they all resemble one another. It is, therefore, important to realise that this cannot possibly be the case. And when this is realised, it does, I think, diminish the plausibility of the whole theory that there is any such thing .... The objection which I feel to the theory is simply that I cannot discover any such thing. I cannot discover that I ever have it before my mind.[6]

Even where he goes on to find a case where he can have a property or universal before his mind –

This, therefore, would be an argument for supposing that the property common and peculiar to all *pairs must* consist in their possession of a universal ....; whereas, in the case of the colours, there is no necessity to suppose this, since in their case the property common and peculiar to them all *may* be merely a disjunctive property defined by reference to immediate resemblance [7]

– he proceeds to remind us of a distinction already made use of in *Principia* – the distinction between being and existing.[8] Universals, like those involved in our comprehension of numbers, and "truths" [9] may be said to *be* in some sense, but only particulars *exist*. Moreover, the attempt to define "properties" in terms of a relation of resemblance was even then a classical move in some nominalistic gambits. Moore's evident concern about universals, like redness, and his suggestion that even universals which *are* do not exist, reflect nominalistic leanings. Furthermore, like the nominalistically inclined classical empiricists Moore tends to confuse a phenomenal quality, like yellow, with particulars that exemplify it, yellow patches. Such confusion is apparent in Moore's celebrated "The Refutation of Idealism," [10] published in the same year as *Principia*. Also, Moore himself says, in the appendix, added in 1952 to *Some Main Problems of Philosophy:*

---

[6] G. E. Moore, *Some Main Problems of Philosophy* (George Allen & Unwin Ltd: London, second impression, 1958), p. 361.

[7] *Ibid.*, p. 368.

[8] *Ibid.*, pp. 372–73.

[9] Moore distinguishes *truths*, not the universal *truth*, from existent particulars and from non-existent universals. Perhaps, on analysis, these would turn out to be non-existent particulars, since he classifies them, along with universals, as non-existents. In that case, while all existents would be particulars, not all particulars would be existents. The distinction between existent and non-existent particulars would undoubtedly be based on the "fact" that non-existent particulars, like universals, would not be temporal entities. (*Ibid.*, p. 372).

[10] "The Refutation of Idealism," reprinted in *Philosophical Studies* (Routledge & Kegan Paul: London, 1951). See pp. 17–19.

"I failed, for some reason or other, to see that the colour of a patch is not identical with the patch in question ...." [11] In the same appendix he mentions another mistake he earlier made:

A second gross mistake which I made was that of supposing anybody to hold that, in a case where we see two patches of exactly the same shade of colour, or one patch of the shade in question, this shade of colour is something which we don't see.... Why should it not be the case (as I now suppose it to be) that whenever I see a white patch, of one and the same shade of white all over, I *also* see that particular shade of white, *of* which that patch happens to be? [12]

His earlier view that perhaps one doesn't *see* the universal but only the particular patch may have contributed to his suspicions about the existence of such universals. Recall, in a passage cited above, his earlier statement to the effect that he cannot discover a universal like white "before" his mind. Yet in both *Principia* and *Some Main Problems of Philosophy* Moore is concerned to give some ontological status to universals. In this vein he holds that not all universals may be eliminated by definition and he does not doubt that there are, in some sense, relational universals. Thus one cannot simply classify Moore as a nominalist, for there appear to be strains of both realism and nominalism in his thought. Why this "double aspect" is there we shall soon see.

Moore does not construe non-natural properties in terms of simple particulars. Non-natural properties, unlike natural ones, are not substantial for him. Goodness would not then be construed in terms of simple particulars like *this yellowness*. Rather, goodness is a *bona fide* universal. This may be the simple but striking difference between natural and non-natural properties. *Only non-natural properties are universals*. Natural ones are not universals at all but are thought of in terms of simple particulars. In the phrase "non-natural property" the adjective "non-natural" would then be superfluous if one equated properties with universals. This conclusion, while perhaps startling, certainly points to a distinction between natural and non-natural properties and thus provides a partial explication of the adjective "non-natural." Natural and non-natural properties are different kinds of entities in somewhat the same sense that a realist might say that this chair is a different kind of thing from any universal it exemplifies. The distinction is far-reaching. For it would involve more than Moore's holding that there are at least three different sorts of entities in his ontology – composite particulars, simple particulars, and non-natural

[11] *Some Main Problems of Philosophy*, p. 374.
[12] *Ibid.*, p. 375.

properties or universals. Such an ontology would also seem to require an additional fundamental tie besides that expressed by "contains" or "is a part of." One would not say that Paul is good by asserting that Paul contains goodness. Rather, the composite particular Paul, if it were good, would *exemplify* goodness. Perhaps simple particulars would also. Exemplification would not hold between two particulars but between a particular and a universal. This structural complication reflects the basic ontological difference between goodness and simple particulars. There would then be two ways of combining terms to make sentences and, thus, of combining entities into facts. One way would involve a term referring to a particular and a term denoting a non-natural property or universal; the other would involve two terms referring to particulars. In this latter case one term would refer to a simple particular or natural property. Thus, as Moore often said, "good" would indeed be a predicate of a different *kind* from "yellow." If by "predicate" one meant either a term that could occupy a certain place in a sentence expressing an exemplification relation or a term that must occupy a certain place in a sentence expressing a containment relation, then we would have two different kinds of predicates. Only the terms of one kind, however, would denote universals. Thus there is a fundamental difference between sentences like "this is yellow" and "this is good." This reflects the difference between the two fundamental ontological ties of exemplifying and containing. But there is still a problem about the ontological status of universals. Before considering it, we might note another facet of Moore's discussion of goodness that jibes with the structural difference between goodness and yellowness that we just considered.

Moore makes frequent and systematic use of the argument that pleasure, for example, may not be identified with good, since we may always ask if pleasure is good. This query may be raised against any attempted identification of a natural property with good. To identify pleasure with good is to assert that pleasure is identical with good, where both "pleasure" and "good" are predicates. With "P" and "G" abbreviating "pleasure" and "good" respectively, this would assert the identity statement "P = G." But in Moore's characteristic query, he is not asking if pleasure is identical with good when he asks if pleasure is good. Rather, he is asking if pleasure exemplifies goodness. And it is precisely because he holds such a query to be "significant" that he questions the identification. Thus he is concerned with a proposition of the form "G (P)." Since a proposition of the form "G (P)" makes sense, Moore concludes that "P = G" is false. But, since "G (P)" makes sense, one may note that "G" and "P" must be terms of different logical types. Consequently, one may conclude that part of Moore's objection to what he calls the naturalistic fallacy rests on a claim that terms like "G" and "P" are of different logical kinds. If one considers pleasure to be a universal, rather than a simple particular, one could look upon goodness as a universal of a higher "type" than pleasure. However, a complication would result from the possibility of its applying to objects that exemplified pleasure, as well as to pleasure. But the logical difference between goodness and pleasure would also be preserved, without this complication, if pleasure were construed along the nominalistic lines we have been discussing, while goodness remained a universal. Speaking of pleasure would then always involve a reference to some particular, either simple or composite. These particulars, in turn, could exemplify goodness. Hence, one could, as Moore argues, always sensibly ask if good is exemplified by pleasure (a simple particular) or by pleasant objects. On the other hand, any proposed identification of goodness with pleasure would then commit a logical blunder. For goodness and pleasure are just different sorts of things.

In saying all this I do not mean to attribute to Moore anything like Russell's theory of types, and I certainly do not wish to suggest that he rejects "P = G" on structural grounds alone. I merely wish to suggest that his abrupt dismissal of all proposed naturalistic identifications of goodness with natural properties may stem, in part, from his feeling that there is a structural difference between terms like "good" and "pleasure." And this feeling is made quite explicit in the nominalistic view that we considered.

Even though Moore may treat natural properties like redness in terms of simple particulars, goodness is clearly a universal for him. What then is its ontological status? He tells us that good is a mere predicate (the universal, not the term) which attaches to objects but is not a substantial part of any object. He also tells us in *Principia* that good doesn't exist.

They (metaphysicians) have always been much occupied, not only with that other class of natural objects which consists in mental facts, but also with the class of objects or properties of objects, which certainly do not exist in time ,are nottherefore parts of Nature, and which, in fact, do not *exist* at all. To this class, as I have said, belongs what we mean by the adjective "good."
.... the assumption that "good" *must* denote some *real* property of things

.... is mainly due to two erroneous doctrines, the first *logical*, the second *epistemological*.[13]

Here he asserts quite clearly the classical nominalistic doctrine that to exist is to exist in time and, consequently, that the property good does not exist. We then have a second notion involved in the concept of a non-natural property. *Non-natural properties do not exist.* The first notion was, to repeat, that non-natural properties are the only universals. From these two contentions it follows that universals do not exist. And this, we noticed, is a theme that Moore explicitly adheres to in 1913 in *Some Main Problems of Philosophy*. But in *Principia*, as in this later work, he distinguishes between *being* and *existing*. Good *is* somehow, – even though it doesn't *exist*. Moore thus explicitly recognizes two sorts of entities – existents and non-existents. Within the first category we have composite particulars and simple particulars. In the second, there are properties and apparently, from the cited passages, certain individuals or particulars as well. Thus the phrase "kind of entity" takes on two meanings for Moore. There are two "kinds of entities" in the sense of particulars and universals. There are also two "kinds of entities" in the sense of existents and non-existents. Thus we have four possible kinds of entities: existent particulars, existent universals, non-existent particulars, non-existent universals. But in *Principia*, only three of these possibilities are realized. For there are no existent universals. Hence, non-existent universals are exemplified not only by non-existent particulars, but by existent ones! Thus there is an ontological tie between existent and non-existent entities. This seems strange. That real particulars exemplify real universals is a familiar philosophical theme. That there are no universals for particulars to exemplify is another. But Moore's view is neither of these, for his nominalism is tempered by the addition of universals, as non-existent entities, to his ontology. A classical realist would hold that a particular, which is in time, exemplifies a universal which is not. Like the realist, Moore retains the exemplification relation and the atemporality of universals; but, identifying, like the nominalist, *existing* with *being in time*, Moore contends that exemplification holds between an existent and a non-existent. This explains why he speaks of good as a "mere predicate." But such a view itself requires explanation. And this returns us to Moore's view that an (existent) composite particular contains its natural properties rather than exemplifying them. This, of course, is the nub of Moore's nominalism in *Principia*, since it is

13 *Principia Ethica*, pp. 110, 140.

plausible to hold, once one has replaced *exemplification* by *contains*, that parts and wholes are the same *sorts of entities*, in both senses of that phrase. For, it might seem strange to say either that a real thing has unreal parts or that *part* of a particular object is not itself a particular object. This much would seem to be involved in the use of *contains* rather than *exemplification*. Thus we must ask two further questions. Why does Moore think in terms of *contains* at all? And, secondly, once he replaces *exemplification* by *contains* for natural properties, why does he retain *exemplification* for non-natural ones? To put it another way, why doesn't a composite particular *contain this goodness* as it *contains this redness*? Or, to put it still differently, why doesn't he construe the so-called non-natural properties, like goodness, in terms of simple particulars? Moreover, a number of further questions arise concerning simple particulars (natural properties). Since simple particulars are temporal entities, how are they related to temporal properties? That is, are temporal properties non-natural properties, and hence non-existent universals, which are exemplified by simple particulars, or are temporal properties themselves natural properties and thus also to be construed in terms of simple particulars? Further, do, for example, two yellow patches contain the same *this yellowness* or would there be more than one such simple particular? And, if the latter, in virtue of what are they both yellownesses? All these questions naturally arise in connection with Moore's nominalism. Yet there are no explicit answers in *Principia*. We will consider these questions next. Before doing so, one further complication in Moore's ontological views is relevant here.

Sometimes Moore suggests that simples only are real, while composites are simply collections of simples. Thus simple particulars would be, ultimately, the only existent entities. But in *Principia* Moore consistently uses "real" as synonymous with "being in time," rather than with "simple" or "simple and in time." Thus natural objects which are composites are existents in the sense of being *natural* or *temporal*. For Moore does not seem concerned with the ontological theme of simplicity in *Principia*, aside from his concern with the simplicity of goodness. Nevertheless Moore is ultimately concerned with simplicity. And we shall see some further strange consequences when that concern is blended with his view that an existent is in time.

(B) CONCEPTS AND OBJECTS IN MOORE'S ONTOLOGY

In Moore's 1899 paper "The Nature of Judgment," we find not only the origin of the ontology I attributed to *Principia* but a basis for answering the questions raised at the end of section (A). In that paper Moore tells us that a *concept* is not something mental but "what Mr. Bradley calls a 'universal meaning' ...." In short, concepts are objective universals and not "subjective ideas." Among concepts we find *red*, *this*, and *now*. Propositions are composed neither of words nor of thoughts but of concepts. Concepts may also be objects of thought. But this merely means that they come into a relation with a thinker and are not dependent upon such a thinker. Further, concepts are incapable of change and hence are immutable. *Existence*, we are told, is also a concept. And, moreover, everything that exists is composed of concepts. Objects, as well as propositions, are thus composites of concepts. In this vein Moore asserts, "It seems necessary then, to regard the world as formed of concepts." [14]

What Moore seems to have in mind in stating all of this is the following view. Recall the square yellow patch named "Paul." The *concept of Paul* is a complex concept composed of simple concepts like yellow and square. The object named "Paul" is also a complex of concepts. It is composed not only of the concepts contained in the *concept of Paul* but of existence as well. Each of these complexes of concepts also contains a relation in which its constitutive concepts stand. It is not quite clear whether these relations differ in the case of objects and concepts of objects, but at times Moore suggests that they do.[15] Let us then refer to the relation involved in the concept of Paul by the term "R_1" and to that relation in the object Paul by the term "R_2." Also, it is not exactly clear whether the object Paul is made up of the concept of Paul and the concept of existence in the relation R_2, or whether the object Paul is composed of the constituent concepts of the concept of Paul together with the concept existence in the relation R_2. The difference would be that in the former case the relation R_1 would also be involved in the structure of the object, whereas in the latter case it would not be. Aside from the difference between R_1 and R_2, objects would differ from concepts of objects in that the former would contain the concept *existence*, while the latter would not. Propositions, too, are complexes of concepts. They consist of concepts in a further relation, say, R_3. Thus Paul, the concept of Paul, and propositions about Paul are all composed, ultimately, of concepts. Existents are

---

[14] G. E. Moore, "The Nature of Judgment," *Mind*, 30, 1899, 182. The ontological status of mind is not discussed by Moore in this paper.

[15] *Ibid.*, 182–3.

those entities which "contain" the concept existence. In this vein
Moore even thinks of existential propositions, as distinct from other
propositions, as existents! For an existential proposition is a complex
of concepts, one of which is the concept existence.

Even the description of an existent as a proposition (a true existential proposition) seems to lose its strangeness, when it is remembered that a proposition is
here to be understood, not as anything subjective .... but as the combination
of concepts which is affirmed.[16]

But why then aren't false existential propositions existents as well?
For they too *contain* existence. One ground for distinguishing them
seems to be that the component concepts of true propositions stand in a
different relation than the components of false propositions. Thus
instead of R_3 being involved in both true and false propositions, there
would be two distinct relations, say R_{3t} and R_{3f}, one of which, R_{3t},
would hold between the constituent concepts of true propositions and
the other, R_{3f}, between those of false propositions.[17] But then a
sentence will signify one propositional entity if it is true, an entity
involving R_{3t}, and another propositional entity if it is false, one
involving R_{3f}. Hence, if propositonal entities provide the meaning for
sentences just as concepts provide the meaning of terms, a sentence
would mean one thing if it were true and another thing if it were false.
Also, if the difference between true and false propositions, as entities,
lies in the relation combining their constitutive concepts, then this
relation is apparently the key to why true existential propositions are
existents and false ones are not. For the concept existence will stand in
one relation to the other conceptual constituents of a true existential
proposition, and in a different relation to those of a false proposition.
But if the combining relation plays such a role, then Moore need not
accept propositions as existents at all. He need only view complexes of
concepts which contain existence and involve the relation R_2 (the
"object relation") as existents. For it certainly seems more cogent to
draw an existential line between objects, on the one hand, and concepts
of objects together with propositions, on the other, than to include
existential propositions with objects. But there is a reason why Moore
does not do this.

All of R_1, R_2, R_{3t}, and R_{3f} give rise to complexes which "contain"
their constituent concepts. Hence all these relations may be confused
with the relation of containment. Since an existent is what *contains*

[16] *Ibid.*, 183.
[17] *Ibid.*, 180.

existence, it might then seem natural to hold that any complex of concepts which "contains" existence is an existent. (If consistent, one would not then balk at false existential propositions.) Thus the notion of *containment* may provide a basis both for the fusing of the various R's and for Moore's consequent belief that some propositions are existents. Moreover, if one confuses the R's with each other and with *contains*, we should not be surprised if sometimes Moore confuses objects with concepts and with propositions. The latter confusion might be involved in Moore's holding existential propositions to be existents. Did not Moore once recount a nightmare in which he could not distinguish propositions from tables? In any case, we shall see the confusion between objects and concepts occur in another context.

Let us assume that Paul has no other properties than being yellow and square. He would then be composed of the concepts *yellow, square, now*, and *existence* (and perhaps also *this*), in the relation R_2. To "picture" Paul's structure, we might refer to "him" by the following complex sign:

(a) R_2 [yellow, square, now, existence].

Similarly, the concept of Paul might be signified by

(b) R_1 [yellow, square].

Recall that Paul might be considered to be composed of *his concept* together with *existence* (and *now*). On this alternative Paul would be represented not by (a) but by

(a') R_2 [R_1 (yellow, square), now, existence].

In either case, (a) or (a'), we can see in what sense Paul is ultimately composed of simple concepts. The inclusion of the concept *now* also shows the temporal character of existent objects.

At this point two alternative interpretations of what Moore says are open to us. We may consider him to hold that there is one basic tie – contains – which is not a concept among concepts, but which relates any complex of concepts to any constituent of that complex. Thus statements asserting that a certain object contains a constituent x and that a certain proposition contains a constituent y would both involve the same sense of "contains." But the constituents in both cases would be "tied" together to make the different complexes by different relations – relations other than containment – R_1, R_2, etc. These R's, like "contains," may be thought of as ontological ties and not concepts – though Moore does sometimes unwarily speak of such relations as if they were concepts among concepts.[18] This contrasts strongly with one who, not holding to the containment pattern, thinks in terms of bare particulars *exemplifying* universals. For this latter pattern does not involve one in speaking of *wholes* which contain *parts*. Hence, in addition to exemplification which connects the particular with the universal, he does not need to speak of a whole which is also related to something as a part. But the whole which is a complex of concepts connected by one of the R's is also related to each of its constituents in that it *contains* them. One who embraces this pattern also requires, in addition to the R's, the containment relation. For the R's relate parts to each other to form the whole; they do not, in turn, relate the whole to each part. The containment pattern thus involves one with two sorts of relations or ties. In the case of exemplification this dual role of the tie does not require a further relation. For what is connected by exemplification to the universal to form a "fact," and what is spoken about in a sentence that ascribes the universal to something is, in both cases, the same bare particular. A corresponding need for a further relation would arise only if one included facts as further entities in one's ontology and then wished to assert that such facts *contained* universals as constituents. For then one would speak of a certain whole, the fact, and not of a bare particular as being connected with a universal, and this would certainly involve a different connection from that of exemplification. In the containment pattern the subject of that relation is always a composite of related concepts. Hence such subjects have a factual aspect; they are, as it were, facts compressed into objects. This contrasts strongly with the case of a bare particular exemplifying a universal in the exemplification pattern. For there, there is a clear distinction between the bare particular and the fact to which it gives rise by exemplifying a property. Thus one may notice, perhaps uncomfortably, that by using *contains* there seems to be a redundancy in assertions like "Paul is yellow." Since yellow is contained in the concept of Paul, this is like saying that a complex of concepts, of which yellow is one, contains yellow. Thus, upon analysis, sentences like "Paul is yellow" may, by the use of *contains*, turn out to be analytic. All of this is perhaps what attracts some to bare particulars and the ontological tie of exemplification.

If one then accepts both the R's and *contains*, one may point out that the R's, rather than *contains*, are the fundamental ties of the pattern since they, so to speak, provide the ontological glue to unite concepts

[18] *Ibid.*, 181.

into composites. But this really adds nothing to what has been said. However, it may lead one to propose an alternative interpretation of what Moore says. Instead of having several different R's and one containment relation, this alternative would seek to get along with several different containment relations and not make use of the R's at all. Or, to put it another way, the R's we have introduced would each express a different sense of "contains." There would not then be any further relation in addition to the R's. But, as it stands, this merely gives a dual role to each of the R's. For they would then function both to relate the parts to each other, and to relate the whole to any part. To remove this complexity one might drop the relation between the whole and any part. Such a one might suggest that to say, for example, "Paul is yellow" is not to say that "Paul contains yellow," but that certain concepts (the others which make up the concept of Paul) stand in a certain relation, R_2, with yellow. This alternative, like the first, is fraught with difficulties that it is not my intention to explore here. We may simple note that in effect this alternative abandons the containment pattern, in that it drops the connection between whole and part. In view of this, and for the easier exposition of what follows, the first alternative will be adopted here.

In connection with all this we might note that (a), above, may alternatively be considered a sentence stating that certain concepts are "tied" by R_2 or a sign referring to Paul. This reflects, again, the factual "aspect" that objects take on in the containment pattern. Even though Moore suggests otherwise, in neither case must R_2 be thought of as a relational concept. For then one either falls heir to a Bradleyian type regress or lapses into the exemplification pattern by holding, in effect, that the other concepts exemplify the relation R_2. To repeat, R_2, like "exemplifies," is a tie and not a concept (albeit relational) among concepts. Be that as it may, the two-fold way in which (a) may be considered leads to a problem which brings us to the heart of Moore's pattern. To get to that problem, consider the sentence "Paul is yellow." We may transcribe this sentence by

(α) Paul C yellow,

where "C" stands for the containment relation. Note that this relation, like the R's, is not a concept among concepts. (α), if true, would also give rise to a propositional entity denoted by

(c) R_{3t} [the concept of Paul, yellow],

and an object, Paul, denoted by (a) or (a'). [Hereafter (a') will be used, since the distinction, once seen, may be forgotten for the ensuing discussion.] The sentence (α) would then be true if there is a certain propositional entity (which, by the way, is really what is true for Moore, since he thinks of propositions, rather than sentences, as being true or false) denoted by (c). Likewise, if we are talking about an object, the truth of the sentence, or proposition, would indicate that the object contains yellow. The same would hold for existential propositions. To say that Paul exists would be to assert

(β) Paul C existence.

This would be the case if there were a propositional entity denoted by

(d) R_{3t} [the concept of Paul, existence] [19]

and an object denoted by (a'). All this shows why Moore sometimes expresses the fact that an object exists in terms of the object's containing existence, and other times by stating that the concept of the object stands in a certain relation to existence.[20] For *in* the existent object we have the concept of it and existence in the relation R_2. This, of course, fits with what was said above about the two-fold way one may look at expressions like (a), (b), (a'), etc. If we take them as signs referring to objects, etc., we would use them as subjects in sentences stating that what they refer to *contains* something. If we take them as sentences, they state that concepts stand in certain relations. Moore speaks of them in both ways. But the use of these alternative phrasings brings us to the problem I mentioned. Actually, the problem does not arise directly in the case of an object like Paul. But suppose we wish to say that the simple concept red exists. One might think that this would be asserted by holding that red and existence stand in the relation R_2. But then what exists is not the concept red but a composite composed of *red, existence*, the relation R_2, and *now*. Speaking in terms of con-

---

[19] Notice that the concept *now* is not included in a propositional entity of this kind. Nor, for that matter, would any other temporal concept be included in either (c) or (d). For propositions do not seem to be temporal entities. This might be the origin of Moore's distinguishing truths (true propositions) from both universals and particulars. (See note 9, above.) Not being concepts like red, propositions are not universals; but, not being temporal, they are not thought of as particulars. This shows how, for Moore, being in time and being a particular go together. But a problem will arise due to his holding that some propositions are existents and that all existents are temporal or particular. A further problem will arise in connection with propositions that contain temporal concepts. To avoid calling such entities "temporal," one might hold that a temporal entity not only contained a temporal concept but contained it in a certain relation to its other concepts – the relation R_2. Recall the above discussion of Moore's "mistake" in holding that existential propositions are existents since they contain the concept existence.

[20] *Ibid.*, 180–81, 183, 189. Moore does not use the term "contains," but speaks of concepts being combined with each other.

tainment makes it even clearer. For only composites can contain anything. Hence, a simple concept like red could not be the subject of a containing relation. *Red cannot then exist,* if one thinks of existents as containing the concept existence. But Moore speaks of the existence of red. Sometimes he seems to mean a particular red patch. But some other times he seems to mean something else.

It was pointed out that a pure existential proposition could only assert the existence of a simple concept; all others involving the *a priori* concepts of substance and attribute. If now we take the existential proposition "Red exists," we have an example of the type required. It is maintained that, when I say this, my meaning is that the concept "red" and the concept "existence" stand in a specific relation both to one another and to the concept of time. I mean that "Red exists now," and thereby imply a distinction from its past and future existence.[21]

Here Moore does not appear to be talking about red patches but about the simple concept red. Yet concepts, recall, are immutable. Hence, there is no need, if we are talking about a simple concept, to distinguish its present, past, and future existence. And, as we just noted, the simplest existent still could not be a simple concept. We could, however, have a complex of concepts composed of the concepts *red, existence,* and *now* in the relation R_2. Such an object would be denoted by

(e) R_2 [red, existence, now].

This object would not be a red patch, since it would have no shape or other property. But neither would it be the concept red, which it would, however, *contain.* Moore may be confusing such an object with the concept red. This confusion could be aided by his sometimes speaking of existents in terms of their concepts standing to existence in the relation R_2. But even so, if we render "Paul exists" by "The concept of Paul stands in the relation R_2 to existence," what then exists (if the sentence is true) is Paul, not his concept. That is, the object Paul exists. However, in the case of Paul, there is clearly a difference between him and his concept. But Moore does not think in terms of the concept of red. He speaks of the *concept red.* There is no distinction between the universal red and a concept of it; to say that red is a concept is to say that it is a universal. But the concept of Paul is not a universal like red. Hence, when one says that red exists, it might be natural to think that one is talking about the concept, especially if one thinks in terms of the concept standing in relation to existence. But on Moore's analysis of existents, when one says that a concept stands

[21] *Ibid.,* 189–90.

in the relation R_2 to existence one does not assert that the concept exists. Rather, what exists is what the concept is "the concept of." Thus, just as when we say Paul exists we are not talking about the concept of Paul, when we say that red exists we can not be talking either about the concept red or about a red patch.[22] Instead we would be talking about a third thing. This third sort of thing, denoted by (e), we will call a "simple object." Being an existent temporal object, such an entity may be considered to be substantial or particular. Hence, such simple objects may be confused with particular patches. Since we have already noted why Moore may confuse simple objects with simple concepts, such simple objects may provide the bridge for his characteristic confusion of simple concepts with particular patches – of red with a red patch. Be that as it may, with the appearance of such simple objects, we may look upon a sentence like "Paul is yellow" in a different light. Instead of holding that Paul contains yellow, one might suggest that Paul contains a simple object denoted by "R_2 [yellow, existence, now]," which will be abbreviated by "$yellow_1$." Thus Paul, being substantial, would be made up of, or contain, substantial parts. The sentence "Paul is yellow" would then be transcribed by

(γ) Paul C $yellow_1$.

Since (γ) provides a basis for thinking of a composite substance like Paul as being composed of substantial parts, it reflects the point we noted much earlier that *contains* relates entities that are both substances and existents. In turn this may be taken to indicate a sort of Aristotelian nominalism or conceptualism in Moore's 1899 paper. We thus have a link with what Moore says in *Principia*. More about this shortly.

The simple object $yellow_1$ might also be said to *contain* the concept yellow, just as Paul *contains* $yellow_1$. But about this we should note two things. First, as an ontological tie between Paul and $yellow_1$, C connects two entities both of which are particulars and existents. But as the tie between $yellow_1$ and yellow, it holds between a particular and a universal, between an existent and a non-existent. For concepts, recall, cannot be existents. This suggests that we might distinguish the

---

[22] At one point Moore says, "I endeavor to show, what I must own appears to me perfectly obvious, that the concept can consistently be described neither as an existent, nor as part of an existent" (*Ibid.*, 181). But just as the first part of his statement (that concepts cannot be *described* as existents) should not be taken as supporting my point that concepts *are not* existents for Moore, the second part, that concepts cannot be *described* as parts of existents, does not weigh against the contention that they are, for Moore, parts of existents. For taking this statement in its context reveals that Moore is arguing that concepts are more basic than existents and, hence, what concepts are cannot be explained by a consideration of the nature of existents.

sense in which Paul contains yellow$_1$ from that in which yellow$_1$ contains yellow. In other words, simple objects "contain" simple concepts in a different sense from that in which complex objects "contain" simple objects. Thus an ontology embracing complex objects, simple objects, and concepts might acknowledge two distinct senses of "contains." This second tie, that between yellow$_1$ and yellow, will be designated by "$C*$." [23]

Second, both C and $C*$ are ordered relations. If we consider the first place in a sentence containing either C or $C*$ as the subject place and the second place as the predicate place, then we see, first, that "yellow" will not occur in the subject place of a sentence expressing a "containing" relation (in either sense); and, second, that "yellow$_1$" can occur in either place. It will occur in the first place in a sentence like "yellow$_1$ $C*$ yellow," and in the second place in "Paul C yellow$_1$." The first point shows, again, why yellow cannot be said to exist; the second point shows in what sense simple objects, like yellow$_1$, might be considered to be properties. Thus we could not have a sentence like "yellow$_1$ $C*$ existence" or "yellow C existence," but we could have "yellow$_1$ C existence." Note that whereas yellow$_1$ is the relevant existent, the concept yellow is what stands in the relation R_2 to existence. But if one thinks in terms of a sentence like "yellow R_2 existence" or "R_2 [yellow, existence]" as stating this fact, we can see why the confusions we discussed earlier arise. On the one hand, one is tempted to confuse yellow with yellow$_1$ and, on the other, R_2 with C.

A question also arises as to whether there is a plurality of simple objects like yellow$_1$ associated with a simple concept like yellow. If there is, then we clearly have a view very much like an Aristotelian nominalism. For then one may hold that the simple object, say yellow$_1$, contained in one yellow patch is different from that, say yellow$_2$, in another yellow patch. Alternatively, if one holds that there is only one such simple object which is contained in all yellow patches, then we have a view somewhat like the extreme "Platonism" of William of Champeaux. To hold to such an entity in addition to the concept yellow would indeed seem pointless since one would then have not only a universal concept, but also a universal particular – whatever that would mean. As Moore's discussion is neither clear nor detailed, one can only attribute views to him. But this version of extreme

---

[23] The distinction between C and $C*$ is suggested simply to contrast Moore's with more traditional variants of the containment pattern. In them, when Paul contains yellow$_1$, the latter does not contain, as a part, the concept yellow but "falls under" it. Here we clearly have a further tie connecting the simple particular with a concept.

realism does not at all seem to be what is involved, even implicitly, in his discussion. The only reason one might have for considering it at all is that Moore does not include either the concept *this* or a spatial concept in a simple object like yellow$_1$. One reason for this might be, again, his fusing simple objects with simple concepts. Yet he might have intended to include a spatial concept in a simple object like yellow$_1$. Thus, when he says

> If now we take the existential proposition "Red exists," .... my meaning is that the concept "red" and the concept "existence" stand in a specific relation both to one another and to the concept of time,[24]

he might simply have neglected to include a spatial concept. For he later says:

> It seems rather to be this: That time alone is sufficient for some sort of experience, since it alone seems to be involved in the simplest kind of existential proposition, *e.g.*, "Pleasure exists"; and that again time and space together will suffice to account for the possibility of other pieces of knowledge.... [25]

A simple object containing the concept red *might* then differ from a simple object which contains the concept pleasure, in that the former also includes a spatial concept whereas the latter does not. For the former, unlike the latter, may be thought to be in space. But in neither case does Moore include the concept *this*. This seems to be due to his reserving that concept for those cases where we would use a phrase like "this paper." For he holds that the simplest kind of existential proposition need not involve the concept of substance, and the inclusion of the concept *this* would seem to do just that.[26] Even without the inclusion of spatial concepts or the concept *this* in simple objects, the fact that simple objects contain temporal concepts would seem to indicate that there would be a plurality of such objects containing the concept yellow.[27] All the simple objects containing the concept yellow

[24] *Ibid.*, 189.

[25] *Ibid.*, 191.

[26] Moore is not accepting a bare substance in his acknowledgment of the concept *this*. For concepts are not substances. His distaste for bare substances could be shown by his not acknowledging simple objects constructed from the concept *this* in the sense in which yellow$_1$ is constructed from yellow.

[27] This is not to say that problems would not arise in trying to distinguish simple objects constructed from the same concept on the basis of time alone. Also, it is quite unlikely that the concepts *now*, *was*, and *will be* will prove adequate for dealing with the philosophical problems involved in time and change. But again, our concern here is not to attempt to make Moore's ontology adequate. We might note that if one attempts to solve the problem of individuation, within Moore's pattern, in terms of different objects containing different spatial and temporal concepts, then one accepts a view reminiscent of the *haecceitas* of Scotus. On the other hand, if one sees the solution to the problem of individuation to lie in there being different existent simple objects (yellow$_1$ as opposed to yellow$_2$, for example), then one adopts a view patterned after Aquinas' *principium individuationis*.

would then be "yellownesses" in virtue of the concept yellow contained in them.

Concerning the attribution to Moore of an ontology embracing such simple objects, we might note what he says in his 1901 paper "Identity."

On the other hand, we have accepted the principle frequently implied in Plato that the idea in a thing may be different from the idea in itself; and we have still to see whether there is any insurmountable objection to this view.

The view we have accepted is that in some cases where two things are truly said to have a common predicate, there exists in each a predicate exactly similar to that which exists in the other, but not numerically identical with it. And I confess I see no objections to this view, except what seem to rest on a bare denial of the difference between conceptual and numerical difference. These two exactly similar things are, I may be told, identical in content: exact similarity means identity in content. I admit that they are so. In that case, my adversary may retort, they are the same thing; there is no difference between them; there are not two but one. But this is merely to beg the point at issue. What I have urged is that many of our judgments plainly imply that there may be *two* things, things having a kind of difference which I call numerical, which yet have not another kind of difference which I call conceptual. And I explain the phrase, identity of content, as applying only to two such things, which have no conceptual difference. The two things, are, I admit, in one sense the same; but that they are not therefore also *one* and the same is just what I have tried to show.[28]

Here Moore explicitly leans to the immanent characters of Plato as distinct from the transcendent forms. The *tallness in Phaedo* is distinct from, though conceptually related to, the form *tallness. If such immanent characters are considered to be substantial,* as they are in *Principia* and in "The Nature of Judgment," *we have the simple objects of Moore's ontology.* Notice too how the simple objects easily provide him with the distinction he asserts between numerical and conceptual identity. Yellow$_1$ and yellow$_2$ would be conceptually identical, in that both are simple objects containing the concept yellow. Yet they are numerically different, in that yellow$_1$ is not the same simple object as yellow$_2$. Thus what he says in his paper "Identity" jibes with the above interpretation of the ontology of his 1899 paper.

The ontology of the 1899 paper may then be summed up as follows. There are two kinds of entities, existents and non-existents; and two basic kinds of ontological ties, the R's, on one hand, and C and C^*, on the other. All existent entities are made up ultimately of simple concepts which are non-existent. Also, all other non-existent entities are likewise reducible to simple concepts. The category of existent entities includes simple objects, like yellow$_1$, and complex objects, like Paul, as well as existential propositions. In addition to simple concepts,

[28] G. E. Moore, "Identity," *Proceedings of the Aristotelian Society*, vol., 1, 1901, 111–112.

the category of non-existent entities includes non-existential propositions, and complex concepts like the concept of Paul. With such an
ontology we can understand why Moore must, sooner or later, explicitly
distinguish between being and existence. For his ontology includes a
variety of non-existent entities among which are the "ultimate" ingredients of the universe. These latter must be given some ontological
status if Moore is not to talk outright nonsense, though his confusion
of simple objects with simple concepts enables him to avoid facing this
problem directly. Yet, as we saw, he does come to distinguish, in
Principia, between being and existence. And we can now see the root
of the view, expressed in *Principia*, that universals do not exist and,
hence, the basis of the ontology implicit in those strange passages cited
from *Principia*.

(C) CONTAINS, EXEMPLIFICATION, AND GOODNESS

Moore's ontology, then, includes existent objects "constructed" of
non-existent concepts. Yet, as we noted, since he confuses simple
concepts with simple objects, he need not consider his view peculiar. In
this vein he tells us that concepts are not adjectives but substantives:

A concept is not in any intelligible sense an 'adjective,' as if there were something
substantive, more ultimate than it. For we must, if we are to be consistent,
describe what appears to be most substantive as no more than a collection of
such supposed adjectives: and thus, in the end, the concept turns out to be the
only substantive or subject, and no one concept either more or less an adjective
than any other.[29]

Since substantial objects are composed of concepts, Moore apparently
thinks that such objects cannot be more substantial than concepts.
That concepts or universals *depend* on objects that exemplify them is a
familiar ontological theme of nominalistically inclined philosophers. It
reflects the idea that what exists, ultimately, is independent. But for
Moore, objects depend on concepts in that they are composed of
concepts. We shall shortly see how the notion of "dependence" enters
into Moore's conception of goodness and into his variation of an
Aristotelian type conceptualism. Here we see not only the importance
of the ontological themes of simplicity and independence for Moore (for
simple concepts, the ultimate ingredients of the universe, are both
simple and independent), but also why he is naturally led to confuse
concepts with their simple objects. This confusion is a consequence of
his considering substantial objects to be composed of simple concepts.

[29] *The Nature of Judgment*, 192–93.

To see why, we need only note that Moore has two notions of a "substantive." First, in nominalistic fashion, a substantive is an existent and, hence, temporal object. Second, a substantive is an "independent" entity, a subject, on which adjectives "depend." Since simple concepts are the entities on which all others "depend," he comes to think of them as substantial existents. And by thus fusing the two notions of a "substantive," he explicitly confuses simple concepts with their simple objects. It is now clear why he says what he does in *Principia*. Properties like yellow in *Principia* are confused "combinations" of the concepts and the simple objects of the 1899 paper. When he speaks, in *Principia*, of natural properties as existing independently in time, he is really speaking of simple objects like yellow₁. We can then see why one might think of Moore as a realist in *Principia* and yet be puzzled by his speaking of properties as temporal substances and of some universals as non-existents. For once one has confused simple objects with universal concepts, what one says may be interpreted as indicating both realism and nominalism.

Before considering how goodness fits into all this, we might note a further classical ontological theme embodied in Moore's discussion. Objects, like Paul, are thought of as composed either of the concept of Paul together with existence (in the relation R_2) or of the simple concepts which make up the concept of Paul together with existence (in the relation R_2). One may then think of Paul as somehow made up of his concept together with existence. This is certainly reminiscent of those who held that existents were composites of essence plus existence. It is then no wonder that Moore says some of the things he does and has some of the problems that he has.

We have seen the answer to the first question asked at the end of section (A), "Why does Moore think in terms of contains rather than of exemplification in *Principia*?" We have also seen the answers to the questions we raised there about "simple particulars" in view of the discussion of the simple objects of the 1899 paper. We will now proceed to the second question: "Why is goodness different from redness and yellowness in that it is exemplified by, rather than contained in, objects?'

In the 1899 paper Moore held that no one concept is "either more or less an adjective than any other." [30] Clearly he had not yet formulated his later view about goodness. Goodness was thus grafted onto an earlier ontological framework. While this marks goodness as a sort of

---

[30] *Ibid.*, 193.

intruder into Moore's ontology, it does not explain why he fitted it in the way he did. But there are several reasons that do.

First, Moore does not think of goodness as an "empirical" property, in that it is not sensible or an object of perception. In this sense it is more like mathematical properties than like red. In the 1899 paper he seems to have distinguished empirical concepts as those which can exist in time.[31] Fusing these two senses of "empirical" may have contributed to his view that goodness cannot exist in time. Hence, it cannot be a substantial part of objects. Consequently, the concept good would not give rise to simple objects as yellow gives rise to $yellow_1$. Thus objects would have to exemplify goodness rather than contain a simple object like, say, $goodness_1$. Since Moore already recognized entities like numbers which did not exist in time and which were not objects of perception, he already had, so to speak, a category in which to place goodness in *Principia*.

Second, recall the difference between "G = P" and "G(P)" that we discussed earlier. Moore is preoccupied by the notion that one can always ask of anything other than goodness, "Is it good?" But if goodness were contained, rather than exemplified, we could not significantly ask of a simple property like red or pleasure if it were good. For we would be asking if these simple qualities contained goodness, but simple qualities do not contain anything at all. Even a simple object like $yellow_1$ could not contain goodness. Hence one could ask only if these simple qualities were identical with goodness. But this is not what Moore believes he is asking. To put the matter another way, one can ask of both simple and composite objects if they are good. The relation between them and goodness, if we are asking the same thing in both cases, cannot then be either C or C^*. Thus something else must be involved. Exemplification is a natural answer.

Third, recall Paul, the square yellow patch mentioned above. Suppose Paul also contained a particular goodness as he contains $yellow_1$ and, say, $square_1$. There would still be a difference. If we "took away" the particular goodness we would still have an ordinary composite object that was a square yellow patch. But if we "took away" either the particular yellowness or the particular squareness of the patch, we wouldn't have an ordinary composite object at all. For square patches must have a color, and colored patches require a shape. We just couldn't have a good square or a good yellow thing where the first had no color and the second no shape. This could lead one to think

[31] *Ibid.*, 187.

that goodness shouldn't be considered a substantial part of Paul in the way in which his yellowness and squareness are such parts. If we recall one of the passages from *Principia* cited above,[32] it does seem that Moore thinks along this line. Note that one isn't merely saying here that Paul would be a different object without his yellownes, but that there couldn't be the *same sort of object*, an ordinary composite object. To see this suppose again Paul to be composed only of the concepts yellow, square, existence, and now. To withdraw yellow would leave something composed of square, existence, and now. This would be the simple object square$_1$. We no longer have a composite particular square patch. However, if Paul also contains goodness and it is withdrawn, we would still have a particular square patch, albeit not a good one. One may then hold that it is not the same square patch since its goodness is somehow "intrinsic" to it; but it would still be a square patch – a particular composite object. Hence it would be the same sort of thing, in that sense, as a good square patch. Not being a substantial part of Paul, goodness must then attach to him as a mere adjective or predicate, for this seems to be the only alternative.[33]

Fourth, the notion of whole and part may enter in yet another way. Moore holds that the goodness of certain "organic" wholes is not reducible to the goodness of their parts. One cannot help but wonder if his concern with this point contributes to his refraining from thinking of goodness as a "part" of a complex object in the sense of being contained in it.

Fifth, some philosophers have held that universals are *dependent* on the particulars which exemplify them. Moore suggests this theme when he speaks of good as an adjective or "mere predicate." Whatever else is involved in this view, it certainly suggests the point that somehow the existence, or perhaps the being, of a universal requires the existence of

---

[32] See note 1 above.

[33] In view of some of the things Moore says in "The Conception of Intrinsic Value" (in *Philosophical Studies*), the "withdrawal" of the goodness from a good object would also necessitate the "withdrawal" of those natural properties it was intrinsically or necessarily connected with. Thus, as he puts it, one could not have two natural objects "exactly alike" in natural properties but differing in value. Hence the withdrawal of Paul's goodness would also necessitate the withdrawal of at least one of his natural properties, say his yellowness. Without his being good Paul would not then be yellow. But the point is that we would not then have a yellow square due to its not containing yellowness, even though the yellowness would be withdrawn due to its intrinsic connection with goodness. In any case to speak of "taking away" or "withdrawing" properties, as Moore does, is to speak metaphorically. In short, the above discussion merely reflects the simple and obvious point that natural properties can combine into objects without goodness, but goodness "requires" natural properties for there to be a good object. This involves the *dependent* nature of goodness, which is discussed further below.

an exemplifying particular – a substance. We noticed above Moore's concern with the adjectival nature of universals or concepts. He also thinks of goodness as being *dependent* on natural qualities. He thinks of it as being dependent on natural qualities. He thinks of it as dependent in two ways. First, he seems to hold that goodness is dependent in the sense that if an object exemplified goodness then it must have, or must be conceived as having, other properties. This is not to say that from its being good one could infer that an object had *certain specific* characteristics (this he expressly denied), but merely that it must have some other characteristics besides goodness. Second, goodness is dependent in the sense that an object's being good follows from the fact that it possesses certain natural properties. But Moore thinks of natural properties as substances. This may well provide a ground for his mixing these various senses of "dependent." Goodness, then, being dependent on the substantial natural properties, would not itself be thought of as substantial. Hence, it becomes *dependent*, in the sense of being a mere adjective or universal. Moore's ontological views provide a natural basis for his mingling these senses of "dependent." If goodness were like redness, then there would be a simple object denoted by "R_2 [good, existence, now]," *i.e.*, $good_1$, the particular goodness in, say, Paul. We would, in Moore's terminology, have a substantive existent goodness without there being any natural properties like yellow, pleasure, etc., to be "dependent" on. Goodness would then be "independent" like yellowness. And, if "independent," it could be conceived of as existing by itself in time. But Moore believes goodness to be "dependent." Hence, there cannot be a simple object like $good_1$, and goodness cannot then be spoken of as being contained in composite objects.

We see then how Moore's 1899 paper provides the basis and explanation for the ontology of *Principia*. Moore might be thought to have nominalistic leanings, in that (a) he has simple objects; (b) concepts are non-existents; and, most important, (c) he confuses concepts with simple objects. This confusion, in turn, explains his attempt to distinguish natural from non-natural properties. In the case of concepts like yellow we have a concept, simple objects, and complex objects. *Non-natural* properties (concepts) *have no simple objects*. Hence, there is nothing to confuse them with. Thus he speaks of them as genuine universals. But not being confused with simple objects, they are, in nominalistic fashion, classified as non-existents. Without this confusion between concepts and their simple objects, Moore would have to recognize two kinds of concepts – those which had simple objects and those which did not. Both kinds of concepts would be nonexistents, though, being entities, they would *be* in some sense. Thus the difference between natural and non-natural properties (concepts) would not be that the first are existents while the second are not; rather, it would be based on the existence of correlated simple objects for the natural ones. The introduction of such "non-natural" concepts gives rise to yet a further ontological tie, namely, exemplification. For when we say of a composite natural object that it is red we are saying that it contains (C) a simple object which, in turn, contains ($C*$) the concept red. But to say of either a simple or a composite object that it is good is to say that it exemplifies goodness. Thus, with concepts like goodness introduced, Moore's ontology embraces three basic kinds of ontological ties: the R's, the C's, and exemplification.

Three further points may be made about Moore's ontology. First, one may consider the need for both C and $C*$ to reflect the inadequacy of an ontology which recognizes simple objects but not universals. For without $C*$ and the universal concepts, one could not say what made yellow$_1$ and yellow$_2$ both yellownesses. Yet his ontology is an original variant of an Aristotelian "conceptualism." For his simple objects do not "fall under" mental concepts; rather, they are *composed* of concepts which are clearly not mind-*dependent* but are the ultimate *independent* entities. In this sense Moore is, of course, far from being a nominalist.

Second, non-natural concepts like goodness are already foreshadowed in the 1899 paper. There, *truth* is considered a property of propositions. Moore does not go into any details concerning the connection between the property truth and true propositions, but it would seem to be that of exemplification rather than either C or $C*$. Hence, *truth* would be a non-natural property like goodness. The only basis for considering *truth* to be contained in true propositions would be if one confused this property with the relation R_{3t} and considered the latter, as Moore does, a *constituent* of a true proposition. But if one does not make this confusion, the relation R_{3t} may be considered the 'true making" element of true propositions, just as good objects would have "good making" characteristics *contained* in them.

Third, one could simplify Moore's ontology by holding that composite objects contained, not simple objects, but concepts. One would not then require simple objects, and would require only one containing relation. But one would also have to abandon the notion that "natural properties" were *substantial, temporal* existents. One would then simply say that there were two basically different ways in which objects combined with concepts. The only difference between natural and non-natural properties would then lie in their different ontological ties to objects. Both ties would be ultimate, and one could not say anything more to "explain" the difference between natural and non-natural properties. But once the simple objects are discarded a relation of containment seems to lose its point. Or rather, its only point might seem to be to enable one to distinguish natural from non-natural properties. For if we have to say that existent objects contain, as parts, entities which are not existent objects, but which are non-existent universal concepts, we may as well revert to exemplification for natural properties as well. Yet, even with simple objects, Moore must ultimately say something like this.[34] Since he confuses simple concepts with simple objects, this alternative does not clearly arise for him. But in any case, the task of this paper was not to justify the distinction between natural and non-natural properties. Rather, it was to show what could have led him to say what he did, and to think he had made the distinction in *Principia*. And if the analysis presented in this paper is plausible, we have seen the ontological roots of Moore's value theory.[35]

[34] For a consideration of the difference between a property like good and a property like yellow without such ontological complications, see my "Phenomena, Value and Objectivity," *Philosophical Quarterly*, 8, 1958, 208–225.

[35] In "The Conception of Intrinsic Value" of 1922, Moore once again tried to distinguish between natural and non-natural properties. He there held that a non-natural property like good, while depending on the "intrinsic nature" of an object in the sense that no two objects could be "exactly alike" in natural properties if one of them had such a non-natural property and the other did not, was not one of the properties one would list in a complete *description* of the object. But he does not tell us, as he admits he cannot, what distinguishes a descriptive property from a property like good. One might then notice that in this later essay the properties Moore considers to be intrinsic descriptive properties are those he once considered to be substantive parts of objects. A possible verbal bridge between the label "descriptive property" and the notion of being a part of an object may be provided by Moore's thinking that to describe something intrinsically is to say what it is. And this is what one would naturally say one does when one lists the parts which an object contains. Also, we may note that in the 1922 paper Moore distinguishes two kinds of necessity; one kind of necessary connection links intrinsic natures with non-natural properties, the other connects such natures with natural properties. Thus the distinction between a natural and a non-natural property is made to rest on there being two kinds of necessary connection, where formerly, as we saw, the distinction depended on there being two ontological ties, exemplification and containment. That Moore still adheres to this structural pattern in 1922 shows how deep the matter lies in his thought.

XII. THE *TRACTATUS*: NOMINALISTIC OR REALISTIC?

EDWIN B. ALLAIRE

The *Tractatus* is nominalistic. This claim, designed by Anscombe and Copi,[1] is now the fashion. It does not deserve to be: the *Tractatus* looks foolish in it. In this paper I want to try a realistic interpretation on the work.[2] Since this interpretation itself is not wholly fitting, much of my concern will be with how and why it fails to fit exactly.

If the *Tractatus* were neatly realistic, it would exhibit these lines: (1) properties as well as particulars are constituents of atomic facts; (2) properties are different in kind from particulars. In other words, if the early Wittgenstein had not been somewhat inhibited by deep and reasonable concerns, he would have *explicitly* analysed 'this is red', asserted truly of a speck in the visual field, as follows: both 'this' and 'red' refer not only to different entities but to different kinds of entities.

According to Anscombe and Copi, the *Tractatus* denies that properties are constituents of atomic facts. In other words, they claim that it denies both (1) and (2). As indicated above, I shall argue that it affirms both (1) and (2). I stress the difference in order to remark on what one might think is another possibility; viz., that it denies (2) but affirms (1). In the case of the *Tractatus*, and perhaps in general, the possibility is illusory. One can argue that Wittgenstein affirms (1) only by showing that he affirms (2). That is so because he provides no examples of properties.

The point of the preceding paragraph can be better expressed by noticing an ambiguity of 'property'. Consider, again, 'this is red'. One might argue that 'this' and 'red' refer to distinct and unanalyzable

---

[1] Anscombe, G.E.M., *An Introduction to Wittgenstein's Tractatus* (London, 1959). Cf. Ch. 7. I.M. Copi, "Objects, Properties and Relations in the *Tractatus*," *Mind*, 67, 1959, 145–165. Two reviewers of Stenius' Wittgenstein's '*Tractatus*' (Oxford, 1960) rely heavily and uncritically on the arguments of Anscombe and Copi. Cf. Richard J. Bernstein, "Wittgenstein's Three Languages," *The Review of Metaphysics*, 15, 1961, 278–298, and Judith Jarvis, "Professor Stenius on the *Tractatus*," *The Journal of Philosophy*, 63, 1961, 584–596.
[2] Though several philosophers, e.g. Bergmann, Stenius, and Ramsey, have stated that the *Tractatus* is realistic, none have argued that it is.

entities and yet deny that they are different in kind. By using 'proper-ty' *in an ordinary or grammatical sense*, one might then say that particulars and properties *exist*, even though they are not different in kind. Since Wittgenstein gives no example of a property in the ordinary sense one can show that he accepts (1) only by showing that he believes that there are properties *in an extraordinary or ontological sense*. In other words, one can show that he is a realist only by showing that he believes that the ontological assay of an atomic fact will reveal differ-ent kinds of existents. If one can show that, as I hope to do, one must then explain, as I also hope to do, why he provides no examples of properties.

I want to begin my argument by offering three nontextual reasons for disbelieving that the *Tractatus* is nominalistic. Being nontextual they are perhaps inconclusive. They are nonetheless impressive. First, shortly before and shortly after the *Tractatus* Wittgenstein holds a realistic position. Second, when speaking in the later works about the *Tractatus*, he suggests that it is realistic. Third, the nominalistic position imputed to the *Tractatus* by Anscombe and Copi is sheer nonsense.

In the recently published *Notebooks* 1914–16, many passages enforce realism. The two that follow are typical.

Could one manage without names? Surely not. Names are necessary for an assertion that *this* thing possesses *that* property.[3]

Relations and properties .... are objects.[4]

In the 1929 paper, "Some Remarks on Logical Form," Wittgenstein is bizarrely realistic.

I only wish to point out the direction in which, I believe, the analysis of visual phenomena is to be looked for and that in this analysis we meet with logical forms quite different from those which ordinary language leads us to expect. The occurrence of numbers in the forms of atomic propositions is .... an .... una-voidable feature of the representation .... Numbers will have to enter these forms when – as we should say in ordinary language – we are dealing with properties which admit of gradation, i.e., properties such as the length of an interval, the pitch of a tone, the brightness or redness of a shade of color, etc. It is characteristic of these properties that one degree of them excludes any other. One shade of color cannot simultaneously have two different degrees of brightness.[5]

For the purpose at hand, these passages need no comment, only

[3] Wittgenstein, L., *Notebooks* 1914–16 (Oxford, 1961), p. 53e.
[4] *Ibid.*, p. 61e.
[5] Wittgenstein, L., "Some Remarks on Logical Form," *Aristotelian Society*, Supp. Vol. IX (1929), pp. 162–171; pp. 166–167.

emphasis: both before and after the *Tractatus* Wittgenstein advocates a bold realism.

Speaking in the 1929 paper about – I presume – the *Tractatus*, Wittgenstein says:

> One might think – and I thought so not so long ago – that a statement expressing the degree of a quality could be analyzed into a product of single statements of quantity and a completing supplementary statement. I maintain that the statement which attributes a degree to a quality cannot further be analyzed.[6]

Without exploring the subtleties and peculiarities of this passage, one can say unreservedly that Wittgenstein once held, presumably at the time of the *Tractatus*, that some properties, those referred to by certain quantity words, are constituents of atomic facts.

In the *Blue Book* he says:

> Talking of a fact as a "complex of objects" springs from this confusion (cf. *Tractatus Logico-philosophicus*). Supposing we asked: "How can one *imagine* what does not exist?" The answer seems to be: "If we do, we imagine the nonexistent combinations of existing elements." A centaur doesn't exist, but a man's head and torso and arms and a horse's legs do exist. "But can't we imagine an object utterly different from any one which exists?" We should be inclined to answer: "No, the elements, the individuals, must exist. If redness, roundness, and sweetness did not exist, we could not imagine them." [7]

This passage, though perhaps less trustworthy than the preceding one, also suggests that at least some of the constituents of atomic facts are properties. Whether or not the passages just quoted bear faithful witness to what Wittgenstein held in the *Tractatus* is not worth arguing. They are at least typical of the way in which he speaks of the earlier work in the later ones. He never speaks of it, at least with respect to the nominalism-realism issue, as Copi and Anscombe do. According to them, the only entities that enter into atomic facts are bare particulars, the sorts of entities Russell claimed to be the referents of logically proper names. Whatever such entities be, and they are elusive at best, they are neither qualities nor qualitied particulars. That is, bare particulars are neither colors nor colored things; they are the entities having or exemplifying the colors. The strangeness of bare particulars aide, the question is: What, upon the Anscombe-Copi interpretation of the *Tractatus*, are properties? They are "configurations of bare particulars." Consider these statements by Anscombe.

---

[6] *Ibid.*, p. 167.
[7] Wittgenstein, L., *The Blue and Brown Books* (Oxford, 1958), p. 31.

Wittgenstein does not speak of 'concepts' or 'universals' as a kind of thing to be found in the world; it is quite clear that for him there is nothing but objects in configuration.[8]

Red is a material property, and therefore formed by a configuration of objects.[9]

This position, i.e., the one attributed to the early Wittgenstein, is nonsense, though not in the sense in which, according to some, all ontological positions are, nor in the less damaging and admittedly queer sense that it is unique, without historical roots or parallels, not even in 17th Century atomism. The position is nonsense – sheer nonsense I said – in that, unlike the traditional ontological positions, it has no rationale watsoever. To lean on the later Wittgenstein, there are no grammatical analogies that can show how the early Wittgenstein got into such a bottle. At least there are none that I can discover. The position is, I submit, pathetically verbal, being words about mere marks on paper. Nor does Anscombe try to make it more than that. She tries to make it neither intelligible – she does not think it is – nor worthy of sympathy.

The above reasons for disbelieving that the *Tractatus* is nominalistic (at least in the sense that it denies that property words refer to unanalyzable entities) are impressive even if inconclusive. Wittgenstein may have been fickle, chasing now nominalism now realism; he may have been a poor guide to his past; he may have been an advocate of sheer nonsense. However, to claim that he was all three demands *very* convincing textual evidence. What is offered by Anscombe and Copi does not convince.

I cannot hope to examine all the textual arguments offered by Anscombe and Copi. Nor would that be worthwhile: the *Tractatus* would be lost in the effort. Accordingly, I shall examine only three of their arguments. Two are formidable; one is not. My reason for examining the latter – it is advanced by Anscombe – is that it is illuminating and will aid me in speaking to the point about the realism of the *Tractatus*.

Consider the following passage from Anscombe.[10]

.... at 2.0231 we learn that the substance of the world – i.e., the objects – *can* only determine a form, not any material properties. For it needs propositions (as opposed to names) to represent material properties; such properties are only formed by 'the configuration of objects.' Red is a material property, and therefore formed by a configuration of objects.

[8] Anscombe, G.E.M., *op. cit.*, p. 99.
[9] *Ibid.*, p. 111.
[10] *Ibid.*, p. 111.

Anscombe's argument is a paraphrase of 2.0231, a stern test for any realistic interpretation.

The substance of the world *can* only determine a form and not any material properties. For these are first presented by the propositions – first formed by the configuration of objects.

As the context (roughly 2.011–2.025) makes clear, the main point of 2.0231 is that there is no logical connection between an entity and the facts in which it actually occurs. 2.0231 is therefore a variant of the thesis of logical atomism. It declares that the constituents of atomic facts are simple. Just as there is no logical connection between two atomic facts, so too there is no logical connection between an entity and the facts in which it actually occurs. There is, however, some "logical" connection between entities and facts. It is this: the *kind* an entity is determines the facts in which it *can* occur. That is what is meant by "the substance of the world can only determine a form." That it can *only* determine the facts in which an entity can occur and not any material properties means, to repeat, that there is no logical connection between the kind an entity is and the specific properties it has.

Wittgenstein himself expresses a similar thought in 2.01231: "In order to know an object, I must know not its external qualities, but its internal qualities." Another expression to this end is 2.0131: "A speck in the visual field need not be red, but it must have a colour." The difference stressed in these passages as well as in 2.0231 may be explained in several ways. For example, the determination that a string is well formed is different from the determination that it is true or false. The former determination is logically prior to, and independent of, the latter one. A person can know what a sentence means without knowing whether it is true or false. Another way of explaining the difference is by saying that it strives to capture the difference between knowing what a word means (what it refers to and the syntactical rules governing its use) and knowing true sentences in which it occurs. Still another way, perhaps the most satisfactory one, is as follows. To represent the formal properties of an object one needs to exhibit only the formation rules governing the sign referring to it; to represent the material properties of an object one needs to exhibit the true sentences in which the sign for it occurs.

In the light of this last expression of the difference between material and formal properties, the first part of the second sentence (of 2.0231) becomes clear. In saying that material properties are first presented by the propositions, Wittgenstein simply means that in order to represent that (e.g.) a speck in the visual field is red one must make a sentence, i.e., put words in combination. It is not enough to give the rules for the word referring to the speck. Now consider the last part of the second sentence, "material properties are first formed by configurations of objects," recalling that it is there to echo the first part. If the last part were expressed linguistically, and mark that Wittgenstein's initial effort is linguistic, there would be no difficulty. It would say just what the first part does. Unhappily it is not expressed linguistically. Nevertheless its meaning ought by now to be clear. The material properties an entity has depends on the entities with which it is combined. The formal properties do not so depend and are, indeed, "internal" to the entity.

In 2.0231 Wittgenstein is enforcing a difference between formal and material properties. In so doing, he first says that the substance (in the sense of unanalyzable entities) of the world determines a form. This means that entities have formal properties which do not depend on their being in configurations but which determine the configurations in which they can occur. He also says that material properties are not so determined, meaning that the specific property an entity has is not determined by its formal property. Attempting to illuminate this difference, he further says that material properties are first presented by the propositions – first formed by the configurations. This means that, unlike the formal properties, the material properties are determined by the configurations in the sense that the material properties are accidental and appear only in configurations. Stated briefly, 2.0231 strives to secure the difference between the fact that a speck must be colored and the fact that a speck is red. The former is logical and depends on the kind the entity is; the latter is not logical and depends on the other entities (e.g., red) with which the speck is combined. (That Wittgenstein speaks of formal properties as internal and material ones as external is merely more of the same.)

2.0231, then, has nothing to do with the question of whether or not properties are constituents of atomic facts. In its obscure way it insists on a difference between the formation rules of a language and true sentences of it. The former show the kinds of entities that can be combined in facts; the latter the entities that are combined. Therefore, the former depend on the formal or internal properties of the entities; the latter on the material or external properties of them. Since 2.0231 is

neutral regarding the nominalism-realism issue, the nominalistic interpretation is without one of its most prominent pillars.[11]

I want now to examine another of Anscombe's arguments, the one
I said was illuminating though not formidable.

> .... if [the elementary proposition] is just a concatenation of names – then it is
> not reproduced by a formula consisting of some letters for names and some
> letters for functions. And this is borne out by many passages. Notably for
> example 3.1431: The nature of the propositional sign becomes very clear, if we
> imagine it as composed of three-dimensional objects .... instead of written
> signs.[12]

Anscombe is arguing that function signs do not occur in the atomic
sentences of Wittgenstein's picture language. That needs no argument,
and even if it did 3.1431 would not bear it out. The entire effort of
that passage is to convince one that sentences are not, as Frege believed
(cf. 3.143), names. Whether or not they are is quite distinct from
whether or not function signs occur in sentences. That lapse aside,
Anscombe's point needs, to repeat, no argument. 4.22 expresses it
openly: elementary propositions are concatenations of names. That
Anscombe argues for what needs no argument reveals how significant
she believes the point to be. For her, its significance is due to a comparison between Frege and Wittgenstein on which she bases much of
her interpretation of the *Tractatus*.

Her comparison emerges in the following passage.[13]

> What has become of Frege's concepts in Wittgenstein's theory? They seem to
> have disappeared; actually, however, instead of making concepts or universals
> into a kind of objects .... Wittgenstein made the gulf between concepts and
> objects much greater than Frege ever made it .... In respect of having argu-
> ments places, concepts go over entirely into logical forms. In the 'completely
> analyzed' proposition .... the Fregean concept, the thing with the holes in it,
> has become simply the logical form.

Anscombe's comparison and the argument she bases on it may be
stated this way. Frege holds that there are concepts as well as objects.
He also holds that the former are represented by functions, the latter
by names. For Frege, an atomic sentence would thus consist of a
function and a name. In contrast, Wittgenstein holds that an atomic
sentence consists only of names. That is her comparison. Her argument
is that since Wittgenstein denies that functions occur in atomic sentences,
he also denies that the sorts of entities Frege calls concepts occur in

---

[11] Sellars has recently attacked the nominalistic interpretation on this same point.
"Naming and Saying," *Philosophy of Science*, 29, 1962, 7–26.

[12] Anscombe, G.E.M., *op. cit.*, p. 100.

[13] *Ibid.*, p. 108.

atomic facts. In other words, since Wittgenstein admits only names into atomic sentences, he grants existence only to the sorts of entities Frege calls objects. (According to Anscombe, these are bare particulars.)

The comparison is shallow; the argument, naive. The comparison is shallow because it fails to explore Wittgenstein's own deep commitment to the propositional-function notation. Exploring that, one finds the true nature of Wittgenstein's disagreement with Frege. The argument is naive because the claim that only names occur in atomic sentences does not entail that properties are not constituents of atomic facts. Nothing whatsoever recommends her silent premiss that Wittgenstein could not have thought that names represent properties.

Let me first explore Wittgenstein's use of the propositional-function notation. Consider 4.126.

Formal concepts cannot, like proper concepts, be presented by a function. For their characteristics, the formal properties, are not expressed by functions. The expression of a formal property is a feature of certain symbols. The mark that signifies the characteristics of a formal concept is .... a characteristic of all symbols whose meanings fall under the concept.

The propositional-function notation is sometimes used as follows. Assume that red is a concept and that '$f_1(x)$', a propositional function, represents it. The objects falling under the concept red are those referred to by the substitution instances of 'x' resulting in true sentences. In 4.126 the notation is not used in that way. 4.126 distinguishes between formal and proper concepts, speaking of the latter as falling under the former which cannot themselves be represented by funtions. Wittgenstein's meaning may be illustrated as follows. Consider again '$f_1(x)$'. It is a function representing the proper concept red. It falls under the formal concept, property, in virtue of having the characteristic mark 'f' which, since it represents no entity, is not a function. It is a variable. 4.126 makes clear therefore that not only does Wittgenstein rely heavily upon the function notation but that he thinks of proper concepts as entities, i.e., as constituents of atomic facts.

In 4.1272 one hears:

.... the variable name 'x' is the proper sign of the pseudo concept object. Whenever it is used otherwise, i.e., as a proper concept word, there arise senseless pseudo propositions. So one cannot, e.g., say 'There are objects' as one says 'There are books.'

Again, Wittgenstein's point is that some concepts, the formal ones, are not represented by signs. Instead, they are represented by variables i.e., the characteristic marks of the substitution instances of them. For example, red, a proper concept, falls under the formal concept property. Therefore, red is represented by a sign which is an instance of the variable representing the pseudo concept property.

Further and stronger evidence for Wittgenstein's adherence to the propositional-function notation is contained in the following passages.

3.3 Only the proposition has a sense; only in the context of a proposition has a name meaning.

3.31 Every part of a proposition which characterizes its sense I call an expression.

3.311 An expression .... is the common characteristic of a class of propositions.

3.312 It is therefore represented by the general form of the propositions which it characterizes, and in this expression is *constant* and everything else *variable*.

3.313 An expression is thus presented by a variable, whose values are the propositions which contain the expression.

Besides leaving no doubt that Wittgenstein makes full use of the function notation, these passages emphasize two of his most significant ideas: first, that no sign can meaningfully occur alone and, second, that *all* signs, those for particulars as well as those for properties, are in one sense functions. The first point is the linguistic counterpart of 2.1022: the thing is independent in so far as it can occur in all *possible* circumstances, but this form of independence is a form of connection with the atomic fact, a form of dependence. Wittgenstein might have expressed the point this way: that entities occur only as constituents of facts is shown by the fact that single signs cannot occur meaningfully in the picture language. The second point, viz., that all signs are in some sense functions, is a little more difficult to expose for it incorporates several themes. Recall that in 2.0131 Wittgenstein says: a speck in the visual field must have a color, a tone a pitch, the object of touch a hardness, etc." In other words, he distinguishes amongst kinds of particulars. His purpose is to stress that some particulars *must* have certain properties. He would also, I suppose, argue that a speck in the visual field cannot have a tone. The implication is that particulars, being of various kinds, are limited as to the other entities (i.e. properties) with which they can combine to make facts. Wittgenstein might have expressed the point this way: that particulars as well as properties are limited as to the combinations in which they can enter is shown by the fact that *all* entities must be represented by functions. For, functions are implicit formation rules and thus reflect the limitations of the entities they represent.

Even though Wittgenstein argues that all entities must be represented by functions he does not deny the distinction between names and functions. However, for him the distinction does not have the same import that it has for Frege. Frege holds that the distinction between functions and names reflects the distinction between two kinds of entities; Wittgenstein holds that it reflects the distinction between two features of entities; more accurately, the name represents the entity; the function, its formal properties. Perhaps I can get Wittgenstein's point across by recalling the distinction between formal and proper concepts.

Formal concepts cannot be represented by functions because they are not entities. Proper concepts can be so represented because they are entities. However, when representing an entity by means of a function one is representing the formal properties of the entity, one is representing the sorts of facts in which the entity can occur. One is not representing the material properties of the entity, one is not representing the other entities with which it is combined. If one wished to do the latter, one would have to make a true sentence, combining the signs referring to the entities combined. And in the sentence no functions, only names (i.e. words) occur. A sentence represents the entity in combination with other entities. A sentence does not represent the formal properties of an entity.

At this point a slight digression is necessary in order to attend to a possible confusion between an entity's form and its formal properties. The form of an entity is its ontological kind, e.g., being a particular or being a property. The form is *shown* by the sign for an entity being a substitution instance of a certain variable. The formal properties of an entity are the kinds with which it can combine in a fact. For example, properties can combine with either particulars or properties of properties. Thus, formal properties are *represented* by functions which are implicit formation rules.

The same distinction can be stated as follows. On the one hand there is the type distinction; on the other, the type rules. In other words, one can distinguish signs according to shapes and then specify which shapes can combine to make sentences. Such a procedure enables one to show, first, what kinds of entities there are, and, second, what kinds can combine in facts. Wittgenstein himself does not state the distinction in this way because he uses functions rather than rules in order to express the rules. One of his deepest reasons for so doing is that he denies logic any ontological status. To express the point differently, he grounds the formation rules on the entities rather than on a logical relation or nexus. (3.334: The rules of logical syntax must follow of themselves, if we only know how every single sign signifies.) The consequence is that every entity must be represented by a function, at least in the meta-language.

Notice that even though an entity's form can show itself in the object language its formal properties cannot. That is because one cannot show in the object language all the sentences in which a sign can occur. On the other hand, one can show by a single occurence, the form or kind of an object; that is shown by the shape of the sign.

The distinction between form and formal property has another root. Wittgenstein implies that particulars as well as properties are of different kinds. For example, there are visual and auditory particulars; color and tone properties. That is, he implies that being a property is a form (2.0131) whereas being a color is a formal property (4.122–4.125). Though he is not very clear about the distinction, its import is not hard to divine. By taking color and visual as formal properties, the function representing red shows that it can combine only with visual particulars. The reason for making formal properties so narrow is to cope with the issues of elementarism and the synthetic a priori. For what I am about neither is relevant. Here I only want to state that the distinction between form and formal properties is compatible with holding that both properties and particulars are constituents of atomic facts. So much for the digression.

Wittgenstein is struggling with the difference between a sign and its rules. More accurately perhaps, he is struggling with the significance of that distinction. The sign occurs in (object-language) sentences; the rules do not. The latter depend on the form and formal properties of the entity and are thus represented by functions (in the metalanguage) which Wittgenstein sees for what they are, implicit formation rules. Nor should it be overlooked that Wittgenstein correctly sees both that functions do not literally occur in sentences and that signs for particulars as well as for properties are governed by rules. In brief, Wittgenstein sees that Frege's distinction between names and functions is muddled.

Before examining Anscombe's argument, I want to stress that Wittgenstein's denial that functions occur in sentences does not constitute a denial that properties are constituents of atomic facts. Indeed, the foregoing examination of his use of the function notation reveals that he affirms that the constituents of atomic facts are not all of the same kind. What he denies is the Fregean distinction between properties (concepts) and particulars.

The jist of Anscombe's argument can be gleaned from the following passage.[14]

the problem of 'universals' can .... be given this form: was Frege right to introduce two wholly different kinds of 'reference' for words, namely objects and concepts. A concept was the reference of a predicate; now the characteristic mark of a predicate is its possession of an argument-place or-places, which could be filled with names of now one, now another object, hence a 'concept' is a universal. In Wittgenstein's fully analysed propositions, we have nothing but a set of argument places filled with the names of objects; there remains no expression that could be regarded as standing for a concept.,

Anscombe's movement of thought is straightforward. First, she states the problem of universals: are there two kinds of objects? Second, she offers a specific syntactical explication of the problem: Are there both names and functions in the language? Third, she claims that since the atomic sentences of Wittgenstein's language do not contain function signs, the atomic facts represented by those sentences do not contain concepts in the sense that they do not contain the entities Frege calls concepts, e.g., the colors.

The argument is astonishingly naive. For example, even if it were the case – and it is not – that Frege's syntactical distinction between names and functions is the only way to explicate the distinction between objects and concepts, it still would not follow that Wittgenstein by denying Frege's distinction denies that the entities called concepts are constituents of atomic facts. Wittgenstein could have thought they were nameable. Of deeper significance is the fact that Frege's distinction is far from sacred. Indeed, Wittgenstein shows it to be mistaken.

Wittgenstein's denial of the Fregean difference between names and functions is of great significance, even if Anscombe fails to reveal it. The significance is this: Wittgenstein denies that Frege is right concerning the difference between particulars and properties; he is affirming that they are more nearly alike than Frege realized. Not only are both kinds of entities limited in their possibilities for combining with other entities, both are unsaturated or incomplete. Let me explain this last. Frege's distinction fosters the terminology that particulars are complete or saturated whereas properties are incomplete or unsaturated. That terminology fosters in turn, whatever the intention be, the claim that particulars are independent, capable of existing alone, whereas properties are dependent. For example, Russell once said that "there is no reason why you should not have a universe consisting of

one particular and nothing else. That is the peculiarity of particulars."
Wittgenstein himself vigorously rejects that idea and thus has further
grounds for rejecting Frege's distinction between names and functions.
At 2.0121 he puts forth his own thesis: "Just as we cannot think of
spatial objects at all apart from space, or temporal objects apart from
time, so we cannot think of *any* object apart from the possibility of its
connection with other things." That theme recurs throughout the
Tractatus. In 2.0122 it is explicated in this way: it is impossible for
words to occur in two different ways, alone and in the proposition.

Though Wittgenstein more often than not emphasizes his rejection
of the Fregean difference between particulars and properties, thereby
suggesting that particulars and properties are the same in kind, he
does at times imply that there is a difference. For example, his discussion of formal concepts rests on just such a difference. (To speak
about the form of an object is without point unless there are different
forms.) In 5.5261 the implication is perhaps clearest.

A completely generalized proposition is like every other proposition composite.
(This is shown by the fact that in '(Ex, φ) (φ, x)' we must mention 'x' and 'φ''
separately. Both stand independently in signifying relations to the world as in
the ungeneralized proposition.)

By distinguishing between 'x' and 'φ' and by emphasizing that even
in ungeneralized propositions both stand independently in signifying
relations to the world, Wittgenstein gives voice to a type distinction,
implying thereby that the referents of the different types are different
in kind. For Wittgenstein of course, the type distinction is between
functions.[15] Nevertheless, in so far as functions fall under different
formal concepts, the consequence is the same.

Wittgenstein's disagreement with Frege concerns the difference
between the referents of subjects and the referents of predicates.
Whereas Frege holds them to be radically different, Wittgenstein holds
them to be more nearly alike. In the *Tractatus*, he sets himself the
task of establishing that. Thus, even though he ocassionally suggests
that there is some difference between properties and particulars, the
difference does not preoccupy him. What does preoccupy him is the
sameness of the kinds. It is therefore not surprising that in the *Tractatus*,
just as in the *Notebooks*, 'object' is used broadly to cover both particulars and properties. In this connection, I want to call attention to a
passage from Moore's notes on Wittgenstein's lectures of 1930–33.

15 Cf., "Types and Formation Rules: A Note on *Tractatus* 3.334," *Analysis*, 21, 1960, 14–16.

[Wittgenstein] went on to say that if we are talking about 'individuals' in Russell's sense (and he actually here mentioned atoms as well as colors, as if they were "individuals" in this sense) [16]

Moore's parenthetical remark expresses astonishment that Wittgenstein should ignore or take lightly the difference between particulars and properties. If I am right regarding the *Tractatus*, Wittgenstein's lack of concern should not astonish us.

Wittgenstein's failure to dwell on the difference between particulars and properties is not the only reason why the *Tractatus* looks slightly odd in the realistic interpretation. A perhaps deeper reason is that Wittgenstein can provide no example of a simple property. This reason can be uncovered by examining one of Copi's arguments for the nominalistic interpretation.[17]

If *any* properties are simple, specific colors ought to be counted among the simplest. If objects are properties and elementary propositions consist of names of objects .... then the propositions ['this is red' and 'this is blue'] must be elementary propositions. But can they both be true? Wittgenstein's answer is unequivocal: "For two colours, e.g., to be at one place in the visual field, is impossible, logically impossible, for it is excluded by the logical structure of colour .... (It is clear that the logical product of two elementary propositions can neither be a tautology nor a contradiction. The assertion that two different colours are at the same place at the same time, is a contradiction.)" (6.3751) It follows that color predications are not elementary propositions, and the implication seems clear that objects are not properties.

Copi's argument is imposing. Thus, I want, first, to try to get clear on what 6.3751 says and, second, to distinguish carefully between the two conclusions Copi believes are implied by it. In 6.3751 Wittgenstein begins by asserting that it is logically impossible for two colors to be, simultaneously, at one place in the visual field. What makes it impossible is "the logical structure of color." After comparing this impossibility with an apparently similar one regarding particulars at the same time at the same place, he further asserts, *parenthetically*, that the logical product of two elementary propositions can be neither a tautology nor a contradiction as well as repeating that the assertion that two colors are at the same place at the same time, is a contradiction.

Now Copi says that "it follows that color predications are not elementary, and the implication seems clear that objects are not properties." With the former there can be no quarrel. That color predications are not elementary does indeed follow from 6.3751. With

---

[16] Moore, G. E., "Wittgenstein's Lectures in 1930–33," *Mind*, 63, 1954, 1–15; 64, 1955, 1–28 and 289–315. Cf. 64, 2–3.
[17] Copi, I. M., *op. cit.*, p. 162.

the latter there can be a quarrel. That objects are not properties does not follow from 6.3751, but rather from that passage *together with* what Copi himself asserts in the first sentence of the quoted passage, viz., that "if *any* properties are simple, specific colors ought to be." For what I am about it is crucial to realize that Copi's first conclusion follows from 6.3751 whereas his second conclusion follows from it only together with a further premiss. I want to contend that Wittgenstein does not accept that premiss. In other words, Wittgenstein does not believe, at least at the time of the *Tractatus*, that if a specific color is not a property, nothing is. He in fact believes that words like 'red' and 'green' can be defined. Before trying to substantiate what I have just said, it might help to get clear on what problem Wittgenstein is struggling with in 6.3751.

The specific problem is: in what sense is 'this is red and this is blue' (where 'this' refers to a speck presently in the visual field) a contradiction? The general problem is: Given the truth-table explication of 'necessary' and 'contradictory', how can one show, as Wittgenstein hopes to, that what the tradition called synthetic-a-priori sentences express contradictions or necessities? No solution is offered in 6.3751. We are told only that the components of conjunctions like 'this is red and this is blue' cannot be elementary. Though "the logical structure of color" is said to preclude such possibilities, that is no solution. It is merely a vague phrase.

Now it is not idle to remark that the nominalistic interpretation does not, in its simple form at least, provide a solution. If 'this is red' is transcribed as an elementary sentence, then the problem has not been solved, regardless of whether properties are or are not constituents of atomic facts. The solution to the problem requires that the transcription of 'this is red' be a molecular sentence which either contains the negation of 'this is blue' or logically entails it. In other words, if I am right regarding the problem raised, but not solved, in 6.3751, colors cannot be mere configurations of particulars.

Of course, that the nominalistic interpretation does not even approach solving the problem raised in 6.3751 does not make it incorrect. However, in so far as the nominalistic interpretation is based on 6.3751, it is dubious. Certainly, it would be better if one could find an interpretation of the *Tractatus* which provides an at least apparent solution to the problem of 6.3751. I suggest that the realistic interpretation does. In particular, I suggest that the denial that 'this is red' is atomic implies that 'red' is not indefinable, i.e., red is not simple, in the sense, not of being a configuration of particulars, but of being analysable into other simpler properties. To this end let me comment again on 6.3751, in particular, on the parenthetical remark contained in it.

In the parenthetical remark Wittgenstein seems to be saying something like this: "and color predications are *not*, as one might think, elementary. They cannot be; if 'contradiction' is explicated by means of the truth tables and 'this is red and this is blue' is a "formal" truth, as all will agree." Now since Wittgenstein does not pursue the matter, does not make an attempt to solve the problem, the parenthetical remark stands as a challenge or, perhaps better, as an admission of a difficulty. The implication, then, is not that properties are configurations of particulars. It is that there are difficulties here which are not yet solved. There is however a hint regarding the direction in which Wittgenstein thinks the solution may be found. The hint is that since red and blue are not simple, 'red' and 'blue' can be defined. This is what is intended by the phrase 'the logical structure of color'. What evidence is there for my claim? The 1929 paper provides excellent evidence. Furthermore, it leads us to a plausible Wittgenstein.

In the confused and, even to its author, disappointing 1929 paper, Wittgenstein makes clear that he once believed color words to be definable.

If statements of degree were analysable – as I used to think – then we could explain this contradiction ['this is red and this is blue'] by saying that the colour R contains all degrees of R and none of B and the colour B contains all degrees of B and none of R.[18]

This passage leaves no doubt that Wittgenstein once hoped to make 'this is red and this is blue' a contradiction by defining the color words in terms of the words referring to the, say, unanalysable shades of them and the addition of the dubious phrase 'and none of....' Regardless of the feasibility of the program, at the time of the *Tractatus* he had hopes for it. But he did not know how to carry it out and may even have been dimly aware that it could not be carried out. Be that as it may, 6.3751 hints at the program, even if its main task is to acknowledge the difficulty.

The difficulty is a profound one, one that played a decisive role in Wittgenstein's eventual rejection of the *Tractatus*.[19] Wittgenstein, hoping to secure the formal character of synthetic-a-priori sentences

---

[18] Wittgenstein, L., "Remarks on Logical Form," pp. 168–169.
[19] Cf. "*Tractatus* 6.3751," *Analysis*, 19, 1959, 100–105.

while explicating 'necessary' and 'contradictory' by means of the truth tables, is forced to suggest that all the apparently indefinable property words are really definable. The suggestion remains just that: he knows neither how to define them nor what the indefinable ones are. Thus, in the *Tractatus* we are offered no examples of simple properties; we are offered no more than a vague program.

Of course, in the 1929 paper Wittgenstein reveals that he sees what Copi sees, viz., that if specific colors are not simple, no properties are. In other words, he sees that the program hinted at in 6.3751 can not be managed. His response is, first, to accept colors as simple, and, second, to argue that the truth table explication of 'necessary' and 'contradictory' is not quite accurate and needs some modification, if one is to accommodate the *formal* character of synthetic-a-priori sentences. The 1929 paper thus marks the onset of his rejection of the *Tractatus*. But he did not see in 1915 what he saw in 1929. If he had, the *Tractatus* would be other than it is.

I have argued that the *Tractatus* is realistic, i.e., that it affirms that the constituents of atomic facts are of at least two kinds. Nevertheless, the realism is subdued; at times disguised. On the one hand, Wittgenstein's assault on the Fregean difference between particulars and properties prompts him to emphasise their sameness at the expense of their difference; on the other, his commitment to the formal character of synthetic-a-priori sentences prohibits him from providing examples of unanalyzable properties. The realism is further subdued because it is not crucial to the major theses of the *Tractatus*. First, the truth-table explication of 'necessary' and 'contradictory' (5.525) insisting as it does only on a specific analysis of the connectives, is independent of the ontological analysis of atomic facts. Second, the picture theory in its limited and apparently superficial form insists only that a sentence and the fact it expresses share a structure. (2.032, 4.0311) Again, the specific structure of the fact makes no difference.

The picture theory has, however, a deeper and far more significant core which does require realism (in the sense of there being different kinds of entities). In so far as the picture theory insists that there is an isomorphism between language and the world a type distinction is demanded. The isomorphism is such that "to a definite logical combination of signs corresponds a definite logical combination of their meanings [i.e., the objects the signs stand for (3.203)]." The picture theory thus asserts that what is possible (well-formed) in the atomic-sentence language is possible in the world.[20] Linguistic possibility is a matter of formation rules which Wittgenstein grounds on the entities (3.334). In so far as the formation rules depend on a type distinction (and in a PM-like language there is nothing else for them to depend on) a difference of kind is clearly implied.

That Wittgenstein is fully aware of what he holds in the *Tractatus* becomes painfully clear when one examines both the 1929 paper and his later efforts. He had to accept realism in order to feel the destructive tension among it, the truth-table explication of necessity, and the formal character of synthetic-a-priori sentences. His coping with that tension helps to explain his later philosophy. Wittgenstein certainly meant what he said in the Preface to the *Investigations*: "Four years ago I had occasion to re-read my first book. . . . It suddenly seemed to me that I should publish those old thoughts and the new ones together: that the latter could be seen in the right light only by contrast with and against the background of my old way of thinking."

20 For an incisive discussion of the picture theory and the several meanings of 'possible' see Gustav Bergmann, "Stenius on the *Tractatus*," *Theoria*, 29, 1963.

XIII. OF MIND AND MYTH

HERBERT HOCHBERG

In recent years Professor Quine has rejected mental entities. Yet, his resulting materialism (physicalism) is a qualified one as he further holds that physical objects are ontological "myths." This somewhat paradoxical view is a consequence of a residual phenomenalism in an eclectic metaphysics that also embraces elements of pragmatism, holism, materialism, neo-Kantianism, and analytical philosophy. To see this we will trace Quine's development from an apparent phenomenalist to a "physical mythologist." This development may be divided into three stages.

In 1948 we find Quine holding that phenomena are of the utmost significance for epistemology. The phenomenalist "conceptual scheme" is "epistemologically fundamental." Physical objects, on the other hand, are only convenient myths, and the physicalistic conceptual scheme is scientifically fundamental rather than philosophically so. At this stage science and philosophy have yet to be merged. One ground for such a merger is soon to be provided by behaviorist psychology. In 1951, the second stage, we find Quine attacking phenomenalism by castigating attempts at phenomenalistic reduction, the thesis that physical object statements can be reconstructed in a phenomenalistic conceptual scheme. It takes only one more year for Quine to advance to the third and final stage by adopting Watsonian behaviorism as a philosophy of mind. Embracing behaviorism, Quine resolves whatever doubt he may still have had by explicitly rejecting phenomena. Yet there are still some phenomenalistic hangovers. They lurk behind his continued reference to "mythology" as well as his use of the term 'experience' at critical points. To a detailed account and analysis of these stages I will shortly turn. First, I will briefly consider some notions that are germane to the analysis.

I

The notion of an improved or "ideal" language is familiar in contemporary philosophical discussion. A formalism like *Principia Mathematica* supplemented by adding certain classes of descriptive signs (and the so-called axiom of extensionality to its primitive sentences) can, upon interpretation, serve as an illustration. Some philosophers conceive of philosophical analysis as consisting of informal commonsensical discourse about the structure and interpretation of such ideal languages. One thus *reconstructs* the traditional philosophical problems as questions about such languages. Not all formalisms are ideal languages. In order for an interpreted formalism to qualify as an ideal language it must fulfill three conditions. (1) It must serve as an adequate tool for the analysis of *all* philosophical problems. That is, all philosophical propositions can be reconstructed as statements about its structure and interpretation. (2) It must, in principle, contain transcriptions of anything nonphilosophical we might want to say. Thus it must enable us to account for all areas of our experience. For example, it should not only contain (schematically) the way in which scientific behaviorists speak about mental contents but it should also reflect the different way in which one speaks about his own experience and that of others. And, it must then show how these two jibe. (3) It may not contain the transcriptions of any of those problematic propositions and uses which give rise to the philosophical problems. What is involved in and intended by (1), (2), and (3) I hope to make more explicit as we proceed.

Quine is not hostile to philosophizing by means of ideal languages, though, as far as I know, he seldom speaks of them as such.[1] However, he would not consider (1), (2), and (3) as the criteria for an interpreted formalism's being an ideal language. Rather, we see his alternative criteria when he writes:

Philosophy is in large part concerned with the theoretical non-genetic underpinnings of scientific theory; with what science could get along with, could be reconstructed by means of, as distinct from what science has historically made use of. If certain problems of ontology, say, or modality, or causality, or contrary-to-fact conditionals, which arise in ordinary language, turn out not to arise in science as reconstituted with the help of formal logic, then those philosophical problems have in an important sense been solved: they have been shown not to be implicated in any necessary foundation of science. Such solutions are

---

[1] One such place is in "The Scope and Language of Science," *The British Journal for the Philosophy of Science*, 8, 1957, 1–17.

good to just the extent that (*a*) philosophy of science is philosophy enough and (*b*) the refashioned logical underpinnings of science do not engender new philosophical problems of their own.[2]

Since we have two conflicting sets of criteria for an ideal language I shall compare and contrast them by pointing out some consequences of each. Since one's philosophy is judged by its fruits, I shall attempt to show that Quine's position suffers by such comparison. Quine's (b) seems similar to (3), even though his (a) conflicts with (1). However the agreement between (b) and (3) is illusory. Let us see how they differ.

Quine's well known conception of ontology, condensed in the cryptic phrase "to be is to be the value of a variable," makes the existential operator the key to ontology. Existential statements in his proposed ideal language involve ontological commitments, or, to put it another way, such statements make ontological assertions. Since, first, he has also told us that the existential operator is a more precise or scientific rendering of the 'there is' of ordinary language and, second, it is by use of this single sign that one says such radically different things as (p$_1$) 'There are no physical objects' and (p$_2$) 'There are no rocket ships in Glenview', we may conclude that Quine's conception of ontology results in the collapsing of the ordinary and the ontological (philosophical) uses of 'exist' into the existential operator. This point is made quite obvious by his sometimes speaking of the ontological commitments of ordinary language. By contrast, one might observe that (p$_1$) represents a problematic use that gives rise to philosophical puzzlement, while (p$_2$) represents an ordinary use that does not. This distinction is indispensable for an adequate analysis of classical ontology. For its neglect will lead one to merely reassert, rather than analyze, traditional ontological assertions. Thus in his proposed ideal language Quine simply restates, even though in symbols, one of the traditional ontological positions – instead of, by means of a symbolism, explicating all of them without accepting any of them in their traditional form. This shows, first, the difference between (3) and (b) and, second, the inadequacy of both Quine's explication of ontology and his criteria expressed in (b). For (b) does not prohibit the assertion, within Quine's ideal language, of statements that give rise to philosophical problems, since it permits the reproduction of the traditional puzzling uses of language. A purported philosophical analysis that results in the reassertion of

---

[2] W. V. Quine, "Mr. Strawson on Logical Theory," *Mind*, 62, 1953, 446.

traditional metaphysical statements provides neither an explication nor an analysis.[3]

In view of (b)'s permitting the assertion of philosophically problematic statements one may well wonder precisely what Quine intends it to exclude. (b) might well be intended to preclude, first, the paradoxes that interest logicians and mathematicians and, second, all philosophical statements and questions that are not reconstructible as ones for, or about, science. This latter would seem to be implicit in his suggestion that "philosophy of science is philosophy enough." Hence classical ontological assertions are permissible if, for Quine, they are the ontological "hypotheses" of the scientist. The scientist thus provides the answer to the classical ontological questions. We can then readily see how the acceptance of behaviorist psychology as *science* helps set the stage for the *philosophical* assertion that there are no mental entities. The behaviorist, we recall, always speaks physicalistically. Quine's criterion (b) for a language's being an ideal one is thus an important point in his ultimate rejection of phenomena. His explication of ontology (referred to hereafter as (o_1)) may be considered to have two parts: first, ontological commitments are made via the use of the existential operator and, second, the answer to the question "What exists?" is given by the ontological commitments of the simplest conceptual scheme that can accomodate all of science:

Ontological questions, under this view, are on a par with questions of natural science ....

Our acceptance of an ontology is, I think, similar in principle to our acceptance of a scientific theory, say a system of physics: we adopt, at least insofar as we are reasonable, the simplest conceptual scheme into which the disordered fragments of raw experience can be fitted and arranged. Our ontology is determined once we have fixed upon the over-all conceptual scheme which is to accomodate science in the broadest sense; .... [4]

Thus it seems that not only is philosophy of science "philosophy enough," but for ontological questions, science is enough.

As distinct from Quine's reconstruction of ontology, (o_1), one might propose that the undefined descriptive signs of a philosopher's ideal language give his existents in the ontological sense of that term. In connection with this latter explication ,(o_2), we note three things.

---

[3] For a detailed analysis of Quine's explication of ontology see three of my papers, "The Ontological Operator," *Philosophy of Science*, 23, 1956, 250–259; "Professor Quine, Pegasus and Dr. Cartwright," *Philosophy of Science*, 24, 1957, 191–203; "On Pegasizing," *Philosophy and Phenomenological Research*, 17, 1957, 551–4.

[4] W. V. Quine, *From a Logical Point of View* (Harvard University Press, Cambridge, 1953), pp. 45, 16–17. Hereafter, I will refer to this book as *FLPV* and footnote quoted passages according to where they occur in the book, rather than in the original papers.

First, we are not concerned with ontological commitments of ordinary languages or sign systems in general. Rather, we are concerned with an explication of classical ontology and, as such, speak only of ontological commitment in connection with an ideal language. Thus a philosopher's answer to the ontological question "What exists?" is reconstructed in terms of the undefined descriptive signs of his (explicit or implicit) *proposed* ideal language. Second, ontology is primarily concerned with kinds of entities, rather than with particular existents, and, further, with existents in the narrow sense of that term which connotes simplicity. That is, one of the traditional ontological motifs is the idea that entities which exist in the ontological sense are neither complexes nor patterns of other entities. This is *one* reason for making the undefined (rather than all of the) descriptive signs carry the ontological burden. Third, one is not involved in making ontological assertions by using the existential operator, since that sign is not, on this view, the key to ontology. Thus one can distinguish between two kinds of uses – philosophical and ordinary – of 'exist'. The former is explicated in terms of the undefined descriptive signs while the latter is reflected in the existential operator. This is not to say either that there are not other metaphysical uses, i.e., "subsistence," which also require explication or that one cannot make further distinctions among the various ordinary uses. The key point is that all the former will be explicated as questions and answers *about* the structure and interpretation of an ideal language, while the latter will be reflected in the various existential statements made *in* the language. Hence one does not reproduce within the language the ontological statements that give rise to the philosophical puzzles. We may then consider a difference between a phenomenalist and a realist to be partially explicated as follows. The former would hold that the undefined descriptive signs of his ideal language refer only to phenomena and properties of such; the latter would insist that such signs refer to physical objects and their properties. The traditional question can then be partially reconstructed as a question about the interpretation of the ideal language. Its answer is given by a consideration of whether or not the proposed alternative ideal languages do in fact fulfill (1), (2), and (3). That is, if it can be argued that a proposed ideal language that is physicalistically interpreted cannot fulfill these criteria but, on the other hand, a phenomenalistically interpreted one can, then the reconstructed question is answered. But notice, in saying all this one neither adopts nor rejects either position in its traditional form. In fact we no longer find ourselves in the predicament of being forced to choose between them. For, upon reconstruction, the common sense cores of the various traditional positions need no longer be incompatible. Thus one can recover these various "cores" without either asserting the puzzling propositions or accepting the extravagances of the classical positions.[5]

II

In his paper "On What There Is" Quine sets forth the position of the first stage.

But simplicity, as a guiding principle in constructing conceptual schemes, is not a clear and unambiguous idea; and it is quite capable of presenting a double or multiple standard. Imagine, for example, that we have devised the most economical set of concepts adequate to the play-by-play reporting of immediate experience. The entities under this scheme – the values of bound variables – are, let us suppose, individual subjective events of sensation or reflection. We should still find, no doubt, that a physicalistic conceptual scheme, purporting to talk about external objects, offers great advantages in simplifying our over-all reports. By bringing together scattered sense events and treating them as perceptions of one object, we reduce the complexity of our stream of experience to a manageable conceptual simplicity. The rule of simplicity is indeed our guiding maxim in assigning sense data to objects: we associate an earlier and a later round sensum with the same so-called penny, or with two different so-called pennies, in obedience to the demands of maximum simplicity in our total world-picture.

Here we have two competing conceptual schemes, a phenomenalistic one and a physicalistic one. Which should prevail? Each has its advantages; each has its special simplicity in its own way. Each, I suggest, deserves to be developed. Each may be said, indeed, to be the more fundamental, though in different senses: the one is epistemologically, the other physically, fundamental....

Physical objects are postulated entities which round out and simplify our account of the flux of experience, just as the introduction of irrational numbers simplifies laws of arithmetic.[6]

These passages make it clear that for Quine phenomenal entities are "epistemologically fundamental" while physical objects are "postulated entities." The difference seems to lie in the fact that phenomenal entities are objects of direct experience while physical objects are not. Thus phenomena are more fundamental in that they and they alone are directly given. Physical objects, not being *given*, are *introduced* (or *postulated*) only in order to round out and simplify our accounts of the *given* phenomena. They are, so to speak, introduced "for the sake of the phenomena." Phenomena, on the other hand, are not introduced

---

[5] For detailed discussions of the role of ideal languages in philosophical analysis see G. Bergmann, *The Metaphysics of Logical Positivism* (Longmans, Green, and Co., 1954); *Meaning and Existence* (University of Wisconsin Press, Madison, 1959).

[6] *FLPV*, pp. 17–18.

for the sake of anything. In fact they are not introduced at all: we simply find them in experience.

What Quine says seems to lie somewhere on a continuum between Berkeley and the neo-Kantians, yet it is hard to say just where. In terms of the explication of ontology expressed in (o_2), Quine's characterization of physical objects as "myths" could be explicated by his (explicitly or implicitly) proposing an ideal language all of whose undefined descriptive signs referred to phenomenal entities and properties of such. The "names" of physical objects, provided there were such, and of the characters they exemplify would then be defined signs. Thus we would have a perfectly clear cut explication of that picturesque phrase, "the myth of physical objects." Such an explication would reflect an essentially Berkeleyan outlook. But this Berkeleyan alternative does not seem to reflect what Quine has in mind. This is implicit in his use of 'postulate' as well as explicit in his doubts concerning the definability of physical object terms by means of phenomenalistic ones. If this is the basis of the mythical character of physical objects, it would seem that phenomena, the data of immediate experience, are not myths. Not being myths, phenomena are surely existents. Thus in the first stage it seems that Quine is primarily concerned, positively, with securing some ontologically respectable status for physical objects; he is not concerned, negatively, with destroying the ontological status of phenomena. Such respectability for physical objects is needed and desired for three reasons. First, due to Quine's commitment to the epistemological priority of phenomena, he holds that physical objects are not objects of direct experience. Hence they are ontologically suspect. Second, even though ontologically suspect, physical objects are needed in Quine's conceptual scheme to accocomodate the statements of science. For, third, phenomenalistic reconstruction cannot be achieved. In short, Quine's conceptual scheme must contain physical object terms that make ontological commitments, but such commitments conflict with his phenomenalistic orientation. This shows that in addition to the two parts of (o_1), which we considered above, Quine apparently also thinks that "to be is to be an object of direct experience." His explication of ontology, at this stage of his thought, is thus really three-fold. Yet this "phenomenalism" puts Quine in a quandary. Since only objects of direct experience exist, and hence are not myths, he, not being a direct realist, must consider physical objects as myths. On the other hand, since a phenomenalistic conceptual scheme cannot literally reconstruct all statements of science, it cannot serve as an ideal language. Hence he must accept a conceptual scheme which "postulates" mythical entities – physical objects. But he does not, as yet, reject directly given existents. Thus, in the first stage Quine apparently adheres to a conceptual scheme committed ontologically to phenomena *and* to physical objects. This seems to be so in spite of the fact that he contrasts a phenomenalistic scheme with a physicalistic one, and not, explicitly, with a "mixed" one. At this stage, a "physicalistic scheme" is for him apparently one which accepts physical objects in addition to phenomena. This interpretation is clearly supported, first, by his speaking of associating sense data with physical objects in a physicalistic conceptual scheme and, second, by his analogy between the physicalistic and phenomenalistic schemes on the one hand and the arithmetic of rational and irrational numbers on the other.

From the point of view of the conceptual scheme of the elementary arithmetic of rational numbers alone, the broader arithmetic of rational and irrational numbers would have the status of a convenient myth, simpler than the literal truth (namely, the arithmetic of rationals) and yet containing that literal truth as a scattered part. Similarly, from a phenomenalistic point of view, the conceptual scheme of physical objects is a convenient myth, simpler than the literal truth and yet containing that literal truth as a scattered part.[7]

Thus a physicalistic scheme, in Quine's terms, contains the phenomenalistic one (i.e., commits one to phenomenal entities) as a part. Yet, due to his phenomenalism he has misgivings; so much so that he is still willing to see to what extent phenomenalistic reconstruction can be achieved.

Let us by all means see how much of the physicalistic conceptual scheme can be reduced to a phenomenalistic one; still, physics also naturally demands pursuing, irreducible *in toto* though it be.[8]

From philosophical-epistemological motives Quine is pulled towards phenomenalism; from "scientific" motives he is pulled towards an ontology aknowledging physical objects. Hence his views contain unreconciled tensions. This is inherent in what I called his threefold explication of ontology: (a) to be is to be the value of a variable, (b) to be is to be an ontological commitment of the "simplest" conceptual scheme adequate to the reconstruction of science, (c) to be is to be an object of direct experience. Given the criterion of ontological commitment expressed in (a) and the failure of phenomenalistic reconstruction, Quine's conceptual scheme cannot satisfy both (b) and (c).

[7] *FLPV*, p. 18.
[8] *FLPV*, p. 19.

The adoption of a complex ontology provides neither a solution nor a reconciliation. Moreover, for one who philosophizes, as I believe Quine does, with Ockham's dictum in mind, a complex ontology can only be a temporary expedient. That this is so is implicit in Quine's discussion of simplicity.

As Quine notes, 'simple' is an ambiguous term. In one sense one may hold that a phenomenalistic scheme is simpler than a physicalistic one in that phenomena are simpler and more fundamental entities. That is, sensa, for example, are *neither posits nor composits*. A second and third sense of 'simple' arise when Quine speaks of simplifying our account of physics by postulating physical objects. One thing he apparently has in mind is something similar to what some mean when they speak of a linguistic structure or scientific theory being simpler than another in some technical sense concerning the kinds of terms and the forms of statements. Another thing he seems to have in mind is a sense of 'simplify' which is synonymous with 'unify'. Just as scientists achieve simplification when they unify different areas or theories by, for example, subsumption of one or more theories under a different theory, so we achieve conceptual simplification by associating different phenomena with one physical object. (A further sense of 'simplify' is involved in assigning phenomena to physical objects according to the "demands of maximum simplicity." But this is irrelevant to our discussion.)

In a fourth and crucial sense one conceptual scheme may be considered simpler than another if it commits one to fewer *kinds* of entities. In this sense neither a phenomenalistic nor a physicalistic (in the usual sense, *i.e.*, one committed only to physical objects) scheme would, as such, be simpler than the other. Both, however, would be simpler than a scheme which acknowledged both kinds of entities. Following Ockham's dictum, Quine would or could be led to seek a simple scheme in this fourth sense of 'simple'. This, I believe, provides *a* key to his ultimately rejecting phenomena, after once having considered them to be "epistemologically fundamental." This point may be seen as follows. As we noted, the Quine of the first stage is confronted with two "opposing" conceptual schemes: one phenomenalistic, the other committed to phenomena and to physical objects. Suppose that both are adequate in that they can both serve for the description of all areas of our experience and for the reconstruction of all physical object statements of the scientist. The phenomenalistic scheme would be simpler in the first and fourth senses of that term, while the complex scheme would be technically simpler. To vacillate between the two because of the technical simplicity of the one would be to show the grossest neglect for both ontology and epistemology. Yet, as I read the above quoted passages of Quine, it seems that he might be swayed, or at least tempted, by such "technical" considerations. Be that as it may, he does not have to face such a choice, since a phenomenalistic scheme is not likely to be adequate. It is not adequate because, we recall, a phenomenalistic reconstruction of the scientist's statements, according to Quine, cannot be achieved. In fact we may even take the third sense of 'simple' that I distinguished – 'simple' as synonymous with 'unify' – to reflect this inadequacy. For, if one could reconstruct physical-object terms in a phenomenalistic reconstruction, then one would achieve the "unification" of various sensa with a single physical "object" without recourse to an ontology embracing physical objects. Thus Quine writes:

The physical conceptual scheme simplifies our account of experience because of the way myriad scattered sense events come to be associated with single so-called objects; still there is no likelihood that each sentence about physical objects can actually be translated, however deviously and complexly, into the phenomenalistic language. Physical objects are postulated entities . . . . [9]

Physical objects are thus postulated not "merely" for technical simplicity but as a necessary condition for the adequate reconstruction of physics. Hence we would not be confronted by two adequate schemes one of which was technically simpler, the other ontologically and epistemologically simpler. Rather, we would have to choose between an adequate and an inadequate scheme. In this sense there is no real choice. Consequently, as we saw, physical objects must be postulated. Thus the only scheme which might be both adequate and ontologically simple would be one committed to an ontology of physical objects alone. In this manner a "new" alternative arises and, for one who seeks ontological simplicity and is more concerned with the need to *literally* reconstruct all statements of science than he is with epistemological problems, the road to materialism is open. But if such a one was once impressed by the epistemological priority of phenomena he must first convince himself that the immediately given and "epistemologically fundamental" is non-existent. Quine seeks to convince himself by attacking phenomenalism. At first he develops his misgivings about phenomenalistic schemes by assaulting literal phenomenalistic recon-struction. Eventually he comes to consider phenomena to be posits like

[9] *FLPV*, p. 18.

physical objects. (To help convince himself of this he will even adopt traditional holistic arguments against phenomena as self-contained givens). Then, alternative schemes of *postulated entities* confront each other. Phenomena are thus no longer epistemologically fundamental. Convinced of this he can then embrace materialism without a bad epistemological conscience. To make doubly sure, as it were, he will even attack epistemology. We may now turn to what I have called the second stage: Quine's well-known attack on the plausibility of phenomenalistic reconstruction.

III

The second stage is explicitly characterized by a marked change of tone rather than by one of doctrine.[11] In the first stage we noted that while Quine did not hold that phenomenalistic reduction could be achieved, he was sympathetic to attempts to carry it out. Now the sympathy has completely disappeared, and belief in such a reconstruction in castigated as "naive" and "dogmatic." With phenomenalism thus dismissed, there is no longer any thought of possible reduction of the mixed ontology of the second stage to a "simpler" ontology of phenomena alone. Physical objects are now firmly incorporated in Quine's ontology:

Physical objects are conceptually imported into the situation as convenient intermediaries– not by definition in terms of experience, but simply as irreducible posits comparable, epistemologically, to the gods of Homer.
    .... But in point of epistemological footing the physical objects and the gods differ only in degree and not in kind. Both sorts of entities enter our conception only as cultural posits. The myth of physical objects is epistemologically superior to most in that it has proved more efficacious than other myths ....[11]

This passage also makes it clear that physical objects are still second-class ontological citizens. As "myths" they are on a par with Homer's gods precisely because, as we noted earlier, they are not objects of direct experience. Thus at this stage Quine apparently still retains his belief in the epistemological primacy of phenomena (experience). Quine's classifying physical objects with Homeric deities goes beyond his fondness for the catching phrase and starting formulation. We have seen how his phenomenalism, his belief that in some sense to be is to be an object of direct experience, makes physical objects postulational entities. On the other hand his requiring an ideal language

---

[10] *However*, see the discussion below concerning the holism implicit in the second stage.
[11] *FLPV*, p.44.

to contain literal reconstructions of all statements of science leads him to reject a phenomenalistic conceptual scheme. Granting this requirement, Quine's rejection of a phenomenalistic ideal language is not debatable. However, the requirement itself is. For one may hold that this requirement reflects the fact that Quine's primary concern is with the actual reconstruction of science and not with the solution of the philosophical problems. We recall that, for Quine, if one's ideal language does not embody these problems he considers them to be solved. If, on the other hand, one views an ideal language as a tool for the analysis and solution of philosophical problems by discourse about it, rather than by mere elimination within it, one need not and, reasonably, will not insist on a complete and literal reconstruction of ordinary language (including that of the scientist). Instead, one may be content with reconstructing, from a phenomenalistic basis, only what is necessary for the analysis of the philosophical puzzles. That is, to put it figuratively, an ideal language is ideal not only in that it is an improved language but that it is, in a sense, a fiction. Thus, for example, not every physical object statement, nor, indeed, all of what we "mean" by any such statement, need be reconstructed in order for us to deal with the philosophical problems surrounding physical identity and the notion of substance. In fact no contemporary phenomenalist who knows what he is about would claim that his ideal language can actually be employed by the scientist. We have, then, two opposed views regarding the nature and purpose of philosophizing by means of an ideal language. As in other things one may, perhaps, judge the two "enterprises" by their fruits. Earlier we noted that Quine's views on ontology result in his mixing philosophical and ordinary uses of 'exist'. Consequently, he is led to repeat, in his ideal language, philosophically problematic assertions. The same tendency may be noted in connection with his criteria for an adequate conceptual scheme (ideal language). He is ultimately led to deny such common-sense things as phenomenal entities. As for physical objects, a supposedly philosophical analysis leads to nothing more definite than the poetic conclusion that physical objects are myths, like the gods of Homer. Thus Quine clearly concludes his analysis with propositions just like those that gave rise to the linguistic turn in philosophy. This outcome, I submit, argues against Quine's conception of analysis. It shows clearly that Quine has either not accepted or not grasped the crucial distinction between ordinary non-philosophical usage and the extraordinary use of language that philosophers are prone to.

In the second stage Quine still faces the dilemma of the first. As we have seen he is led to include both mythical physical objects and directly given phenomenal entities in his ontology. But if one is still at heart in the classical tradition and concerned with ontological simplicity, he has to choose eventually between phenomenalism and realism. The dilemma is finally resolved – after a fashion – when he embraces Watsonian behaviorism as a philosophy of mind. This step is a natural one to take in view of Quine's criteria for an adequate conceptual scheme. For, to many in the empiricist-analytic tradition, behaviorism is equivalent to scientific psychology. Hence one may be a behaviorist and, in principle, be able to say all that a scientist may have to say about "mind." Since, for Quine, all we are concerned with when we construct a conceptual scheme are the statements of the scientist, we can see how his criteria for an adequate conceptual scheme may lead him to adopt behaviorism as a philosophy of mind. This is a further fruit of his conception of the philosophical enterprise. As a philosophical behaviorist, Quine may then explicity reject phenomena. Yet, he will still call physical objects myths. For, as we shall see, while Quine the behaviorist may have disposed of phenomenal entities, he has not completely disposed of Quine the phenomenalist.

IV

The third stage is proclaimed in Quine's paper "On Mental Entities" when he writes

I suggest that it is a mistake to seek an immediately evident reality, somehow more immediately evident than the realm of external objects.[12]

With this statement he cancels the epistemological priority of phenomena. When we recall that "epistemological priority" once attracted him to a phenomenalistic conceptual scheme, it is no surprise to find that he quickly proceeds to reject phenomena.

Epistemologists have wanted to posit a realm of sense data, situated somehow just me-ward of the physical stimulus, for fear of circularity: to view the physical stimulation rather than the sense datum as the end point of scientific evidence would be to make physical science rest for its evidence on physical science. But if with Neurath we accept this circularity, simply recognizing that the science of science is a science, then we dispose of the epistemological motive for assuming a realm of sense data.[13]

---

[12] W. V. Quine, "On Mental Entities," *Proceedings of the American Academy of Arts and Sciences*, 80, 3, 202. I will refer to this paper as *OME*.

[13] *OME*, 202.

Nor, in view of Quine's concern with "science" throughout all this, need we be surprised when he "replaces" phenomena in the scientifically adequate manner of behaviorist psychology.

> To repudiate mental entities is not to deny that we sense or even that we are conscious; it is merely to report and try to describe these facts without assuming entities of a mental kind.
> .... we construe consciousness as a faculty of responding to one's own responses. The responses here are, or can be construed as, physical behaviour.[14]

The contrasting of epistemology, on the one hand, with a "science of science," on the other, is rather strange. The science of science is apparently behaviorist psychology (perhaps "science of scientists" would be more apt). Yet behavior scientists, as scientists, are concerned with discovering lawful connections between items of overt behavior. They are not, as physicists are not, concerned with philosophical problems – either epistemological or ontological. As such neither behavior science nor physics provides answers to philosophical questions. Thus, properly understood, behavior science is not a philosophy of mind – just as phenomenalism is not an experimental science. Yet Quine speaks as if he advocated the replacement of epistemology by a science. Perception psychology construed along behavioristic lines becomes an alternative to phenomenalism. Thus Quine refuses to recognize that phenomenalists at least saw certain philosophical questions to which the psychology of perception has no answer. As we earlier saw that he does not distinguish between philosophical and ordinary usage, we now see that he mixes scientific with philosophical questions. By accepting the circularity he mentions, Quine therefore rejects epistemology, as it is ordinarily understood. He thus accepts uncritically the universe of the physicalistic behaviorist. Any question as to how we know all the things the scientist tells us is omitted. This rejection of philosophy, though strange, is not surprising. For Quine once, we recall, held phenomena to be epistemologically fundamental. Now he rejects phenomena, in favor of postulated physical objects. How could he do that in good conscience if he retained the epistemological questions? So, in rejecting phenomena, Quine simultaneously rejects epistemology. It suggests the ploy of one who, not being able to refute Berkeley, seeks to forget him. This rejection of philosophy in favor of science is what I find strange.[15] Yet my attitude reflects a certain conception of philosophy that Quine does not share. For,

---

[14] *OME*, 203.
[15] Recall that in a passage quoted above Quine seemed to contrast physics with phenomenalism. See note 8.

as we saw, in view of his criteria for an adequate conceptual scheme, behaviorist psychology may provide a philosophical answer to a philosophical question (or set of such). This is the fruit of his conception of philosophy, which led him to reject phenomenalistic reconstruction in the second stage, that Quine enjoys in the third stage. All this is not, of course, to be construed as an attack on either science or, specifically, behaviorist psychology. It is merely to suggest that behavior science is not to be mistaken for a philosophical position.

One who makes such a "mistake" either rejects philosophy or embraces materialism or, more often, does both (though, of course, not usually explicitly). I shall not here rehearse the classical objections that Quine thus inherits. What we should note, however, is the complications that ensue by his insisting on the mythical status of material objects. For with phenomena banished, we are faced with a world whose only entities are mythical. This brings us to another strange consequence of Quine's rejection of phenomena.

In the third stage sensa become posits, posits less warranted than physical objects. This is a radical change from the first stage, though, again, not surprising in view of Quine's rejection of epistemology. However, it is extremely paradoxical. An ontological posit may be warranted if it is necessary for the simplification and ordering of our immediate data – sensa and other phenomenal entities. A posit surely is not warranted if it is not so needed. This, we know, is the strategy of ontological postulation. Now, if one holds that phenomena are given, as the Quine of the first stage did, then it is obviously nonsense to say that such givens are unnecessary posits (or even necessary posits). On the other hand, if one rejects phenomena as given, then what is it that we produce order among by making ontological posits? Since there are no longer phenomena, either as given or as posits, all that is left are posited physical things. This is the real circularity that Quine accepts. *We posit physical objects to order posited physical objects.* This puzzling circularity is understandable, genetically, when we recall that the "method" of ontological postulation was formulated in Quine's phenomenalistic first stage. For then he had directly given phenomena whose ordering seemed to require posited physical objects. Without such givens the method of ontological postulation is both pointless and paradoxical. Consequently, so is the ontology that he is ultimately led to adopt by use of this "method."

We have seen how Quine has been led to such a strange position. But we may reasonably wonder why he accepts it. A possible explanation lies in his use, at crucial points, of the term 'experience.'

The linguistic material is an interlocked system which is tied here and there to experience....

The statement that there is the planet may be keyed with our sense experience by our seeing the planet, or by our merely noting perturbations in the orbits of other planets. And even the statement that there is a table right here may be keyed with our sense experience through *or* sight *or* hearsay.

.... how the overall system will continue to work in connection with experience.[16]

What does 'experience' mean in such passages? If, in spite of Quine's possible protestations to the contrary, he is still thinking of experience in terms of phenomena, then the position of the third stage is blatantly inconsistent. Yet such lapses would make plausible both his retention of the terminology of ontological postulation and his failure to realize the paradoxical consummation of his views. What Quine should, and at places does, hold is that experience is to be construed in terms of items of overt behavior and physical stimulation. But to do this is to explicitly assert the paradox we noted above. For to speak of experience in terms of overt behavior and physical stimulation is to speak physicalistically. Hence we are back to postulating physical objects to order postulated physical objects. Quine's use of the term 'experience' thus enables him to castigate phenomenalists and to propose, unmindful of its absurd consequences, his mythological materialism. Actually, Quine's overlooking the consequences of his view may have been aided by an expository device.

....I do not want to force the issue of recognizing experience as an entity or composite of entities. I have talked up to now as if there were such entities; I had to talk some language and I uncritically talked this one. But the history of the mind-body problem bears witness to the awkwardness of the practice.[17]

Perhaps his "uncritical" linguistic habits are in some measure responsible for what, I suggest, is an uncritical philosophy. For, in the first stage he accepted phenomena, in the third he speaks, at places, as if he did. It may be that he takes himself too literally when, in the third stage, he ties language to "experience."

Quine's well-known contention that a language need only be tied to "experience" at certain points does nothing to alleviate the problem. In fact, if anything, such talk dramatically illustrates his dilemma. Consider a language, L, which, as we say, contains physical object terms, but no terms that refer to phenomenal objects or properties of such. Some, but not all, of such terms (or statements containing them) are coordinated to terms (statements) in a language, L', whose terms

[16] *OME*, 198, 199, 200.
[17] *OME*, 202.

refer to "experiences." Thus L is "interpreted" by means of L', much like certain abstract calculi of the theoretical scientist are partially interpreted into empirical concepts (statements). For one who accepted phenomenal entities referred to by the terms of L', or perhaps characterized by the statements of L', this would seem, on first sight, to be a plausible suggestion. Instead of requiring that all physical object terms (statements) be defined (reconstructed), in this case in L', by means of phenomenal terms (statements), one now would only require a partial interpretation of L by means of L'. But for Quine "experience" is physicalistically construed. Hence the terms of L' are also physical-object terms. This is, once again, the circularity he accepts. But it is a vicious circle. For the whole problem was to "tie" physical object terms to something other than physical object terms. To drive home the point, one need only ask what would be gained toward reducing the abstract character of an uninterpreted symbolic system if we provided a "coordinating dictionary" in terms of another uninterpreted system. (This analogy may suggest a connection between Quine's calling physical objects myths and his thinking of a language as partially tied to experience. Recall that certain scientists and philosophers of science sometimes speak of some of the terms of a partially interpreted calculus as "referring" to "fictional entities," and Quine also speaks, at places, of "positing" microscopic entities).

Aside from the above mentioned difficulties of Quine's position, there is a further point to note concerning his behaviorism. First, recall that he rejected a phenomenalistic conceptual scheme because a complete and literal reconstruction of physical object statements can not be achieved in it. Reductionism, he contended, is a naive dogma. Yet, is it not strangely inconsistent for him to reject the phenomenalistic reconstruction of statements about "experience"? For the behavioristic reconstruction, like the phenomenalistic one, is a reconstruction only in part and in principle. *It is just as "naive and dogmatic" to hold that the one is literally feasible as it is to contend that the other is.* Quine should then, for consistency's sake, reject behaviorism as well as phenomenalism. Yet the behaviorist, with his partial reconstruction, says everything about minds that can nowadays be said "scientifically." Perhaps this reflects Quine's concern with science rather than with epistemology. In any case, he, inconsistently, rejects phenomena twice – once because of an incomplete reconstruction in terms of them; once in favor of an incomplete reconstruction of them.

In a later paper Quine seems to suggest an answer to such an objection when he writes:

Contrary to popular belief, such a physical ontology has a place also for states of mind. An inspiration or a hallucination can .... be identified with its host for the duration. The feasibility of this artificial identification of any mental seizure, x, with the corresponding time-slice x′ of its physical host, may be seen by reflecting on the following simple manoeuvre. Where P is any predicate which we might want to apply to x, let us explain P′ as true of x′ if and only if P is true of x. Whatever may have been looked upon as evidence, cause, or consequence of P, as applied to x, counts now for P′ as applied to x′. This parallelism, taken together with the extensionality of scientific language, enables us to drop the old P and x from our theory and get on with just P′ and x′, rechristened as P and x. Such, in effect, is the identification. It leaves our mentalistic idioms fairly intact, but reconciles them with a physical ontology.[18]

If we take the closing sentences of this passage literally, it seems that the mind-body problem is solved by "rechristening" physical things with mentalistic terms. For, this procedure leads to a physicalistic ontology which preserves the "mentalistic idiom." The basis for this rechristening is that the physical state is present if and only if the mental one is. Moreover, if we know of no such physical state we merely postulate one. Further, since we need not know what this physical state is, we "explain" it in terms of the mental one. Then we eliminate the mental one. This procedure makes no literal sense to me, since we require the mental state, and the assertion about it, to explain what it is we are saying when we assert the postulated physical state. What can we then possibly mean by holding that after we have used the mentalistic assertion to explain the physical one we "rechristen" the physical state by the mentalistic idiom? For without such a mentalistic state and assertion we have no idea what we are saying when we assert the physicalistic proposition. It seems that Quine is suggesting we do not need mental entities in an ontology after we have made use of them to explain what we say when we speak physicalistically. In short, without 'Px' we do not know what it is we are asserting when we use 'P′x″. But to say that we are asserting 'Px' surely will not do, since this means that we either have not purged our phenomenalistic terms from the language or have interpreted a physical-object term in terms of phenomenalistic ones, perhaps making use of a phenomenalistic conceptual scheme. It is one thing to say that 'P′x″ and 'Px' say the "same" thing when we offer the former as a reconstruction of the latter in a physicalistic scheme. It is quite another thing, and a patently illegitimate one for a physicalist, to then seek to provide meaning for 'P′x″ by asserting that it says the "same" thing as 'Px'. Yet this is what Quine seems to be doing by his extension of the

---

[18] "The Scope and Language of Science," p. 15.

"method of postulation." For, according to him, we simply posit that there is a property P' such that 'P'x'' asserts what 'Px' asserts. This use of posits replaces the behaviorist's attempt to at least formulate such a property. A natural candidate for such a property, as Quine recognizes, would be a characterization of a unique state of the nervous system associated with a certain mental state. But this returns us to what is programmatic in the behaviorist's thesis, as well as to what is problematic philosophically.[19] So, in effect, all Quine has said is that if we have no properties on hand to make our relevant biconditional statements true, we simply posit that there are such. The phenomenalist too might profit from this new use of "posits" in philosophical analysis. Consider the sentence (S_1) 'This is a chair'. We may take a sentence (S_2), asserting that there are chair percepts (visual and/or tactile) which fulfill a certain *posited* complex relational property R, such that (S_2) is true if and only if (S_1) is. The evidence for (S_2) is exactly what we would consider evidence for (S_1). Thus we no longer need physical object statements like (S_1). Perhaps in this manner the phenomenalist may get rid of all physical object statements. Yet the phenomenalist, in his own terms, cannot specify the meaning of 'R', just as Quine cannot do so for 'P''. For, if 'R' is undefined, what it refers to must be presented in experience; if 'R' is a defined term, its definition must be specified. Quine might overlook, or not recognize, this difficulty, because of his holistic conception of meaning – his view that language as a whole, rather than terms or sentences, is the "unit of meaning." One aspect of this question we have already considered in discussing Quine's talk of "experience," to which his conceptual scheme is tied. Another aspect is the issue of holism itself. This brings us to another thread of his argument against sensa.

V

In addition to his Watsonian meditations, Quine provides two further arguments for rejecting sensa. The first attack concerns memory.

Our present data of our own past experiences are, on this theory, some sort of faint present replicas of past sense impressions; faint echoes of past sensation accompanying the blare of present sensation. Now it takes little soul-searching

[19] There is, of course, an issue connected with the use some philosophers make of discovered or speculative (not postulated, in Quine's sense) correlations between mental and physical states, in their attempts to disavow mental entities. But this takes us beyond Quine's particular version of physicalism. For a critical examination of a less sophisticated attempt to use such correlations to establish "identities" between the mental and the physical see my "Physicalism, Behaviorism and Phenomena," *Philosophy of Science*, 26, 2, 1959, 93–103.

to persuade oneself that such double impressions, dim against bright, are rather the exception than the rule. Ordinarily we do not remember the trapezoidal sensory surface of a desk, as a color patch extending across the lower half of the visual field; what we remember is *that* there was a desk meeting such-and-such approximate specifications of form and size in three-dimensional space. Memory is just as much a product of the past positing of extra-sensory objects as it is a datum for the positing of past sense data.[20]

The arguments may be taken in two ways. First, Quine could be contending that a phenomenalistic conceptual scheme is inadequate for the reconstruction of memory statements in that physical object terms are required in some of them. The argument requires him to hold, as he does, that statements involving such terms are not reconstructible. To answer this argument one would, of course, have to present a pattern for reconstructing memory statements within the framework of a phenomenalistic conceptual scheme. One would also have to argue, along the lines I mentioned earlier, that schematic reconstruction of memory statements, as of physical object statements, was sufficient. Here, I merely note that a contemporary phenomenalist need not limit himself to the somewhat Humean apparatus of *vivid* and *faint* data in dealing with the problem of memory.[21] Second, Quine could be suggesting that a phenomenalistic reconstruction of memory statements won't do since we do not speak in sense-data terms in ordinary language. That is, Quine could be arguing along lines similar to those used by ordinary language analysts. If this is so, it is interesting to recall his earlier rejection of epistemology in connection with his arguing in the style of a movement that systematically rejects all philosophical questions.

The second attack seeks to dismiss sensa as "tenuous abstractions."

It would be increasingly apparent from the findings of the Gestalt psychologists, if it were not quite apparent from everyday experience, that our selective awareness of present sensory surfaces is a function of present purposes and past conceptualizations. The contribution of reason cannot be viewed as limited merely to conceptualizing a presented pageant of experience and positing objects behind it; for this activity reacts, by selection and emphasis, on the qualitative make-up of the pageant itself in its succeeding portions. It is not an instructive oversimplification, but a basic falsification, to represent cognition as a discernment of regularities in an unadulterated stream of experience.[22]

In the above quoted passage Quine seems to assert three things. (1) Sensa have causes, in particular our "reason" and the psychological sets with which we confront the stream of experience, and these causes

---

[20] OME, 201.
[21] For example, see G. Bergmann, "Some Reflections on Time," in *Il Tempo* (Archivio di Filosofia, 1958), reprinted in *Meaning and Existence*.
[22] *OME*, 201.

partly determine the qualitative character of the sensa. (2) Sensa are "abstracted out" from a complex stream of experience. As such they are abstract entities. (3) Due to (1) and (2) there are no "pure" sense data. Hence the reality of sensa is suspect.

Concerning (1), aside from the Kantian flavor, we may note that the transition from the quite commonsensical observation that data have causes "outside" of "raw experience" to the banishing of such data as ontological entities is patently illegitimate. The results of perception psychology which show that we bring a "set" to a perceptual situation and that this set may causally determine what we perceive does not in any way provide evidence against the ontology or epistemology of the phenomenalist. The point is not whether or not our data have causes, speaking commonsensically (scientifically, if you will), but whether or not we "have" such data. If there is now a red sensum with which I am acquainted, then it is a fact that there is something red. Whether or not the scientist can discover certain correlations involving my reports of it, my perceptual set when I "have" it, my brain states, etc., has nothing at all to do with whether or not there is such a datum. There is also a suggestion of the holistic pattern in (1), but this comes out much more explicitly in (2). For (2) is reminiscent indeed of the familiar Hegelian-pragmatic antipathy to "vicious abstractions" from the holistic character of experience. According to this pattern, when we "abstract" sensa from the flux of experience we falsify experience which simply doesn't present itself in an atomistic fashion. One may wonder why Quine adopts, at this stage, the Hegelian pattern. The explanation is, I believe, twofold. First, we saw that part of his strategy in rejecting phenomena in the third stage is to consider them as posits rather than as givens. Once they are considered to be posits, he can reject them as unnecessary. This procedure would hardly make sense, as we noted, for objects of direct acquaintance. This being so, Quine seeks arguments against sensa being objects of direct acquaintance. The holistic tradition provides such ready made arguments against the "self-contained given." Second, Quine had already incorporated the holistic pattern into his philosophy in the second stage. In the best known piece of that stage he had linked the dogma of reductionism with a second "dogma of empiricism" – the synthetic-analytic dichotomy. Moreover, and more important ,he implicitly saw a connection between this dichotomy and the thesis of logical atomism.

The dogma of reductionism survives in the supposition that each statement, taken in isolation from its fellows, can admit of confirmation or infirmation at all. My countersuggestion, issuing essentially from Carnap's doctrine of the physical world in the *Aufbau*, is that our statements about the external world face the tribunal of sense experience not individually but only as a corporate body.

The dogma of reductionism even in its attenuated form, is intimately connected with the other dogma – that there is a cleavage between the analytic and the synthetic. We have found ourselves led, indeed, from the latter problem to the former through the verification theory of meaning. More directly, the one dogma clearly supports the other in this way: as long as it is taken to be significant in general to speak of the confirmation and infirmation of a statement, it seems significant to speak of a limiting kind of statement which is vacuously confirmed, *ipso facto*, come what may; and such a statement is analytic.

. . . . But what I am now urging is that even in taking the statement as unit we have drawn our grid too finely. The unit of empirical significance is the whole of science.[23]

In short, the meaning of any term or statement as well as the truth of any statement must be considered in the contextual setting of the total conceptual scheme. This is, of course, the holistic pattern and the rejection of logical atomism. Thus Quine's linking, in the second stage, of the two "dogmas" of phenomenalistic reduction and the synthetic-analytic dichotomy lead him to adopt the holistic pattern. Following this pattern and rejecting logical atomism, he then, in the third stage, may consider phenomena to be "abstractions" and not self-contained, directly given objects of experience. Then, as we saw, phenomena, being abstractions and not directly givens, become, for him, posits. But, under the impetus of his materialism, they are unnecessary posits. Hence they are banished from his ontology. We thus see how a combination of "scientific materialism" and Hegelian holism combine to form a two-pronged attack that, for Quine, obliterates phenomena. But then, the combination of materialism and holism is not new. What is in this context new in Quine's concern with the mythological character of physical objects. This, we saw, is a result of his early commitment to a phenomenalism which lingers on to complicate his materialism. Perhaps by still labelling physical objects "myths" Quine manages to placate an earlier concern with what is "epistemologically fundamental."

[23] *FLPV*, pp. 41, 42.

XIV. THE PHILOSOPHY OF JOHN DEWEY * 1

MAY BRODBECK

John Dewey's "instrumentalism" was at one time the most influential philosophy in America, both among the many and among the few. Our whole climate of opinion was shaped by his ideas. Social thought, political and legal theory and practice, historical method, and, especially, educational doctrine, all reflected Dewey's thought. Its direct impact on technical philosophy, never quite as great as elsewhere, is today vanishingly small. Where instrumentalist-pragmatist ideas do exist, the influence of Dewey is at best oblique, with his name hardly ever invoked. The influence of his thought in other areas, while still of some strength, is not only waning but often explicitly renounced. What was the nature of the philosophical system that came to be known, not without reason, as the characteristically American philosophy? What was the source of its attraction for American intellectuals and why do they now turn away from it?

Dewey's philosophy moves, as it were, on two levels. On one, it consists of certain attitudes towards man, nature, and society. It insists that man and all his works are part of the natural order, accessible to study just like anything else, with no need of appealing to any extra- or supernatural realm either for the sake of explanation or for the sake of salvation of man and his world. In this, instrumentalism is naturalistic. It is humanistic in its belief that man is the measure

* An Italian translation of this essay appeared in the October 1959 issue of *Rivista di Filosofia*. Its publisher and editors, Casa Editrice Taylor, Torino, and Professors Nicola Abbagnano and Norberto Bobbio have kindly authorized publication of the English original in *The Indian Journal of Philosophy* 3, 1961, 69–101. Reprinted by permission.

1 This paper owes a great deal to discussions with Professor Gustav Bergmann. Scattered throughout his work will be found many illuminating, critical comments on the philosophy of instrumentalism. In the present extended study of Dewey's philosophy I have drawn a little from the section on Dewey in my "Philosophy in America: 1900–1950" in *American Non-Fiction*, 1900–1950 by M. Brodbeck., *et al.*, H. Regnery Co., Chicago, 1952, and from my "The New Rationalism: Dewey's Theory of Induction," *The Journal of Philosophy* 46, 1949, 781–91. A part of this essay was read as the opening paper of a symposium held for the Dewey centenary at the annual meeting of the American Philosophical Association at Madison, May 1959.

of all things, that good and evil relate to actual interests and desires of men. It is melioristic in its ardent advocacy of social reform. Temperamentally, despite significant differences, instrumentalism is, among other things, also the heir of the eighteenth century. Like the men of the great Enlightenment, instrumentalists take a healthy-minded view of man and his fate. They see only the smilling aspects of human nature. They also share the Enlightenment's confidence that man can, by applying his intelligence, make life on this earth, which is the only life we have, worth living. Politically, instrumentalism is liberal democratic, insisting as it does that the good society can be built only by the spontaneous, active participation of all. To a very large number of Americans today much of this is almost painfully trite. And a great number of Dewey's writings do seem to be labouring the commonplace. Yet, in fairness, it should be pointed out that Dewey, born in 1859, the year in which the *Origin of Species* appeared, lived his young manhood when these things were not all taken for granted. That they are today is in large measure due to the efforts of Dewey and of the generation he soon came to lead. But beneath this broad creed, this *Weltanschauung*, there is a second, deeper level to Dewey's philosophy. For he elaborated at length technical theories of truth, value, and reality which were all very important as the theoretical vehicle of his influence. It is to this theoretical underpinning that I wish to devote myself in this paper.

I

John Dewey's *Logic: The Theory of Inquiry* which, as he himself quite correctly believed, contained the heart of his philosophy was published in 1938. This was quite some years after philosophy had, under the influence of Moore, Russell, and the logical positivists, taken a linguistic turn. Dewey, of course, never executed this turn. No doubt this was partly because his philosophy was in all essentials formed many years before the new stress on philosophizing by means of language began to make itself felt. And, as the *Logic* only too plainly shows, Dewey never really grasped the new logic that came into prominence in 1910 and was, in large measure, the basis of the new philosophy or, at least, of one very important branch of it. Yet, with this very branch, the logical positivists who followed the cues of Russell and Wittgenstein, he had very much in common. They shared Dewey's naturalistic, humanistic, and scientific temper of mind. Like Dewey, they urged the futility of the quest for certainty. Finally, like Dewey, they too rejected traditional metaphysics. Some of them even did so on the same scientistic grounds, believing, like Dewey, that no problem not solvable by science was a real problem. Yet, despite these areas of agreement, Dewey never relented in his battle against the linguistic philosophers. There were indeed differences of surface that fed this hostility. The representatives of the linguistic turn practised an analytical, formal method which Dewey, steeped in context and continuity, found offensive and viciously abstractive. Yet, as recent developments have shown, this was a resolvable surface difference.[2] And so it was viewed by those of Dewey's followers who formed a *rapprochement* with the positivists. But Dewey, in full grasp of the implications of his own thought, never smiled on this union. He saw that beneath the ideological agreement, there lay profound differences between his own views and those of the linguistic philosophers of his day. There were, ironically, basic metaphysical differences between the anti-metaphysical instrumentalist and linguistic camps. Those linguists who believed that the traditional philosophical positions had to be not so much abandoned as reformulated expressed their metaphysical commitments quite explicitly as 'reconstructed' philosophical theses; with others, they were implicit and unexamined assumptions, usually of a materialistic and realistic kind. But, examined or unexamined, reconstructed or traditional, the philosophical views of the linguistic philosophers were, without exception, anathema to Dewey. For, in one way or another, they recaptured some or all of the traditional philosophical distinctions between reason and experience, deduction and induction, mind and body, subjective and objective, knower and known, value and fact. Nor is this surprising. All these dualisms are either in some sense phenomenally given and, therefore, the only legitimate starting point of all critical philosophy since Descartes; or they are, at least, traditional elaborations of what is thus given and, therefore, though perhaps confused and uncritical, not without *some* legitimate core. Yet we all know how passionately Dewey rejects, because of what he insists is their unhealthy initial dualism, all the traditional problems; how fervidly he condemns all philosophies that start from them or, like Moore, Russell, and the positivists, at least acknowledge that there is something to be clarified behind them. But the denial of a philosophical proposition is itself a philosophical proposi-

---

[2] See "The Revolt against Logical Atomism" by G. Bergmann, *The Philosophical Quarterly* 7, 1957, 323–39 and 8, 1958, 1–13.

tion. The elaborate rationale Dewey constructed to overcome all the classical dualisms is, of course, itself an ingenious metaphysical construction. And, although Dewey never executed the linguistic turn, his work lends itself admirably to analysis by modern methods.

According to those who philosophize by means of language, the philosophers who made such silly claims as that time is unreal or only bodies (or only minds) exist were the victims of linguistic confusion. They were either giving old words, like "real" and "unreal," strange and private meanings, or they were pushed by a misleading grammatical form into bizarre positions that could have been avoided if they had thought to distinguish grammatical from logical form. This distinction led some linguistic philosophers to the notion of an improved or ideal language in which, unlike in ordinary language, the two forms coincide. They then speak commonsensically about the structure and interpretation of the artificial language. In other words, once the structure has been built, one does not just throw away the ladder and gaze in dumb wonder. Instead, one describes the structure and what it represents by talking about in. All philosophical propositions are reconstructed as statements about this ideal language. Traditional epistemological realism thus becomes the statement that the undefined primitive terms of the ideal language refer to physical objects. Nominalism, the view that no undefined terms name properties of things. Traditional materialism, the view that no undefined terms name anything mental. Thus, by using a language that ideally avoids the snares of ordinary speech, one points out the categorial features of the world. In itself, the method implies no philosophical position. Only the syntax and interpretation of the suggested ideal language reveals a metaphysics. In the *Logic* Dewey constructs and talks about what he clearly conceives to be the ideal language. For his 'final judgement' presumably contains, as the ideal language should, everything one would want to say either in common sense or in science. And, in it, linguistic form gives way to what Dewey conceives to be true logical form.[3] Dewey's discourse about the propositions and terms making up final judgement, about their structure and interpretation reveals his ontology, epistemology, and theory of value. As far as the method goes, this is all as it should be. Whether or not the metaphysics thus revealed makes his 'final judgment' a reasonable candidate for the ideal language is another question.

---

[3] *Logic: The Theory of Inquiry*, pp. 290–292. Unless otherwise mentioned, all page references are to this work.

Dewey's notion of 'final judgment' makes esoteric use of the Aristotelian syllogism. But the basic idea is clear. The 'root-metaphor' of Dewey's system is an ideal world-wide axiomatic system. For in final judgement, propositions are arranged in their true 'logical' order, in contrast to their merely temporal order in inquiry. This logical order has, as an axiomatic system should, premisses and conclusion. However, Dewey's notion of the 'logical', and his quaint view that deduction is productive of essential novelty, preserve final judgement from being the 'viciously abstractive' structure envisaged by those formalists, as he would call them, who interpret theories as hypothetico-deductive systems.[4] Be that as it may, 'logical', for Dewey, means 'functional'. [5] The so-called logical order is the order that reveals how, in the course of inquiry, some propositions function as evidence or 'ground' for others. The justifying propositions always come later in the course of inquiry than those they justify and this is reflected in the syllogism that is final judgement. The true logical order or 'context of justification' is thus also, as Dewey sees it, a temporal order. However, it differs from the actual course of inquiry, or the 'context of discovery', in being free of all propositions tentatively considered only to be eventually discarded. Thus purged of irrelevancies, final judgement reflects the temporal and logical structure of completed inquiry. In it is revealed the continuity of earlier and later stages of inquiry, each stage having an appropriate propositional form associated with it. Clearly, Dewey thus combines a causal or psycho-sociological analysis with what is ordinarily called logical analysis. Just as clearly, this is not a marriage made in heaven. Yet in this union lies the secret, Dewey believes, to overcoming all the classical dualisms. In particular, it realizes what he himself frequently affirmed to be his major motive in developing the philosophy of instrumentalism. It successfully obliterates the dualism between fact and value, between, as he put it, 'something called "science" on the one hand and something called "morals" on the other'.[6] This, as we know, is a considerable feat. How was it accomplished, and at what philosophical price?

Dewey's ontology and epistemology of fact and value rest on the universe, as he conceives it, containing three different levels. The

---

[4] However, as will be seen later, Dewey's final judgment is considerably more abstract and formalistic, in a sense that can be made precise, than the so-called 'formalist's' hypothetico-deductive system.

[5] P. 288.

[6] 'From Absolutism to Experimentalism', *Contemporary American Philosophy*, Vol. II, p. 23, New York, 1930.

universe of discourse and the universe of experience are two of these levels. In other words, we have language and, as we ordinarily say, what language speaks about. But what we ordinarily say is not what Dewey says. For Dewey's universe of discourse does not talk about the universe of experience. It does not for the very good reason that the latter, we are informed, is ineffable, indescribable in words.[7] It is also unique and perconceptual, but that amounts to the same thing. Dewey does not try to describe the indescribable. Fortunately, there is still a third level, namely, the process of inquiry. It transpires that this is what the universe of discourse is about. There is, among other things, an apparent inconsistency in this. For surely the process of inquiry is part of the world of experience. Dewey himself insisted, and rightly so, that man is inseparable from his environment. Yet, the inconsistency is only apparent, for, as I shall try to show, propositions talk even about the process only obliquely or at a certain distance, as it were. Yet it is by, in at least some sense, speaking about the process of inquiry, instead of about what we are inquiring into that Dewey believes he avoids ontological commitment. He characteristically settles ontological issues by placing things in the ongoing process. This is most obvious in his interpretation of the predicate, that is, the term that, as we ordinarily say, names a character or property of things.

Dewey vehemently rejects the 'customary position' on predication, according to which we ascribe an attribute, quality, or pattern of qualities to a particular that is found or given in experience. Sentences of the form 'a is F' are customarily so interpreted that 'a' names an individual or particular, while 'F' names a quality exemplified by that individual. 'This is red' asserts that an entity (sense-datum or physical object), characterized by spatial-temporal individuality, exemplifies a certain universal. It has the form of a statement of individual fact. Individual facts occur in causal contexts, of course. There are causes for their occurrence and sometimes these causes are things we do. They, in turn, cause the occurrence of other facts, including things we ourselves may do. Yet they are self-contained in the sense that their truth or falsity, when 'F' names a sense quality, does not depend upon anything else now or in the future, except a's being F. This interpretation implies a realistic epistemology in the sense that the meaning and truth of, say, 'This is red' is different from and independent of the meaning and truth of, say, 'Jones knows or observes that this is red'. Whatever adjustments may be made eventually in our system of

[7] *Logic*, Chapter 8, *passim*.

propositions, *some* statements of individual fact are always the ultimate
court of appeal. The decision to reject, for instance, 'This is a pink
elephant' will be based on laws *and* on the so-called 'certainty' of some
other statements, like 'This is intangible'. The 'certainty' of such
statements is psychological only. We are certain about them. We know
what it means to doubt the truth of other statements, only by comparing them with these. Logically, in the customary sense of 'logical',
statements of individual fact are, of course, not necessary, since they
are not tautological. Again, it is we who are certain, not the statements.
Their indubiety derives merely from the way we know them, directly,
without inference. Proponents of the customary view have not, to be
sure, always been free of confusing and misleading remarks on the
score of 'certainty'. Perhaps this is why Dewey identifies sense-data
sentences with the intuitive, the *a priori*, and, therefore, the unacceptable.[8] But the main burden of Dewey's attack is against the whole
notion of a self-contained individual fact. For this notion is belied,
Dewey believes, by the continuity inherent in the process of inquiry.
How then does he interpret '*a* if *F*', so as to preserve this continuity?

That no stage of inquiry can be understood apart from its context in
the continuum of inquiry is uncontroversial. Behavior, especially the
behavior of scientists, is hardly random. There are all kinds of causal
connexions between the various steps in any inquiry. It is rather less
truistic to say, as Dewey does, that 'continuity is the only principle by
which certain fundamentally important logical forms can be understood'. [9] He holds that no proposition *is* a proposition in isolation,
because no event *is* an event in isolation from other events. Causally
indeed, as just mentioned, no event is isolated from all others (though
it surely is from some others). But what a thing is and what happens to
it are not the same thing. In ordinary scientific description and explanation, we cannot describe a process or change without also speaking
about what it is that proceeds or changes. Not so for Dewey. But then
for him, we cannot even describe what a thing is. What then is it that
his propositions are *about*?

The process of inquiry divides for Dewey into an earlier, empirical
stage and a later, rational stage. The former is represented in final
judgement by a hierarchy of so-called 'existential' propositions. The
latter, by a single form of 'nonexistential' proposition. Let us begin by
ascending the existential hierarchy. The very first step in inquiry is

---

[8] P. 154.
[9] P. 247.

represented in final judgement by a proposition, like 'This is sweet', that attributes, as we ordinarily say, a property to an individual. But this one linguistic form, call it '*a* is *F*', conceals, Dewey explains, two different 'logical' forms. The first, or most rudimentary, he calls the particular proposition; the next stage is represented by the singular. The particular proposition begins inquiry by supplying a datum, thus setting a problem. The singular proposition goes one step further, determining *this* to be one of a kind.[10] It therefore represents what in some contexts is itself a solution. In other words, the singular proposition differs from the particular chiefly in that it is not limited to a here and now but makes a prediction. Dewey here appears to be distinguishing between what non-instrumentalists refer to as the differenc between sense-data statements (and phenomenal descriptions of more complex percepts) and perceptual judgements. It is the difference between 'This is sweet', on the one hand, and 'This is sugar', on the other. However, Dewey most emphatically rejects the identification of his particular and singular propositions with sense-data statements and perceptual judgements, respectively. He does so because he rejects three closely connected views, namely, the sense-data analysis of particular propositions; the notion that anything is given 'ready-made' to inquiry; and the existence of immediate, noninferential knowledge.[11] These, of course, are all basically realistic doctrines. If they are all rejected, what can be the nature of predication in propositions of the linguistic form '*a* if *F*'? To anyone familiar with the idealistic tradition, Dewey's answer has a most familiar ring.

Inquiry begins, according to Dewey, with a concrete, unique, ineffable, and inexhaustible situation. At this stage, the situation is neutral, knowing neither universal nor particular, neither fact nor value. It is indeterminate, for the particular which by limiting it determines it has not yet come into being. Conceptualization or predication is the progressive determination of the indeterminate. The subject of the particular proposition with which inquiry begins is a mere artifact of language, for the operation of producing the quality that is neither found nor given has not yet been carried out. Thus it comes about that the true logical form of 'This is red' is the truncated 'becoming red'. 'Becoming red' does not quite describe a change taking place in the phenomenal here and now, for such immediate experience of the specious present is indescribable. Rather, it designates an operation

[10] Pp. 289ff.
[11] Pp. 139, 154, *passim.*

that must be performed in order to 'institute' the particular or 'this' by selecting it out of a larger field. Such selection is a truly creative process because, before inquiry begins, the 'this' has no 'definite characterization'. It becomes 'definitely characterized' when, in Dewey's words, 'activities involving techniques and organs of observation' are carried out. Whenever this is done, the quality that will give 'this' a definite characterization 'proceeds', as he says, 'from an operation performed by means of a sense organ'. This operation is expressed by the rudimentary predicate 'becoming red'. [12] By producing this quality a subject has been provided for the next stage of inquiry as represented by the singular proposition. This subject is that aspect of the whole that has just been delimited, thus setting a problem. The process of predication is now carried one step further. The predicate of the singular proposition designates the act or 'operation' of incorporating a broader context into the process. This predicate goes beyond change occurring in the specious present for it is a sign of traits not yet present, but which will be brought about by the appropriate operations.

Dewey has insisted that his particular and singular propositions, together with their predicates, are 'hypotheses'. In what sense are they hypothetical? At least part of the tradition that Dewey attacks holds that statements about physical objects are inductively grounded in sense-data statements. The former, being inductions, are 'hypotheses' in a sense that the latter are not. Dewey rejects this analysis, since it implies that there is some immediate, noninferential knowledge. For, though statements about, say, dogs involve inference, statements about canoid patches do not. There is another reason why he cannot accept the inductive nature of singular propositions. 'Hypothesis' means, for Dewey, 'operation'. For Dewey's inquirer or, as he would probably prefer to say, the inquiry creates or produces not only the 'datum' but also the 'thing' or physical object. Both are the results of operations. Yet Dewey's thing or physical object is a 'hypothesis'. The point is that to him 'hypothesis' does not signify what it does to most other philosophers, namely, a proposition or belief inductively arrived at. Rather the term has, I submit, the specific idealistic flavour of 'positing' in the sense in which the Fichtean subject 'posits' the object. Such positing or hypothesizing is regarded as a creative determination of the concrete and preconceptual or, what amounts to the same, of the ineffably unique. Only by such hypothesizing or positing does the subject (of the singular proposition) emerge. By going beyond the here-and-now,

[12] Pp. 127, 289, 291.

a broader strain or slice of the universe is conceptually determined. But there is also, in truly idealistic fashion, the price one has to pay whenever one thus delimits the concrete universal in proceeding on the road to abstraction. Conceptualization impoverishes the given by fitting it into a kind. Such fitting, for Dewey as for the idealists, is forever inadequate and, in this further sense, but hypothetical. 'Hypothesis' is, of course, one of the good words of the empiricist tradition. This accident is probably one among the many factors responsible for Dewey's appeal to the empirical and scientific temper of the age. By now, we tend to take the word 'hypothesis' in its traditional inductive meaning. And Dewey's phraseology is so ambiguous and crowded with words like continuity and function that only after close analysis is it clear that he uses 'hypothesis' in the manner of a tradition inimical to empiricism, namely, the tradition of German idealism. For Dewey holds, in common with the idealists, that the character of what is known is so deeply affected by the process of knowing that knowing must be said to make its objects. He explicitly rejects an empiricism that accepts a 'world already constructed and determined', replacing it with a world constructed by the inquirer. Traditional empiricist doctrines. like that of Mill, went astray because they based themselves on 'antecedent' rather than 'consequent' existence. Dewey felt that this left no place for essential novelty in the world. Only if it is recognized that knowing is an active participant in what is known, so that facts result from the process of inquiry, can novelty appear. A verbal transition is made from an indeterminate situation to an indeterministic world, made so casually as to pass almost unnoticed, in the interests of a universe which is still in the making and, so, unpredictable.

The Archimedean point of Dewey's system is his denial of the given, in that basic phenomenal sense of givenness in which realists and phenomenalists alike recognize that there is something given to us, which, *qua* givenness, is neither producible nor modifiable by us. In Dewey's terms, when inquiry starts, the situation as such is completely indeterminate. It becomes determinate only as the process includes into itself ever-broadening contexts. The quality first 'instituted" by the particular proposition is swept into a broader context by classifying it as one of a kind. This kind is the predicate of the singular proposition. A partial solution to the problem has thus been provided. Not only is such a solution partial, it is also tentative, since the classification expressed by the singular proposition must be justified. For the realist, such 'justification' would rest on direct observation; the phenomenalist would have recourse to induction from such observation. Neither of these methods are open to Dewey, for they allegedly permit nothing new to be brought forth. Instead, the singular must be placed in a still broader context. Since Dewey denies the given, he must shift the burden of 'proof' for what is expressed by each propositional form from the present or past to the future. Accordingly, the singular is justified by a proposition that follows it in the course of inquiry. After the singular comes the generic proposition which performs its justifying function by expanding the context. The generic has the linguistic form of a generalized proposition, like 'All whales are mammals'. It states a connexion among those kinds already mentioned in the singular. Though it has been suggested by a conjunction of singulars, it is no mere summary of them nor, of course, is it in the ordinary sense an inductive generalization from them. Yet, the generic says more than the singulars from which it arises. Only by thus saying more, by including more of the context, can it 'ground' new statements about singulars. Since it is no mere inductive generalization, how does the generic perform this function?

On any nonrationalistic interpretation, a generalized proposition asserts that all *instances* of one kind of character are also *instances* of another kind. The rationalistic traditions, on the other hand, both idealistic and Aristotelian, interpret the general proposition to assert a connexion among the *characters* themselves. The Aristotelian intuits this connexion. For the idealist, who considers the self-sufficient particular to be appearance only, all statements must be about characters or 'meanings', or connexions among such, within the unfolding whole or concrete universal. Dewey, curiously, combines both these rationalistic interpretations. The intuitionism of Aristotle's real definition is perpetuated in his notion of how the generic contrives to say more than a conjunction of singulars. If process and evolution are admitted, then one is, for Dewey, no longer an Aristotelian and saved from all false metaphysics. Classification of a thing as one of a kind can only be 'grounded', he believes, by nonoverlapping definitions that determine inclusive and exhaustive kinds. Bats are not rightly called birds, nor whales fish, despite their flying and swimming propensities. To avoid these errors of classification, we must know more, so Dewey believes, than can be learned from a mere conjunction of singulars. Now, a system of zoology that teaches that bats are birds is undoubtedly less advanced than one that does not contain this proposition. Noninstrumentalist philosophers have their own way of explaining what could be meant by one scientific statement or system being better or more advanced than another. In the course of their explanation, some realists might have recourse to non-inductive knowledge of relations between characters. Thus they would, and consistently could, incorporate an Aristotelian element into their analysis. Yet it is curious that Dewey too virtually duplicates within his nonrealistic system the doctrine of genera, species, and real definitions. Dewey's idea is roughly this. If an individual is a member of a class, that is explicitly all there is to it. Implicitly, however, a great deal more is meant when asserting the singular '*a* is *F*'. Implicitly, *a* is also *G* and not *H*. The generic proposition expresses a connexion among kinds that has been suggested by a large number of singulars. If it were an ordinary inductive generalization from these singulars, it would, Dewey believes, merely repeat what is 'already known'. To escape this redundancy, each generic proposition must be embedded into a system of other generic propositions. Thus gathered together, each is what none is alone, namely, more than a mere summary of statements about singulars. In other words, if one deals with a multitude of classes within one universe of discourse, then the possibility of variegated and neatly arranged relations of exclusion and inclusion arises. One can create a system; and a system means to the idealist a 'logical' system. So it does for Dewey. It is this flavour of system or 'logic' that, he believes, provides the super-inductive sanction for a neatly laid out system of interrelated characters in which all kinds of inferences are possible and in which birds have more in common than the incidental attribute that they fly.[13]

By creating a system, the indeterminate has been made still more determinate. As far as this expanding context as a determiner of the 'situation' is concerned, we are face to face with the holism that is so prominent throughout Dewey's work. There is no doubt a profound structural affinity between holism and idealism. Hegelianism, in particular, is unequivocally a holistic doctrine. But, then, as is shown by the case of Gestalt theory, holism as such is not necessarily idealistic. What makes Dewey's contextualism idealistic is the fact that the efficacious agency in the progressive determination of the indeterminate is the process and the process only. The process thus conceived is the homologue of the unfolding of the Hegelian absolute. The 'situation' on the other hand which, after a fashion, takes the place of

[13] Pp. 268f, 294f.

the given has many features of the concrete universal. Since the context forever expands – inquiry is, by its nature, unending – the situation is, like the concrete universal, inexhaustible.

The empirical stage of inquiry culminates with the generic proposition. It is the last in the hierarchy of 'existential' propositions. But it is in no sense final for it, too, must be 'grounded'. We must know whether the relation of kinds it expresses is *really* so inclusive and exclusive as to be nonoverlapping. In order to adequately 'ground' the generic proposition, inquiry enters into its rational stage, with the formulation of the 'non-existential' universal proposition. Like the generic, the universal has the linguistic form of a generalization. But, as in the case of the particular and singular, this common linguistic form conceals two different 'logical' forms. There are two important differences between the generic and the universal, as Dewey interprets them. The first difference lies in the nature of their terms. Just as the particular and the singular are systematically ambiguous because their constituent terms refer to different kinds of things, so too are the generic and the universal. The terms of the generic are the same as the predicates of the singular. Since they name operations for bringing about existential kinds or 'traits' Dewey also calls them material means. Since they go beyond the here and now, Dewey also calls them 'potentialities'. Reflecting on these material means, other possibilities or 'meanings' occur to the inquirer.[14] In this way a potentiality gives rise to an 'abstract possibility' by the psychological process of association. As possibilities only they are 'non-existential'. These possible means or meanings are procedural rather than material. They do not name operations actually to be performed but rather are about or prescribe such operations. They are thus twice removed from the existential, so to speak. Material means as statements of operations *to be* performed are at first remove, while procedural means as the possible kinds or 'modes' of such operations are at second remove. These possible modes of operation are, for Dewey, the only true universals, hence the propositions in which they occur as terms are the only truly 'universal' propositions.

For all philosophers who are not Hegelians, any word that doesn't refer to an individual object, person, or event – all words except proper

---

14 All readers of Dewey are familiar with his irrepressible and doubtless unconscious punning. Thus he proceeds verbally from "object" to "objective," from "something proposed" to "proposition," from the indeterminate to the undetermined and, among others, from "means" to "meaning."

names and demonstratives – is general, that is, a universal, of which
particular things are instances. Therefore, their logic, which is the
logic of our everyday language, could not distinguish between generalized sentences, in the way that Dewey does. In other words, propositions about existential kinds and propositions about 'possible' kinds
are assimilated to the same form by modern logic, because they *have*
the same form, namely, that of a generalized proposition. That such
propositions are also sometimes called 'universal' has of course nothing
to do with their terms, but only with their generalized form. Dewey's
inability to accept this doctrine stems, on the one hand, from an
inadequate grasp of what logicians mean by 'form' and, on the other,
from a special metaphysical view regarding the nature of universals.
The latter, in turn, derives from his 'postulate of continuity' which, as a
postulate, apparently stands in no need of justification. For the idealists
the Idea or Absolute unfolds itself in a continuous series of more and
more adequate 'meanings'. For Dewey, the process of inquiry generates
a continuous series of propositions, from the particular through the
singular and generic to the universal. As a logician, the so-called
'formalist' would say that what takes place when Dewey's paradigm
'This is sweet' is once interpreted as a particular and once as a singular
proposition is a shift in reference of the subject or 'this'. But this view
is unacceptable to Dewey, since in either case the 'this' is, for him, an
'instituted' element, with the singular proposition going a bit further
and determining 'this' to be one of a kind. Continuity of function must
be expressed, therefore, in the predicate rather than the subject of
propositions. Since, for Dewey as for the idealists, the self-sufficient
particular is merely an artifact of language, there is indeed no other
path open to him. That is, shifting reference of and differentiation
among predicates is the only way in which he can reflect in the terms
of the proposition the continuity of propositions as a whole. To show
this continuity, he distinguishes a sequence of attributes representing a
passage from the unique to the general. The quality as it 'proceeds
from a sense organ' is unique, but when it is used as a sign of other
qualities, as when classified as one of a kind, it becomes progressively
more general, until at the point where from it every other attribute
with which it is accompanied, or of which it is a sign, can be deduced
it becomes truly universal. The predicate of a particular proposition is
thus a mere 'quality', the singular and the still later generic propositions both possess names of kinds or 'traits' as predicates; the universal proposition, finally, expresses a relation between 'properties' or

'categories'. [15] All terms and, through them, all sentences are thus systematically ambiguous. And the true 'logical' form of a proposition, as distinguished from its merely linguistic form, derives from the degree of generality of the quality that it is about. This, in turn, depends upon the context of the inquiry in which it occurs and is revealed by the function, as a sign, which it fulfils in inquiry.[16] Of *this* form nothing is revealed, of course, by its form as the so-called 'formalists' understand that term, whether they are Aristotelians or moderns.

Dewey's use of continuity as a dodge for granting ontological status as a universal to the quality as such, apart from its function in inquiry, is part of the pattern that I suggested typifies his treatment of all ontological issues. The universal is not really denied; instead, its locus is shifted onto the process by making it a function instead of a form. For Dewey the quality as such is never a universal. What he calls the universal is the conceptual, that is, for him, the procedural, which is all bound up with inquiry and has as such no ontological status. In other words, when we decide, on two subsequent occasions, to characterize situations as red, we do not, according to Dewey, recognize two instances of the same ontological character. Instead, we institute the identical procedure or operation. This procedure is the locus of the universal. As he tells us, the 'abuse of abstractions' is corrected by 'noting that their referents are possible modes of operating'. [17] The only true universal is a mode of operation, a way of acting. This analysis of the universal, in the ordinary meaning of the term, is indicative of Dewey's functionalist and biological bias. Whatever merit it may have along these lines, philosophically it is patently and obviously inadequate. For, if there are no universals what would it mean to say that the procedure in the two cases was the 'same' or, to say the same thing differently, how are we ever to know that the two operations are both instances of the same universal? Clearly, we are faced with an infinite regress.

Dewey's belief that the terms of the universal proposition are more general than the terms of the generic is only one reason he discerns an important difference between them. There is still another. One of Dewey's sharpest disagreements with traditional empiricism is his rejection of the dichotomy between the empirical (factual, synthetic) and the rational (formal, analytic) and, correlatively, between induction

[15] Pp. 292, 254.
[16] Pp. 293, 250.
[17] P. 352.

and deduction.[18] This rejection follows the pattern already mentioned: substitution of an essentially causal description of the process of inquiry, in the Darwinist-functionalist vein, for structural analysis of the results of this process. The empirical and the rational, we are told, are merely different aspects of inquiry. They represent, respectively, the earlier and the later stages of scientific method. Upon such a view the distinction between induction and deduction becomes, curiously enough, a matter of *history*, rather than of logic or the theory of knowledge. The earlier stage of the process of inquiry yields merely empirical or contingent truth, while the later or rational stage yields necessary truth. The empirical stage culminates in Dewey's generic propositions. These are, at least in some sense, generalizations from a large number of events actually occurring and, as such, are 'open to nullification'. [19] So we see that they are what everybody else calls a natural law. Dewey points out that they have 'existential reference' and '*at best* a high order of probability'. [20] But he is not willing to let it go at that. To take these propositions out of what, in one of the most remarkable passages in the *Logic*, is called their 'precarious form', [21] the distinction between the generic and the universal propositions is introduced. Only the former are afflicted with the frailness of induction, as empiricists understand that process. The latter remedy this unhappy state of affairs. The generic represents what he calls a 'relatively incomplete *empirical* state of inquiry'; final judgement cannot be made until a *necessary* and *inherent* relation between the events observation has noted to be correlated can be shown. In Dewey's terminology, a *reason* must be found for the observed conjunction of events, before we can tell that it is inherent and necessary.[22] The universal proposition supplies this reason. The very use of the word 'reason' in a causal context is, of course, highly suspect to empiricists. However, even one who, as most philosophers who call themselves empiricists, feels repugnance towards all demands for inherence and necessity may charitably interpret Dewey's insistence that a reason be found for an observed correlation. One could conceivably maintain that this is Dewey's way of giving an account of scientific *explanation* or theory construction. A theory, for empiricists, is a deductively organized system of physical laws. And we say that we have explained or, if you

---

[18] Pp. 305, 427.
[19] P. 379.
[20] Pp. 296, 226, 200, 256, 279.
[21] P. 379.
[22] Pp. 193, 279, 304f.

will, given the reason for a law, if we can state another, usually more general, law or set of laws from which this and other ones may be derived. In this sense we say that Newton's law of gravitation explains or is the 'reason' for Galileo's and Kepler's laws. But, unfortunately, this cannot be what Dewey means. Certainly, it is not what he says. Let me explain.

Dewey's universal propositions are taken to be postulates, representing certain stipulations and demands inquiry must satisfy. In this sense they are, in his terminology, 'operationally *a priori*'. [23] The genuine empiricist strain in Dewey's thought is revealed in the recognition that these demands are the result of previous successful inquiries and are, thus, learned through experience. However – and this is very strange and shows also how far Dewey is from, say, the Millian sort of empiricism – these postulates, learned through experience, are not in the ordinary sense 'empirical'. That is to say, they do not have the characteristics empiricists, in the broadest sense of the term, attribute to natural laws. For, according to Dewey, they are not, as the tradition has it, contingent, inductive, or merely probable. Dewey's 'universal proposition' is not afflicted with any of these infirmities; it is necessarily true. This, in fact, is its distinctive character. The "if .... then ...." hypothetical form of these privileged propositions – their merely verbal form, that is, to which, according to Dewey, all non-instrumentalist logicians cleave – conceals what Dewey calls their 'true logical form', which is that of a *definition*.[24] Thus, universal propositions (laws of nature!) are 'analytic' in the full Kantian sense of the word, for they represent an analysis of a conception into its component parts, as in 'A white horse is white'. And what examples does Dewey himself give of such 'analytic' physical laws? 'All men are mortal' and the Newtonian law of gravitation![25] On the empiricist analysis, these two laws represent extensions or extrapolations to all men and to all bodies of certain regularities observed to hold in a limited number of cases. They are thus contingent, probable, or, what means the same, merely inductive.

Now, there is a perfectly meaningful and harmless interpretation one can give to the view that empirical laws are 'operationally *a priori* with respect to further inquiry'. In principle, every experiment tests all the relevant hypotheses, but for the purposes of any particular

---

[23] Pp. 14, 377, 379.
[24] Pp. 272, 301, 256, 296, *passim*.
[25] Pp. 312–313, 256.

research problem most of these hypotheses are taken for granted. Further, there may be so much converging evidence for a certain law, or this law may occupy so fundamental a place in a well-confirmed theory, that when something happens which seems to throw doubt upon its truth, rather than simply give it up, the scientist will look for interfering factors, or decide that perhaps his initial and boundary conditions were not those for which the law in question was affirmed to hold. A new planet was discovered because the physicists were loath to abandon Newton's law of gravitation in the face of what appeared to be counter-evidence. In a *psychological* sense, but only in a psychological sense, some laws of physics may, at some time, be called necessary. To attribute this sort of necessity to a law is to make a statement about the *behavior* of scientists in specified kinds of situations. The logical status of the law as such remains synthetic or contingent. It does not become 'more and more' analytic, as we become more and more confident of its truth. A vitiating transition from 'operationally *a priori*' to *a priori* in the sense of analytic is intimately connected with – perhaps, I should even say, a part of – Dewey's characteristic equivocation between two levels of analysis: the level of bio-sociological analysis, essentially causal, descriptive of the process of inquiry, on the one hand, and the level of structural or methodological analysis of the results of such inquiry, on the other.

Yet Dewey is not content to claim that a universal proposition is logically necessary because it is operationally *a priori*. He goes further and tells us that the non-existential, necessary, universal proposition has a *form* that is different from that of the existential or contingent proposition. Here he uses, for once, though erroneously, the term 'form' in the usual, non-Pickwickian sense of linguistic structure. The universal proposition, which supplies the reason for, or 'grounds' of, the generic has the form of a *definition*. It is 'non-existential in reference and stands for a necessary relation which follows, by definition, from analysis of a conception'. [26] Thus, the justification, or ground, as Dewey calls it – it will be recalled that for the classical idealist 'ground' refers to the antecedent in a necessary implication – of the empirical law is furnished, not by experience, not by another empirical law, but by a tautology! The occurrence of this tautology 'retains its kinship with the organic', [27] as Dewey puts it or, as I would say, is causally related to empirical laws, by the fact that it is *suggested* by them. But

[26] P. 296, *passim*.
[27] P. 300.

this causal tie between the definitional and the factual as occurrents or events is not the only 'reason' Dewey confounds these two levels. Another is one of his characteristic verbal transitions. This one has the following basis: stated as hypothetical conditionals, the laws of science and Dewey's generic propositions express the 'necessary conditions' for the occurrence of some event. In the expression 'If A, then B', B is a necessary condition for the existence of A: if not B, then not A. However, it marks a high stage of scientific achievement when we can state not only necessary, but also necessary and sufficient conditions. That is, it is desirable that we should be able to say not only 'If A, then B,' but also 'If and *only* if A, then B'. Knowledge of necessary and sufficient conditions means that we can state a material equivalence between propositions: whenever one is true the other will be true and conversely. Such an equivalence is not a definition; the concepts are independently defined. There is nothing *logically* necessary about the relationship. Dewey places much stress on the desirability of fulfilling the criteria of necessary and sufficient conditions or of exhaustiveness and exclusiveness, as he usually says,[28] and the process by which this takes place is as follows, according to him: first we have the generic proposition which expresses in a contingent proposition only the necessary conditions for the occurrence of an event; then we keep on looking until we have the necessary and sufficient conditions. From 'necessary and sufficient' in the material, *factual* sense Dewey makes the transition to '*necessary*' and, moreover, to 'logically necessary'. For only the universal, definitional, non-existential proposition satisfies the criteria of necessary and sufficient condition. It is by such verbal magic that the material equivalence is transformed into a formal, definitional equivalence. By piling synthetic upon synthetic, fact upon fact, he arrives at the analytic! Unfortunately, this won't do, for, as already stressed, no amount of converging evidence can convert the factual, empirical, or synthetic into the verbal, tautological, or analytic.

In order to understand what Dewey means by induction, we must give the other the half of the story. For Dewey stresses that the process goes in two directions, from the generic to the universal and back again. The generic suggests the universal in two ways: first, it leads to definitions devised as a result of inductive knowledge, in the usual sense; second, the necessary conditions indicated by the generic lead the inquirer to conjecture that perhaps they are both necessary and sufficient. Verbally, such a hypothesis takes the form of a universal proposition,

[28] Pp. 188–189, 307, 309.

which, since it is a mere hypothesis or suggested possibility, is non-existential. But the non-existential is also the logically necessary and definitional. Deduction or reasoning may then be used to elicit all the implications of this universal proposition in conjunction with other universal propositions. In this way a system is formed,[29] which, as is hardly necessary to point out, is wholly definitional and tautological. By developing such implications, new hypotheses are suggested as possibilities. If such a hypothesis is tested, it gives rise to a new generic proposition which, in turn, may warrant a new conceptualization or universal proposition, and so on, and so on. The process is a weaving back and forth between the two realms of the existential and the non-existential. With each successive oscillation the system of meanings, or deductively connected universal propositions, expands by the addition of new definitions. *This* 'to-and-fro movement', [30] to use Dewey's own description, is his substitute for the empiricist's account of systematic, theory-producing and theory-controlled induction. But theory, as the empiricist understands it, does not move on an ontological plane different from, to use Dewey's term, that of the generic. Nor is theory, for the empiricist, all definitional, tautological, and, therefore, necessary. In other words, although theory rationalizes the 'generic' in the sense of systematizing it, it is not rationalistic in the sense of logically necessary, as it is in Dewey's system of universal propositions.

To show conclusively that Deweyan induction is not induction in the usual sense at all, let me ask one further question. Suppose the generic proposition suggested by the system of meanings is not verified in experience. What happens? Non-pragmatists would, of course, say that such failure redirects inquiry to new and different inductive hypotheses. Dewey does not say this. Instead, we are told that in such a case 'one or the other of the involved *universal propositions* must be revised and reformulated'. [31] Here we stand before the secret of induction revealed: *Induction*, for Dewey, *is revision and reformulation* (of universal propositions) *through redefinition*, into which we are jolted through contact with the recalcitrant existential. What is, thus, at best a loose and rather superficial account of one of the *results* of inductive discovery – the formation of new definitions – is offered as an account of induction itself.

The oscillation between the existential and the non-existential,

[29] Pp. 300–301, 111–112.
[30] P. 427.
[31] Pp. 272, 384.

between the factual and the tautological, is, Dewey insists, a continuous process, without end. Given the intrinsic logic of the system *and* Dewey's cultural hostility to all quests for certainty, we understand his insistence that there cannot be an end to inquiry. For, if there were such an end, the untenability or, if you please, the essential rationalism of his system would be manifest. To see this, let us assume what, according to Dewey, must not be assumed, namely, that the process of inquiry has run its course. At this point the system of meanings has reached closure and comprehends in its totality the whole of science. Nevertheless, it would still be a definitional system! In other words, the whole of our knowledge is, ideally speaking, purely logical or, as a non-pragmatist would say, analytic. This, of course, is rationalism at its most uncompromising extreme. It may seem that I am overinterpreting, yet Dewey says as much himself in certain comments on the Aristotelian syllogism.

The Aristotelian syllogism, according to Dewey, has the merit of revealing the structure of final judgement. The logical form of this final judgement, we are told, is that of a universal, non-existential proposition as major premiss, a matter-of-fact, or generic proposition, as minor premiss, and a second universal proposition as conclusion.[32] If we interpret the syllogism temporally, *as Dewey does*, it will be seen that this accords with my description of the oscillatory process whereby the universal grounds the generic, which in turn suggests a new universal. Now, while the generic proposition has the same verbal form as the universal proposition, it is *really*, according to Dewey – who rejects the classical account of induction – *only* a 'some' proposition.[33] The syllogism is, therefore, invalid, since a universal conclusion cannot be derived from an 'existential' premiss. Dewey sees this, of course, and grants that the structure of final judgement as occurring in the process of inquiry is invalid, *but*, he says, we are striving towards a goal. The *ideal* of science is final judgement made up *entirely* of universal propositions, with no matter-of-fact minor premiss![34] That's what Dewey means when he says that judgement is not only necessary and definitional, but is also normative and prescriptive. *The achievement of tautological equivalence is viewed by Dewey as a normative, regulative principle of inquiry*, anticipated, no matter how crudely, by Aristotle's doctrine of the syllogism. A superficial student of Dewey's might very

---

[32] P. 323.
[33] P. 380.
[34] Pp. 324, 303, 319.

well be led by his verbalisms to mistake his theory for what it is not, namely, a description of the axiomatic method which has played such a prominent role in the science of the last half-century and of which empiricists make so much. As I believe to have shown, the similarity is superficial indeed. All the 'operational' and pseudo-psychological 'grounding' apart, the decisive difference is, of course, that, for Dewey, not only the deductions from the premisses but the premisses *themselves* are tautological. Such rationalism is, of course, completely unacceptable to any nonidealistic philosopher. I personally am convinced that, explicitly, it would not have been acceptable to Dewey either. Yet, despite its naturalistic trappings, rationalism is the ineluctable consequence of his elaborate and, in many ways, ingenious construction.

II

Since the predicate or universal is always a 'mode of operating', all propositions are statements of operations to be performed. They thus do not declare anything in the ordinary sense of the word. Instead of describing existence, they tell us what should be done if we want, eventually, to say something about existence. In other words, they direct the process of inquiry and talk about *it*, instead of about its subject-matter. It is one of the peculiar fascinations of Dewey's work that he is always reaching for the existential, but never quite succeeds in laying hold of it. Although they do not describe anything antecedently there, the operations are to be performed, of course, for the purpose of making changes in the existential material. It might seem that after we have carried out this transformation, then, at long last, we can make a purely declarative statement to the effect that this is the way things are. They would be whatever they were because of our operations, yet we could eventually describe what had been wrought. Unfortunately, all declaratives are statements of operations *to be* performed and so, everlastingly, our reach is fated to exceed our grasp. Tantalus – not, as some would have it, Prometheus – is the classical hero who presides over the Deweyan enterprise. Naturally, if direct experience is ineffable, if there is no noninferential knowledge, then we can never say that something is the case, for ultimately all such declarations must receive their justification in knowledge gained not verbally, by reference to other propositions, but by experience. If 'this is red' never refers to an individual self-contained fact, though of course with causes and effects, but always to a future action, then, indeed, the existential if forever beyond our grasp. Final judgment reflects a process in which we cannot say what, if anything, proceeds, nor where it is when it gets where it is going.

If declaratives aren't really declaratives, what are they? They are all, Dewey reveals, disguised evaluations.[35] Here we have the first of Dewey's two major gambits for resolving the dreaded dualism between fact and value, between 'something called morals' and 'something called science'. Operations are performed for a purpose. They are means to an end. All propositions therefore assert a relation between means and consequences. Thus it is that the concept of causality is 'teleological through and through'. [36] The 'effect' or consequence is a desired end, hence something valued. The cause or means is also a value, because it is instrumental to an end and also because, in another context, it may itself be an end. 'Declaratives' therefore tell us what it is *best* to do to achieve the end, which in turn is a means to a further end, and so on, and so on. We can no more say 'This is good' and mean that here and now is something valued, than we can say 'This is red' and mean that here and now a certain quality is presented to sensation. Both alike are 'appraisals'. These relationships of means to ends are, for Dewey, the only legitimate objects of knowledge; only they are 'cognitive'. Since it is the scientist who investigates means and ends, it is he who can tell us what it is best to do, what end is 'worth attaining'. [37] By thus playing fast and loose with the word 'end', a science of value is happily assured. Ideals and standards, like facts, are 'generalized results' of inquiry. Again, ontological status is avoided by casting 'value' onto the process. Value is not merely subjectively in us, nor is it entirely objective; it emerges from the process of inquiry. Anthropologically, there is nothing controversial about all this. The end of inquiry *is* something the scientist values; he does want to find the effects or 'consequences'. But *what* he finds, what the laws declare, are not '*teleological*' statements of his motives. But confusion of the psychology of the researcher with the object of his research is, of course, only one price that is exacted for that unhappy marriage of bio-sociological analysis with structural or philosophical description.

Dewey's second gambit for overcoming the dualism between fact and value is much more fundamental. Only the *relation* between means and ends in cognitive; neither is in itself. If Dewey's universe

[35] Pp. 174, 179.
[36] P. 462.
[37] P. 503.

of discourse actually described the world, then the use of the term
'cognitive' would be most inappropriate, for this of course is an epithet
of psychology not of physics. Knowing is a property of the mind that
knows, and says nothing about the properties of the thing known. Not
so for Dewey. But then, his universe of discourse is about the process of
inquiry, the acts of knowing, and never about what is thus known,
either fact or value. Either fact or value. For if the *evaluative*, the
relations between means and ends, resides only in the process of inquiry,
value, true value in itself, resides elsewhere. Roast pork that is obtained
by burning down houses is not a value in the evaluative sense, because
this is a poor means to that end. But why did men go about finding less
extreme methods of preparing it? Because, of course, it tasted good, it
was enjoyed. This value or enjoyment, being an immediate quality is,
once more, indescribable, according to Dewey, and therefore, not
cognitive. Inquiry starts with the qualitative, ineffable, unique,
preconceptual situation. There too it ends. This is what Dewey means
by saying that final judgement has '*direct* existential import'. [38] Not,
as we have seen, because it describes existence, but because by closing
inquiry it brings us face to face with the unique, preconceptual,
ineffable, qualitative whole. The achievement of the qualitative, the
'having' or 'enjoying' of the indescribable unique situation is an end
in a double sense of that term. It is both the finish or close of inquiry
and it is the purpose of the whole enterprise. Means, we recall, are also
'meanings'. And, indeed, when inquiry has run its course it terminates,
as we saw, in a system of meanings. The 'universal' propositions which
are the goal of inquiry express this relation of 'meanings'. Such
'meanings' are held to be the end-product of inquiry.[39] But, *about the
word 'meaning' there hangs a moral flavour*. For 'meaning' may be used
in the sense of the meaningful, the humanly significant, as contrasted
with the blind, the 'merely mechanical' or meaningless. So it is for
Dewey. The 'unified whole' that is the desired result of inquiry is both a
logical whole, a coherent system of universal propositions, and an
organic whole of 'shared' meanings with ethical and aesthetic significance. Just as the 'end' of inquiry is an end in the sense of termination
or close and an 'end' in the sense of purpose, so there is a logical
'meaning' and a psychological, value-laden 'meaning'. These are not
parallel results of inquiry, but are one and the same result. It is a
tautology in Dewey's system to say that inquiry is instrumental to

[38] P. 120.
[39] P. 327, *passim*.

values, for, by definition, value is the outcome of inquiry. The end of inquiry in order to be an end in the sense of 'close' must be the value, the consummation, the fulfilment, otherwise there is no proper termination. The universe of discourse is merely instrumental to this indescribable enjoyment. Professor Murphy, in his contribution to the Schilpp volume, has clearly expressed this aspect of Dewey's thought:

He regards [knowing] as a use of ideas as signs of possible future experiences and means for effecting the transition to such experiences in a satisfactory manner. These future experiences, insofar as they terminate inquiry, will not be cases of 'knowing', i.e., of the use of given experiences as signs of something else. Hence what justifies cognition is not anything in the same sense 'known' at all, but the occurrence of a non-cognitive satisfaction, and the goodness of cognition in its own primary aim or intent, is determined by its use in bringing about such experiences.[40]

Here we have the roots of a fundamental anti-intellectualism, Dewey's affinity with romanticism. The objects of knowledge, such as they are, do not exist in their own right but are justified by their ability to lead to the precognitive, the preconceptual, the ineffable. The supremacy of the 'enjoyed', of the 'had', over the known is repeatedly stressed by Dewey. 'Scientific subject-matter', as he put it, 'is intermediate, not final and complete in itself'. [41] And in his *Rejoinder* in the Schilpp volume he reaffirmed and left no possible doubt regarding the end to which scientific subject matter is only intermediate:

A typical illustration of what I mean by .... noncognitive experiences is found in my not infrequent statements to the effect that the assumption of the ubiquity of cognitive experience inevitably results in the disparagement of things experienced by way of love, desire, hope, fear, and other traits characteristic of human individuality.[42]

Is it really true that these characteristic human traits are *disparaged* if one insists, as nonidealists do, that he who has, say, loved *knows*, really knows, what love is, while one who never has does not? Be that as it may, Dewey believes that values are not imposed *ab extra*, nor are they subjective, because they inhere in the qualitative, subrelational substratum which 'gives the cognitive its *import*'. The value, in the sense of the enjoyed, has not the same status as fact, but a higher status; it is that for which the whole enterprise is undertaken and which is its consummation.

It is, I trust, clear by now that Dewey unifies fact and value, not, as is sometimes said, by objectifying values but, rather, by subjectifying

[40] *The Philosophy of John Dewey*, edited by P. A. Schilpp, p. 208.
[41] *Logic*, p. 66.
[42] Schilpp, *op. cit.*, p. 548.

both fact and value. In Dewey's terms, when inquiry begins the precognitive situation is indeterminate; it becomes determinate by a process of transformation and modification in which the 'cognitive' or physical objects and events emerge, are 'instituted' or 'brought into existence'. Apart from inquiry, there is neither knowledge nor value, because there is nothing to be known or valued, because, in turn, nothing has been instituted. The process is the ontological locus of fact and value, as it is also the locus of knower and known, subject and object, the rational and the empirical. Thus absorbed into the process, these distinctions reflect no irreducible categorial features of the world. All experienced diversity is displaced from the world's substance to us, from the things themselves to the method by which we know them.

The philosophical dividing line during Dewey's formative years ran between idealistic philosophies on the one hand and realistic-positivistic ones, more or less in the style of Hamilton and the Mills, on the other. Dewey felt that the implications of the realistic-positivistic systems led eventually, by their intrinsic logic, to a severance of fact and value in a sense and of a kind the idealists were unable to accept. Nor was Dewey himself or, for that matter, his culture, in spite of its 'materialistic' leanings, able to accept it. On the other hand, Dewey also must have felt that the idealistic rationale for subordinating fact to value was, because of its ineradicable anthropomorphism, unable to maintain itself in the face of the modern temper and the results of science. This put him in a conflict situation which, the probable social value of his thought as easing an ideological transition notwithstanding, he was unable to solve intellectually. To say the same thing differently, to avoid an unbearable choice, Dewey makes sure that there be no choice from the outset. If only 'facts' – in the sense in which science uses the term – are 'objectively' given while values are 'subjective' and created by us, why then, let us abolish the given or, rather, let us create it as the Fichtean subject creates both his facts and his values. To overcome the difference in the ontological status of knower and known, to eliminate the dreaded dualism between object and subject, that makes our valuations shivering exiles in a cold world of fact, ontological status is denied to both sides of the dichotomy. This is why, in the last analysis, the process and the process alone becomes the real and the given becomes the ineffable, the unique, the concrete. Here, in this unformed, inexhaustible mass, all the traditional dualisms are dissolved; from it they rise as mere artifacts of the process of inquiry, to be triumphantly redissolved when that process has run its course. Here, in particular, fact and value rest in undisturbed harmony; from it they issue *pari passu* and with equal right as inquiry creates them. The efficacious agency in the progressive determination of the indeterminate is the process which, since we live in an age of science and have the Darwinian fallacy at our disposal, becomes the biosocial process of inquiry.

Dewey's philosophy, I believe to have shown, is in essence Hegelian. In form, it is partly Darwinian, when philosophical Darwinism is understood as it should be understood, namely, as a moment in the movement of Hegelian thought through the nineteenth century. Everyone knows how Darwinian theory served to reinforce romantic evolutionism. Thoroughly steeped in that tradition, Dewey repeated the pattern, grafting biological theory on to Hegelianism to construct a beguilingly up-to-date version of the idealistic structure. How did such a system come to be, at least for a long time, the 'characteristically American' philosophy? Until this century, the characteristic American outlook, to whatever extent one may sensibly speak of such a thing, was the hardheaded realism of the Puritan dualistic and individualistic tradition. God, not man, had created the world. God, not man, had decreed the right and the wrong. Facts were intractable facts, whether they were moral, physical, or social. And each man could prove his superiority over his fellows by turning these hard facts to his own advantage in a land of unlimited opportunity. Success was thus always the reward of merit, moral and intellectual.

But this mythology could not long persist. The growing prestige of science broke the back of theological influence. The disclosures of the 'muckrakers' cast disrepute on the premiss that success was always to the righteous and innately superior. The influx of Europe's poor and their segregation into the lowest social and economic strata starkly revealed that the brave ideal of equality of opportunity remained as yet only an ideal. These things all fed into the growing social reform movement in a country whose physical and economic resources could easily afford a large measure of such reform. Religion was displaced by a faith in science. 'Rugged individualism' gave way to the ideal of group effort and state planning. The philosophy of John Dewey provided a theoretical rationale and justification for the social idealism of the reformers. Through his philosophy their goals received welcome 'scientific' sanction. For despite Dewey's forever reiterated denunciation of ethical absolutisms, his philosophy is not, despite superficial similarities, just another brand of ethical relativism. Science, for

Dewey, is not a method for learning about what is already there, but is instead a way of changing the world. As long as inquiry proceeds scientifically, change in the right direction is guaranteed, for, as I pointed out before, by definition values are the outcome of inquiry. By identifying value with whatever results from the scientific manipulation of society, Dewey and his disciples convinced themselves that their own values are not imposed, that they merely tell us, scientifically, all about the natural ways of value. Instrumentalism, like idealism, anchors the good in the world. In this there is no difference. The difference is that the world, the real, is not the Absolute but the evolutionary process. So it comes about that in a word sufficiently plastic the future cannot but be better than the past.

How confidently one can set about the reformer's task if fact and value alike are created by us! As products of the social process, the Deweyan 'fact' and 'value' are and yet are not made by any single individual; they are at once 'objective', yet, since growing and changing, not absolute. Dewey set out to deny that there are any absolute moral ends already given and to which we must conform. In order to do this, he denied that there is any hard fact, any universe, moral or physical, given ready-made and to which we must also conform, in another sense of that word. It is no wonder that this philosophy captured the imagination and loyalty of those who were urgently bent on the urgent task of social reform. It is even less wonder that this philosophy, based on a wish and a hope, could not long endure – not even in America. In our time it is clear as never before that science serves the evil forces in man and society at least as well as it serves the good. This realization has had at least one salutary effect. The scientistic attempt to 'objectify' values is seen as no less a wish-fulfilment rationalization than the narcissistic ego-projection of Hegelianism. Man the doer is no more omnipotent than man the thinker. Some hard facts must be faced. A great power does not go away just because we do not officially recognize it. What is and what ought to be remain asunder. Only by facing the former, can we act intelligently about the latter. By casting everything onto the process, instrumentalism at once denies the very notion of 'fact' and of personal responsibility for moral decision. Can any reflective person who has survived the past quarter of a century lightly embrace such an ontology? Thus it is that in a sobered America instrumentalism is now on the wane.

INDEX

DATE DUE